Science Against
CRIME

Science Against
CRIME

Marshall Cavendish

Editor Yvonne Deutch
Designer Eddie Pitcher
Picture Co-ordinator Annette Zeff
Picture Researcher Mark Dartford

Published by Marshall Cavendish House
58, Old Compton Street,
London W1V 5PA

First printed 1982

Printed in Italy

ISBN 0 85685 902 8

*The Publishers would like to thank
Doctor Ray Williams, Director,
and Ken Creer, head of the
Photographic Department of the
Metropolitan Police Forensic
Laboratory, for help in supplying
information and photographic
material used in this book.*

*Contributors to
the case histories include:*
John Clute
Emma Fisher
Angus Hall
Elizabeth Herr
Frances Kennett
Bernard Knight
Sarah Litvinoff
Robin Odell
Frank Symth

Endpapers: *Examining
fingerprints with a magnifying
glass. Identification of prints is
an important part of the work in
a forensic science laboratory.*

Title page: *The role of the
camera in criminal investigation was quickly recognised by
the great French expert,
Alphonse Bertillon. He devised
this ladder and camera for taking photographs at the scene of
a crime.*

Contents page: *A blood-
stained piece of glass is removed
for examination in the laboratory by a specially trained scenes
of crime officer* (left). *Ballistics
is a specialist skill in itself. Here
a gun is being test-fired by an
examiner wearing protective
equipment for his ears* (right).

FOREWORD

Forensic science is an umbrella term for a branch of science which has many constituent parts. There is probably as much confusion about what a forensic scientist is, as about the work he does. Historically, scientific matters associated with crime detection were almost solely the province of pathologists who carried out 'non-medical' investigations on a somewhat ad hoc basis. Although in some countries the pathologist is still in virtual overall charge of the scientific aspects of an investigation, in most cases the investigator can call upon a variety of experts to assist him according to the needs of the problem he has to solve.

A case of murder, for example, could involve, in the first instance, a police surgeon who certifies death and makes a preliminary examination of the body. The forensic pathologist completes the examination and arranges for the body to be moved to a mortuary where he will conduct a post mortem examination. Meanwhile, police photographers, fingerprint and scenes of crime officers will be making a detailed search of the scene for clues. In complicated cases a scientist from a crime laboratory will often accompany the pathologist and be on hand to assist and advise the police scenes of crime team in the interpretation of what is found.

Long after the event the painstaking work goes on – in the pathologist's laboratory, with microscope sections of tissue removed from the body; in the fingerprint bureau, with marks taken from the scene and vast indexes of fingerprints from known criminals; and in the crime laboratory itself, with microscopic fragments of cloth fibres and paint flakes, with bullets and bloodstains, and a host of other bits and pieces besides.

Diversification among a number of specialists is a necessary and logical development of the investigator's use of science against crime. It has been brought about largely by the tremendous advances in science and technology during the last century and the realization that no one person, be he investigator or expert, can 'go it alone'. Perhaps disappointingly, the popular polymath image of the forensic scientist created by crime novels and television characters, bears little resemblance to the truth. It is only by drawing upon the very different and special knowledge of the medically qualified expert, the forensic toxicologist, the ballistics expert, the forensic biologist and the forensic chemist, among others, that a properly integrated response to crime can be orchestrated by the investigator. Forensic science is truly multidisciplinary in its methods, and the application of its methods requires a team effort on the part of the experts involved.

Crime is a complex interaction of people and things at different points in time and space, and crime detection is a high grade intellectual pursuit. The physical residues of crime – the fibres and the glass, the blood and the tyre marks – all hold vital secrets about what has happened. It is the forensic scientist's job to make them give up their secrets, to interpret the data and to tell the story that is revealed.

A glance at the many examples of classic cases in this book will show that the partnership between science and crime detection is not new. Forensic science is almost as old as crime itself and, even if it is not quite the "oldest profession", then it must surely be the second oldest!

R.E. Stockdale
Oxfordshire
February, 1982

CONTENTS

CRIMINAL IDENTIFICATION

Every day we perform prodigious feats of identification. We notice and identify members of our family and our friends. We leave the house and we identify our neighbours. We notice if any strangers are in the neighbourhood and, perhaps the following day, we will *identify* a stranger as the same person we saw the day before. Our confidence in our identification of a stranger increases in the measure that he becomes less of a stranger until the day comes when he is so much part of our memory patterns that we cease consciously to apply any great attention to the act of identification.

Below: *The English engraver, Thomas Bewick, used his fingerprint to authenticate his work.*

We need not see a person in the flesh to identify him. We may do it from a photograph. The American President, the Queen of England, the Pope are all known to millions of people who have never seen them in the flesh. Although newspaper photographs which show us these celebrities are sometimes provided with captions which may condition our minds to accepting that they are who they are supposed to be, in many cases we would be able to identify them without the label. Here we see the importance of context. We *expect* to see the American President figuring in many newpaper pictures (particularly if the caption says so) in the same way that we *expect* to see members of our family in our house. Thus, the problem of identifying them requires little effort.

Now, take them out of context. The new visitor next door who is sitting in the (familiar) front garden looks just like the Pope although, in the absence of any other clues, we would probably be satisfied with the 'looks like' conclusion. Similarly, the healthy old man pictured on the front of the holiday brochure, shark fishing in the South Pacific, looks very like Grandpa. If you'd seen him in the front garden you'd have been satisfied straightaway that it *was* Grandpa. So these are two of the main features of visual identification – familiarity and context.

See anyone you know?

Now, let's make it a little more difficult. Imagine your friend gives you an old army photograph of a company of soldiers and asks if you can locate a *named* mutual friend. This may be made more difficult because these questions are often asked years after the event and memory dims. Perhaps you know the friend as he is today and your difficulty is remembering what he looked like (if you knew) 20 years ago. The problem would be made even more difficult if the question were framed in the form 'see anyone you know?' Here the less help you get from the context the more familiarity you need with the subject. Look at the photograph of the excited

Right: *Even the most famous face can 'disappear' in a crowd. In this picture a well-known person is almost swamped by the surrounding well-wishers.*

crowd. See anyone you know? So we now have, in addition to familiarity and context, a third important aspect – attention.

If you spend a summer afternoon strolling in a big city you may 'see' several thousand persons without 'identifying' any of them. If, however, one of the thousands speaks to you, using your name, your attention will quicken and you will quite likely identify a friend or acquaintance of, perhaps, years ago. Here you will be helped by familiarity, or is it context?

He speaks with a North American accent so – it's Joe Brown. Perhaps he helps you along a little: "the last time was in Rooney's bar, remember?" It may sound rather obvious to say you can identify people better if you are given a clue who they are but here lies a basic division in identification procedures. On the one hand we have the problem of establishing a stated (or expected) identity as true or false, and on the other hand we have the problem of identifying someone in the absence of clues or statements.

1—RIGHT THUMB	2—RIGHT FORE	3—RIGH
6—LEFT THUMB	7—LEFT FORE	8—LEF
1—RIGHT THUMB	2—RIGHT FORE	3—RIG
6—LEFT THUMB	7—LEFT FORE	8—LE

Whose fingerprints?

Look closely at the two sets of fingerprints on this page. You are now carrying out the basic process of comparison of two identities. Can you find any points of similarity? Do you think they came from the same person? The answer lies in the photograph of the twin girls. What you have just seen are fingerprints of both hands of these identical twins. So here we have done two things. We have demonstrated the difference of fingerprints of different individuals and, at the same time, we have demolished the widely held belief that identical twins have the same finger prints.

Thus, even people with identical genes (the hereditary instructions we receive from our parents in our physical make-up) have different fingerprints. The fingerprint pattern and detail are established in the unborn child in the mother's womb and they remain constant until death except, of course, for ageing changes and injury, which, although they may give difficulties, do not change the essential nature of the fingerprint. Let us now transfer our attention to the scene of a murder. Here the detective may find a fingerprint which he suspects belongs to the killer (on the handle of a knife, for example). If he has an idea of who the killer might be then the process of checking the prints may turn out to be fairly simple – he is checking against a stated, or suspected, identity. If, however, the detective has no idea who the killer is, then the process of checking the fingerprint becomes much more difficult. (See the chapter on Fingerprints.)

Blood group identification

There may be another type of evidence of interest at the same murder scene. The victim was stabbed to death and it is quite possible that the killer got some of the victim's blood on him. If a suspect is arrested, and bloodstains are found on his clothing, what can be established from this? The obvious first step is to establish if the blood is human. If it is, then the next question to consider is how can we 'characterize' or 'individualize' it.

This is a field of study which has occupied forensic scientists for about 70 years and quite enormous advances have been made. The blood of each of us carries a great number of genetically determined factors in many different 'blood group' systems. Chapter two gives further information on this field of study but, in outline, the progress made mainly by European and North American scientists in this field allows us to divide the blood of individuals into millions of combinations of different blood group factors.

Probably the only cases where these blood group combinations do not differ, from individual to individual, is in the case of identical twins such as

MIDDLE	4—RIGHT RING	5—RIGHT LITTLE

MIDDLE	9—LEFT RING	10—LEFT LITTLE

MIDDLE	4—RIGHT RING	5—RIGHT LITTLE

MIDDLE	9—LEFT RING	10—LEFT LITTLE

the blood group combination of the victim occurs in x% of the population at large (usually a small fraction of 1%). Perhaps someday blood group evidence will have the same probative value as fingerprints but much research still requires to be done.

The rules of identification

All the examples given up to now show the contrast between the completely unknown identity and the stated or suspected identity. Two rules may be stated: first, in all cases of human identification the new data from the case in question must be checked against data already held and, second, the process is much easier if a stated or suspected identity is supplied.

One might say that, in some cases, a data collection might not exist but this is not true. To enable the problem to be formulated, no matter how subjectively, some data must be available and it is this which forms the basis of all identification procedures irrespective of their size and complexity in the developed form.

mentioned earlier. (Since the twins were distinguished by their fingerprints then we can see that fingerprints have a greater characterizing power than blood groups.) If the laboratory has examined the bloodstains on the suspect's clothing then the lab report would probably take the form of a statement that the blood is of the same group combination as the victim, but of a different blood group combination from the suspect. The evidential value of this finding would then be assessed by saying that

Voice prints

Human beings have been using identification procedures since they appeared on the surface of the earth. The family, or tribe doubtless identified members or strangers by the same processes. In some cases they identified the strangers by the way they spoke. When, in the Old Testament story (Judges XII 6) Jephthah wished to distinguish his own followers from the Ephraimites as they passed Jordan he asked each person to pronounce 'Shibboleth'. Since the Ephraimites pronounced the word 'Sibboleth' (without the 'h') the necessary identification was done.

This was an elementary example of the analysis of speech patterns. A far more complex example occurred recently in the hunt for Peter William Sutcliffe, the so called 'Yorkshire Ripper'. This man, in just over five years between July 1975 and November 1980 killed 13 women at random and attempted to kill seven more.

The Ripper tape

A huge police hunt was mounted and, after a four years fruitless investigation, the chief investigating officer received a cassette tape, purporting to come from the killer, deriding him for his lack of success. Because of the information contained on the tape and in associated letters it was decided that the speaker very probably *was* the 'Yorkshire Ripper'. A huge publicity campaign was mounted during which time anyone could dial a special telephone number to listen to the tape. Anyone who thought they recognized the voice was asked to contact the police.

Linguistic experts were called in to examine the tape and they decided that the speaker grew up in the town of Sunderland in North East England. Local people were consulted and they agreed that the voice was that of a Sunderland man and that he probably came from the Castletown district of Sunderland. Here we note that the people who added the final refinement to the voice diagnosis were the natives of Sunderland themselves.

The 'Yorkshire Ripper' was arrested in January 1981. He proved to be a Bradford man with a Bradford accent and he had no known connection with the tape. The hoaxer who sent the tape is, at

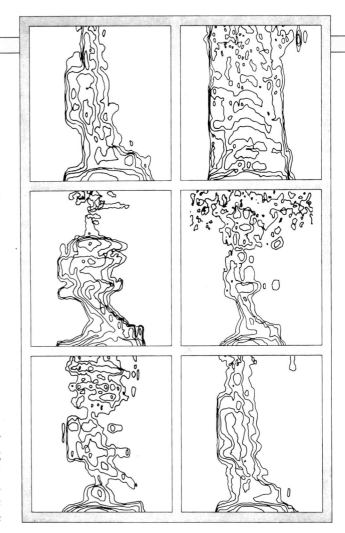

Above: *These voice prints are records of five people saying "you". One person says it twice in a normal and also a falsetto tone. The resulting voice prints look very similar* (upper left and lower right).
Opposite top: *A voice print machine is designed to produce patterns known as "speech spectrograms".*
Opposite below: *The diagram shows how sound is produced, and how male and female voices differ.*

the time of writing, still at large. This action in sending the tape diverted the police from more useful channels of investigation and allowed the Yorkshire Ripper to carry out three more murders and two more attempts before he was finally caught. Police efforts to find the hoaxer continue. When they do, two substantial pieces of evidence will be his voice pattern and the handwriting from the package of the tape and from anonymous letters sent by him to the police.

'Speech spectrograms'

The value of voice patterns in crime investigation is a complicated and controversial field, first brought into the limelight by the experiments, in 1963, of Lawrence G. Kersta at his laboratory in Somerville, New Jersey. The technique has been, since that date, the subject of much research and discussion. Essentially, the method is to examine and compare the 'speech spectrograms' of chosen words and phrases.

This is carried out by reproducing the speech pitch and intensities at intervals of a fraction of a second and comparing the resultant 'speech spectrograms' of the same words when recorded from two different sources. These may be, for example, a recorded telephone call from a blackmailer and a recording made from the voice of a suspect. The Michigan State Police have been using this method with success for investigative purposes since 1968.

However, the method is still very subjective and open to various objections which seem to show that voiceprints are not peculiar to the individual in the same way fingerprints are, despite the fact that they obviously have a good degree of individuality. However, as an investigative tool for the detective, there is little doubt that they are here to stay. Regarding their use as evidence in Courts of Law

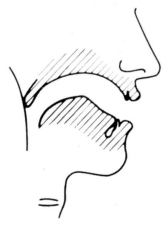

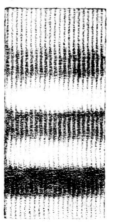

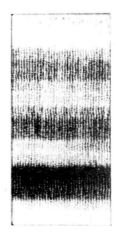

PROFILE   MALE VOICE   FEMALE VOICE

the position is by no means as certain and a committee has been set up in Washington to review the method and to report on its acceptability as an identification technique. Active research on the application of advanced instrumental techniques and statistical methods is being applied to voiceprints at the Forensic Science Institute of the Bundeskriminalamt at Wiesbaden.

Tooth and nail!

Teeth are a remarkably useful means of identification in some cases, particularly those where the identity of a corpse is in question and where little recognizable may be left of the soft tissues upon which we depend for identification (via facial features and fingerprints). Such circumstances may arise during aircraft disasters or where a body is not found until a long time after death. Here the comparison of the teeth of the victim can be made with existing dental charts or X-ray photographs. Both natural features and the nature of dental repair work can be enormously useful as discussed in the chapter on Dentistry.

Even fingernails are peculiar to the individual. Look at your own and see the striations which pass longitudinally from the base to the top (these become more visible as you get older). Now, imagine a criminal clipping his nails at the scene of a crime, the clippings being found by an astute detective, then being shown to match the fingernails of a suspect. Too far-fetched, you might think, but it has been known to happen. Lip prints give another physical attribute which have been shown to be constant to the individual. Research in this field has been carried out in Japan with interesting results. Bone structure can also provide the means of identification, particularly when hospital X-ray records are available. These may show sufficient detail to allow identification of a skeleton either by identifying healed injury or by the general and detailed external and internal structure of the bone. A good example of this is the identification carried out in

Right: *The assembled Bluebell Woods skeleton.*
Opposite left: *The post-mortem skull X-ray.*
Opposite right: *The skull X-ray taken in 1967 showing points of similarity with fig. 2.*

England in the Bluebell Woods case examined by the forensic scientists Russell Stockdale and J.A.J. Ferris.

The Bluebell Woods case

In 1971, while he was birdwatching in the Bluebell Woods near Morpeth in Northumberland, a young boy found a bone near a fox hole, and took it home with him. As his mother was a trained nurse, she recognized that it was human, and got in touch with

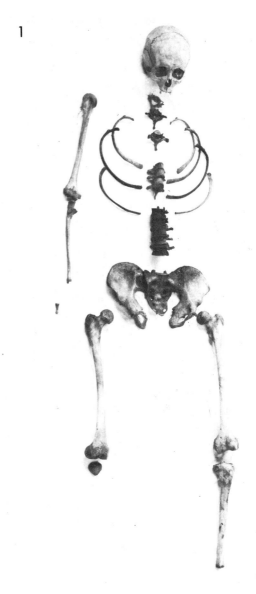

1

the police. Although the area was searched, nothing else was found.

In the meantime N.R. Lee of the Northern Forensic Science Laboratory had examined the bone, which was a left tibia. He estimated that it belonged to a 25 year old adult, and that death had occurred less than three years previously.

About a month later, the Bluebell Woods yielded another find, about half a mile from the original site. Two youths found an almost complete human skull. This time a wide-ranging and intensive search was conducted. The hunt resulted in 28 human bones, some fragments of a man's clothing; also a pair of shoes with the socks inside them (but no foot bones).

The bones all seemed to come from one body, and were assembled into a partial skeleton (fig. 1). A complete examination was made of the bones and the teeth, and the approximate height of the body while living was assessed using orthodox measurement formulae. While alive, the person

would have been around 5ft 4½in (plus or minus 1¾in). Police missing persons files turned up details of a 27 year old patient from a local mental hospital who had disappeared about 9 months previously. The clinical details from his hospital notes tallied with the findings of the forensic scientists, including comparisons of skull X-rays taken by the hospital in 1967. Using one of the X-rays, at least 16 points of similarity were found (figs. 2 and 3), providing positive identification.

But how did he die? There was no evidence of violence on the remains, and, since the shoes and socks were found beside a small river, there was a distinct possibility that he might have drowned. On microscopic examination of bone marrow from the left femur, diatomous material of the type *Navicula* was discovered. Although this is not regarded as final proof of drowning, the presence of diatoms in an enclosed area of the body such as bone marrow would be enough to supply presumptive evidence that the young man had indeed drowned.

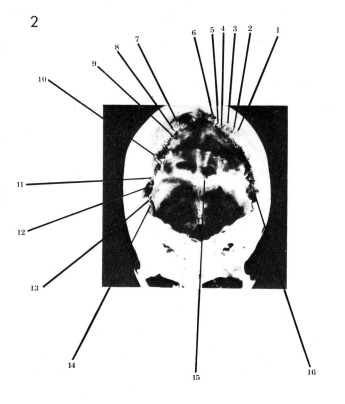

2

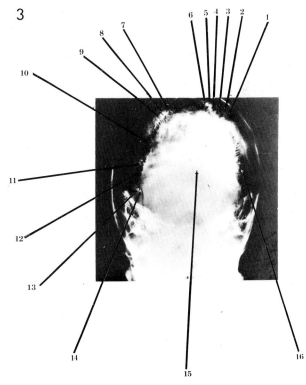

3

MURDERER EXTRAORDINAIRE
Dr. Marcel Petiot

On the face of it, there was no shortage of evidence against Dr Marcel Petiot, murderer extraordinary. When his trial opened in Paris on 18 March 1946 several tonnes of suitcases containing his victims' curiously unidentifiable clothes lined one wall of the courtroom. And that was before one visited No 21 Rue Lesueur, to which a fire and a foul stench had called the police just two years previously.

How many bodies were scattered about this once elegant, but now chaotic three storey house, no one was ever able to determine. Police Commissaire George Massu (the real life original of Simenon's Maigret) had not dared hazard a guess that spring day in 1944 when called to the doctor's house by his colleagues. He had seen the manure pit, filled with quicklime, which crunched underfoot from the quantity of bones dispersed in it. He had inspected another pile of quicklime in the garage, and noted a detached human scalp in its contents. And then there was the sack on the stairs, from whose contents only a foot and some organs were missing.

In the two years it took to catch and bring the doctor to trial the most distinguished forensic scientists in France had sifted the contents of No 21, but, strangely, emerged little the wiser. Bearded Dr Petiot, kindly general practitioner, ex major and — on his account — hero of the Resistance, would face his accusers with astonishing wit and audacity and plead innocence. The case remains as an example of how hard it can be to connect a corpse to a murderer if the latter has been really thorough in his work and can lie his way out of trouble with manic aplomb.

Dr Petiot, owner of No 21, had been thorough. The forensic team, aided by two professors of natural history expert in the assembly of skeletons, put together enough pieces to be certain of ten victims, five men and five women. But unfortunately there were a lot of pieces left over, including 22 toothbrushes (used), three trash cans full of bone fragments too small to identify, 5 kg of human hair — and more than ten scalps. Worse, there was grisly evidence to connect the debris at No 21 with a tide of human remains that had been found floating in the Seine during the last two years — nine severed heads among them.

They too had been made unidentifiable, by the expert removal of face and scalp and the stripping of their fingerprints. But the connection lay in the fact that two thighs, from No 21 and the Seine, bore puncture marks which the head of the forensic team, Dr Paul, swiftly recognized. A pathologist, unlike a surgeon, does not lay down his scalpel when taking a break: he parks it on a convenient part of his client's anatomy.

The thoroughness of the murderer's work won the grudging respect of those who laboured to reassemble it. The dismemberment of the bodies showed a great attention to detail and a knowledge of anatomy that was expert if unorthodox. Long

bones had been broken — probably in a door jamb, speculated Dr Paul — to disguise any deformities that could lead to identification. And all this was before incineration in the stove and scattering in quicklime had added to the destruction. Baffled, the experts sought for (and never found) any trace of the means of death. There were no bullets, no

Below: *The Petiot trial. The piles of suitcases in the background are filled with his victims' belongings — one source of identification.*

poisons, not even any fingerprints. Nor, in the quantity of suitcases and possessions, was there any address or personal identification.

For Parisians, when the news broke, the chamber of horrors at No 21 was a gruesome entertainment of compelling fascination. How had so many, noticed by so few, vanished from the face of the earth? Some estimates put the total at 60. And above all, what was the secret of the triangular room?

The triangular room had two doors. One led from the doctor's consulting room (the only cosily furnished room in the gloomy house). Once inside the room you noticed that there was no handle on the inside. The other door had a bell beside it. Commissaire Massu forced the door open: it was mounted flat against a brick wall. The bell wires led nowhere.

Eight iron rings were mounted on one wall. Apart from a naked light bulb hung from the ceiling, that was all. Did Dr Petiot's patients, after a friendly consultation and perhaps an injection to calm their nerves, enter this room to meet their doom? Were they strung up from the iron rings to die at leisure? When Massu removed the wallpaper he found a spyhole that gave a good view of the rings — and anyone who might have been strung up there. But the wallpaper had been in position for years. On the other side of the wall, the whitewash was unmarked by any ladder or hand used to climb up to view in. This small mystery was typical.

When the greasy smoke from No 21 first alerted its neighbours and brought the police, they couldn't get in, but enquired at neighbours, who gave them Dr Petiot's home number. "I'll be there in fifteen minutes," Petiot promised. And he was, on a green bicycle. Hardly the response of a guilty man.

Meanwhile, dazed firemen had reeled out of the house after finding a stove roaring out of control with a slim hand trailing from the open door. They had already stumbled over two skeletons, a staircase littered with skulls, and sides of flesh, rib cages broken open like the wrecks of ancient ships.

The man on the bicycle was alone in his cool command of the situation. Identifying himself as the *brother* of the owner of No 21 (a typical Petiot touch) the good doctor said: "This is a serious matter. It might cost my head." And then, while the fumes of the burning horrors of No 21 rose around them he explained: "Je suis chef d'une groupe de Résistance." The bodies were those of Germans and traitors. He had 300 files at home to destroy before the Germans found them. In wartime Paris, when so many people disappeared without trace, he was

Above: *Petiot in the dock.*

convincing. With a wink and a nod, Marcel Petiot remounted his bicycle and pedalled away.

It took months to catch up with him.

The trial, when it arrived, was flamboyant (Petiot himself had promised his jailors it would be 'wonderful', 'amusing'). For the defence was Renet Floriot, that brilliant specialist in apparently hopeless cases. When Floriot bent his hornrimmed spectacles on a client he saw not a human being but a challenge to his legal skills.

With Floriot behind them, people had walked out of the court after stealing 20 million francs. Teamed with the amazing doctor, the pair would reduce the court to hysteria and near apoplexy.

Petiot was unabashed by prosecuting counsel's rehearsal of his early life and crimes — an accepted opening gambit in French courts. So he had tortured kittens as a child? Had been in and out of mental hospitals? Had qualified as a doctor in doubtful circumstances and risen to the status of country mayor with the aid of such little tricks as fusing the town's electricity supply when his opponent was due to speak? Petiot could produce plenty of witnesses to state that unlike other mayors he had fixed the town sewage system — and unlike other doctors he would cycle miles to see a sick baby. None of this mattered: the court was agog for the doctor's explanation of the pile of corpses at No 21. "What about the bodies at rue Lesueur?" asked the state prosecutor, Leser. "I was very annoyed," said Petiot briskly. "I didn't want that sort of thing in my house."

The explanation, said Petiot, was simple. During the war, he had been running an intrepid Resis-

tance group, called Fly-Tox (after the name of a well known insect repellant). No one in court had heard of the group? Well, that proved how successful it was. Could he not produce some of his colleagues? No, that might endanger them — after all, he, Petiot was in danger, despite his heroism, at the hands of you people who are just collaborators and Nazi-lovers.

Fly-Tox was devoted to good works. At great risk to himself, Petiot had arranged the escape abroad of countless people to South America and elsewhere. Where are all these people? asked the prosecution, who had been interviewing their equally countless relatives and been endeavouring to track the escapees' careers after the day they had certainly presented themselves to Dr Petiot with large sums of money to pay their passage — and all their wealth in suitcases.

Goodness knew where they were now — but many had written letters or telegrammed home. That was true: the prosecution was sure Petiot had written these letters himself and they produced a graphologist to prove it. For the defence, Floriot demolished the pompous expert at a stroke. "Can you tell me if what I have just written is what I truly believe?" he asked the distinguished M. Rougemont. The note read: "Monsieur Rougemont is a distinguished scholar who never makes mistakes."

But these were diversions. There was a solid core of corpses that the police had identified from the debris at No 21 and there were facts to prove their demise followed soon after a visit to the doctor. No problem: Petiot admitted their slaughter. They were, he explained, traitors and Gestapo spies who had been sent to penetrate his Resistance group. He deserved a medal for dispatching them. How could anyone think otherwise? Had not he, Petiot, been a prisoner of the Gestapo during the war and been tortured (which was true)? As for the extra corpses; they must have been left there by his unnameable colleagues.

The outcome of the case was inevitable because the jurors (and everyone else) knew in their guts that Dr Petiot was guilty as hell and they sent him down on May 25 1946 to the guillotine. Yet despite all the grisly remains, no one ever discovered how he had done it, why he had done it — or, in most cases, to whom he had done it. The case remains one of the massive failures of science to combat diligent and wholesale butchery, because Petiot was convicted on sentiment alone.

He faced the guillotine with sardonic aplomb. And according to one photographer's account he was still smiling after his head left the scene.

Facial recognition techniques

The best currently available record of facial appearance is a good photograph. Failing this, attempts to provide substitutes may be made. These substitutes can take the form of recorded verbal descriptions, artists' impressions stemming from verbal descriptions (it's not often a good artist actually witnesses a crime and can produce a useful drawing) or facial assembly techniques. These assembly techniques, of which one of the best known is the Photofit, depend upon an experienced operator assembling the major facial features (lips, nose, hairline etc) into a composite under the guidance of an eyewitness.

The finished product will reflect the recollection of the witness, his ability to put it into words, the comprehension of the operator, or artist, and finally, his ability to produce a finished product which the witness agrees is a fair reproduction of his sense impressions at the scene. Many facial assembly techniques have been proposed each leading to a more or less accurate physical representation of the recollections of eyewitnesses. Penry's 'Photofit' is a good example of this.

Other systems

Amongst other systems used are the Identikit assembly method where line drawings of facial features are brought together to give a facial picture. This facial outline method has recently been refined using a computer technique where the final composite appears on a video display unit (VDU) and where the various constituent characteristics are computer stored. Convenient though the outline method is, it suffers from at least one drawback in that all information used is in two dimensions only. This means that only *outline* information can be recorded whereas eyewitness evidence is at least three dimensions.

The eyewitness sees the dimensions, length, breadth and depth. If we add to this extra 'dimensions' such as that of colour, texture and so on it can be seen that two dimensional reproduction cannot possibly use all the information available. To overcome this problem, methods such as the Photofit system have been proposed where the assembly of facial characteristics enjoys the added dimension of 'tone' (that is the distribution of light and dark available in black and white photographs).

Feature assembly method

This assembly method was first conceived by Detective Constable Albert Simpson, of the Nottingham City Police, England in 1955. Simpson's

Below: *Facial recognition techniques include the Identikit system shown here which combines line drawings of different facial features.*

idea was to assemble, on a pocket mechanical device to be carried by all police officers, a composite photograph where each feature could be described according to an accepted code, which would then be circulated to other police officers. The actual assembly would then be carried out by each individual police officer.

Simpson's method was years ahead of its time. The advent of computer techniques with their enormous capacity for information storage and recall, colour television and microwave radio transmission leaves little doubt in the writer's mind that if Simpson's idea comes to fruition, it will be in the form of pocket colour television receivers, programmed not by the police officer carrying it but by a central agency. However, the idea did have an immediate spinoff in that it led to production of the widely used Photofit method.

Computerization
Facial analysis and assembly methods are of great potential value in crime detection. Photographs of criminals taken either in custody or during the commission of a crime provide great potential for identification when associated with computer methods of information storage and assessment. Although much is said nowadays of the inaccessibility of science to the ordinary man it seems that here is a problem amenable to the approach of the home science enthusiast. Computer techniques are becoming more accessible, photographs and video methods are easily available and all these associated with some originality and mathematical ability may well provide a variety of useful solutions to this crime investigation problem.

Handwriting analysis
Surprisingly, handwriting identification provides a similar problem to facial recognition techniques. However, handwriting characteristics are different in the sense that they are rather more easily modifiable than facial features. Despite this, handwriting examination has been the source of many successes in crime detection. It does however require the profound expertise resulting from long experience and the critical approach.

Handwriting opinions originating from the non-specialist can have disastrous consequences as shown by the involvement of the great French identification expert, Bertillon, in the Dreyfus affair (See page 28). Surprisingly, one does not even have to know the language in which script is handwritten! It seems that the same principles may be applied in any language.

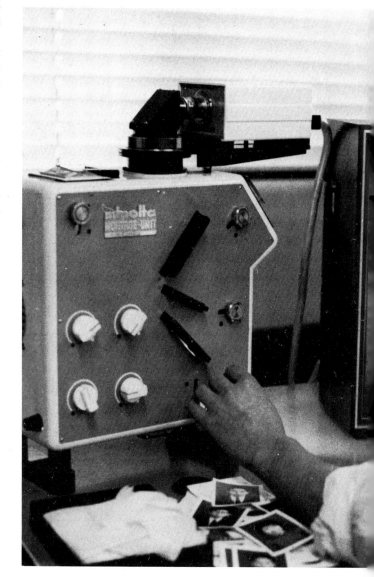

Right: The latest advances in facial recognition techniques incorporate electronics as shown in this Japanese VDU system.

Analysing human hair

Human hair, particularly head hair, figures in many criminal cases. Currently the evidential value of such hair transfer is dependent upon microscopic comparison. The information produced is of comparatively limited value. Some Canadian work on the analysis of the chemical constitution of the hair was at one time thought to be extremely promising but the initial promise has not been maintained. However, some fairly recent work, also in Canada, on the use of microscopic visual features in hair may indicate the way forward in this area of research.

This work involves the visual microscopic assessment of various hair characteristics and the subjective allocation of the head hair into a particular slot in a classification system designed for the purpose. Statistical calculation then yields an estimate of the relative commonness or uncommonness of the hair in question.

The method, however, contains a basic difficulty (some would say a basic flaw). This difficulty relates to allocating different classes by the subjective examination of things which are continuously variable. In other words how can we be sure that a second operator will make the same classification as the first operator? The only way to find out how effective such a method is is by the application of 'blind trials'. These are tests where the examiner is asked to classify a set of hairs where the true result is known only to the tester. Such trials are in common use in forensic science laboratories throughout the world and it seems likely that they may soon be extended on an international basis.

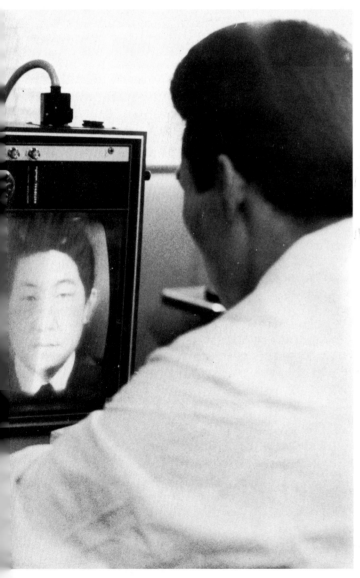

Above: *William Henry Podmore* (left) *and his victim Vivian Messiter* (right). *The 1930 murder case made headlines in the English press because of the brutality of the crime. In his examination of the body, the great pathologist Sir Bernard Spilsbury found two eyebrow hairs on the murder weapon which matched those of Messiter. Although this merely confirmed that a hammer was in fact used to kill Messiter, the press ran the headline "Two hairs hanged this man". There was plenty of other evidence pointing to Podmore, but the two hairs certainly helped.*

Pioneers in identification techniques

We have talked at length about visual recognition and it is surprising to realize that little more than 100 years ago this was the only method in use for the identification of habitual criminals or 'recidivists'. When a person was arrested for a crime it was common for him to give a false identity. If the police were not able to establish the true identity of the criminal this often meant that he would escape with a light sentence as a first offender or that he could avoid being charged with crimes he had committed in another part of the country.

A common method of establishing identity was for detectives regularly to visit prisons and watch the prisoners so as to imprint their faces on the memory. This method was commonly used by the Inspectors of the French Sûreté since its establishment by the famous criminal-turned-policeman, Eugène François Vidocq, in 1810.

Vidocq, by his knowledge of the criminal fraternity of France, enjoyed a most successful career for 23 years, during which time he set up a most effective system of crime detection (mainly run by ex-criminals). Vidocq maintained extensive records for the identification of criminals and these included drawings and descriptions of their appearances and their methods of work. Around the middle of the nineteenth century, photography began to be applied to criminal record purposes and this was a substantial step forward.

Below: Eugène Vidocq founded the Paris Sûreté in the early nineteenth century. His identification system included drawings and other extensive records of criminals, such as details of their characteristic working habits.

Alphonse Bertillon

However, identification record systems still lacked one major and necessary feature. Nowhere was there available a key which would allow the swift sorting of such information. The massive accumulation of personal records necessitated an army of clerks to administer it and, as the number of records increased, so did the number of clerks. It was against the background of this groaning and rickety system that a remarkable Frenchman emerged, Alphonse Bertillon. From all accounts Bertillon was a social misfit. Despite coming from a family of distinguished scientists, in his youth Bertillon showed no promise of following in the family footsteps. Expelled from several schools, he passed some time as an apprentice clerk in a bank before being sacked. Finally, through the influence of his father, he obtained a job as a junior records clerk in the Sûreté.

His job was to complete the record cards of convicted criminals and to determine if an arrested criminal already had a record for previous offences. The system of personal records had largely outlived its initial usefulness and soon the youthful Bertillon (he was appointed at the age of 25) began to realize the futility of his job. Great mountains of dust-covered criminal records were being increased by the addition of further cards. These yielded little profit save the assurance of the continued employment of the army of clerks who serviced them.

Bertillon's experiments

Within a few months of his appointment Bertillon was experimenting with classification systems based on facial features cut from criminal record photographs. He became the target for the jokes of his fellow clerks who thought it greatly amusing to see their new colleague cutting out individual noses or ears and then comparing them in montage, side by side. Here Bertillon's obsessive determination asserted itself. One has only to imagine the position of a young man thrust into a 70 year old system which, in its heyday as a backup for the remarkable Vidocq and his successors, had been a powerful weapon in the fight against crime.

Despite all this Bertillon carried on doggedly with his experiments. He remembered, from his childhood, the interest of his doctor father in the work of the Belgian biometrician Quételét. Quételét's hypothesis was that no two human beings had the same physical measurements. Thus, if the height of an individual were measured together with a selection of other measurements from the enormous number possible (for example, circumference of head, length of feet, length of ears), then the combination of measurements resulting would be highly characteristic of the individual. The more features measured then the

Below left: A wanted notice issued in Boston in 1898 published the Bertillon measurements of the wanted man. The inventor of this system, Alphonse Bertillon (below right) revolutionized the Paris Sûreté's approach to criminal identification.

more characteristic the combination would be until the stage was reached when the odds against coincidence would be so high that for practical purposes the combination of measurements would be unique.

The reader will immediately see the greater chance of coincidence when related individuals are involved. Obviously, with the case of identical twins the greatest difficulty would be presented but there are visual physical differences even between identical twins. However, one might think that for *practical* purposes the identical twin case would give little difficulty! Bertillon spotted the potential value of Quételét's work in criminal identification and so he set about proving his point.

An interesting digression is appropriate here. Although there is little doubt that Bertillon's idea occurred to him independently, what he didn't know was that nineteen years earlier Stevens, Director of the Louvain prison in Belgium, had proposed anthropometry, physical measurement, as a system for classifying and identifying individuals. Stevens had even gone so far as to suggest the measurements which should be used. He proposed, amongst others, the length of the ears, the length of the feet and the circumference of the head. Stevens' ideas, however, were not adopted. Possibly he did not have the same determination as Bertillon!

An exactly parallel situation had occurred two years earlier in 1877 when William Herschel, an official of the British colonial authority in India, had attempted to persuade the Inspector General of Prisons in Bengal to adopt fingerprinting for criminal record purposes. However, like the Belgian Stevens, Herschel obviously was not blessed, or perhaps cursed, with the same degree of determination as Bertillon.

The 'portrait parlé'
Bertillon went about proving his point firstly by obtaining permission to measure convicts brought in for registration. He measured height, length of feet, arms and fingers. Before long he was convinced that his system held the key to the problem of identification in the Paris Sûreté. In October 1879 Bertillon sent a report on his system

to the head of the Sûreté. It was rejected. He tried exerting influence through his eminent father with no success. In the event he had to wait another three years before authority gave him an opportunity to carry out a trial of his system.

When he got the chance it was of such a grudging variety that fainter hearts would not have even tried. With the assistance of two clerks he was given three months, from December 1882 to February 1883, to prove his point. What had to happen, for Bertillon to succeed, was for a criminal to be caught, sentenced, measured by Bertillon, serve his sentence, be released then be rearrested for another crime and measured by Bertillon, all within the three months allowed.

On February 29 1883, with only two weeks to go, Bertillon took the measurements of a thief called Dupont. Going to his index Bertillon retrieved a card, bearing the same measurements of a criminal named Martin who had been measured two months previously. They were the same man and Bertillon's system of identification was launched!

The decline of Bertillonage
In Bertillon's hands the system went from strength to strength over the next few years but the seeds of its decay were already planted. A workable system of fingerprints classification was in use in Argentina in 1891 and when, in 1892, a murder was detected by fingerprints in that country this proved the death blow of the Bertillon system in countries other than France. Apart from rearguard action, fingerprints took over from *Bertillonage*. An amusing sidelight is provided by the appointment, in 1893, of a British Government committee to enquire into the use of identification methods including both Bertillon's system and fingerprints. The committee recommended *both*. It made no difference! By 1900 the British had changed their minds and fingerprints totally displaced anthropometry in the United Kingdom. It seems that even the famous British gift for compromise fell before the onslaught of fingerprints.

Opposite: *A page from* The Illustrated London News, *June 30 1928, discusses the role of Bertillon's 'word portraits' in scientific detection.*

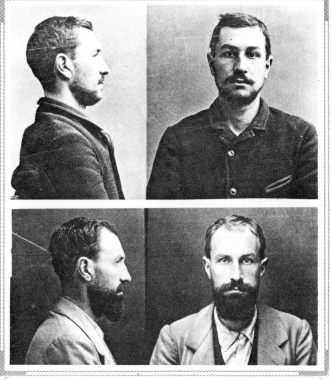

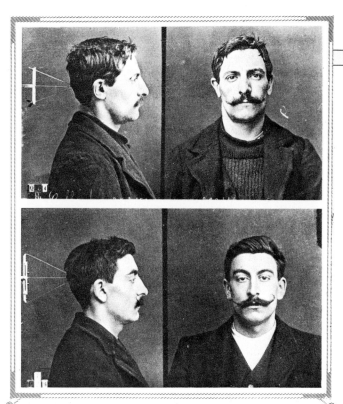

FIG. 3. IDENTITY REVEALED (DESPITE BEARD) BY THE SPIRAL LOBE OF THE EAR AND THE FACIAL ANGLE: BERTILLON PHOTOGRAPHS (FULL-FACE AND PROFILE) OF THE SAME MAN AT TEN YEARS' INTERVAL.

FIG. 4. MISTAKEN IDENTITY ESTABLISHED BY DIFFERENCES IN THE EARS, NOSE, AND "ADAM'S APPLE": BERTILLON PHOTOGRAPHS (FULL-FACE AND PROFILE) OF TWO DIFFERENT MEN EASILY MISTAKEN FOR EACH OTHER

FIG. 5. A CLASS FOR DETECTIVES HELD AT THE HEADQUARTERS OF THE PARIS POLICE: DEMONSTRATIONS OF M. BERTILLON'S ANTHROPOMETRIC CHART (SEEN IN THE LEFT BACKGROUND) OF PHYSICAL CHARACTERISTICS TERMED *LE PORTRAIT PARLÉ* "THE WORD-PORTRAIT" ILLUSTRATED BY PHOTOGRAPHS AND BLACKBOARD DRAWINGS

Thus, we can see how events can be conditioned not only by chance but also by the determination of individuals. Bertillon was a remarkable man and his work in crime investigation, particularly crime scene investigation, exerts an influence even today. It was Bertillon's concept of the *portrait parlé* (the comparison of the individual features of faces mentioned earlier) that stimulated Detective Simpson to propose in 1955 the system which was to become Penry's 'Photofit'.

Today the anthropometric system as proposed by Bertillon is considered an outdated oddity but there are signs that the basic ideas underlying the system are remarkably resilient. Modern work in Switzerland describes the application of techniques of measurement of the human form in questions of disputed paternity. Measurements of the mother and child are carried out and the results compared with measurements from the body of the alleged father using defined mathematical rules. The method is claimed to be complementary to blood-grouping methods.

Famous identification disputes

Both Bertillon's anthropometry system and the fingerprint system were produced too late to be of any value in the famous 'Tichborne Claimant' case in England (see the case history in this chapter). The physical evidence produced consisted of the comparison of photographs and portraits of the Claimant and Roger Tichborne but not in a systematic fashion such as used by Bertillon.

Perhaps the material available was not sufficient to allow a definite decision, but the existence of such a method would have ensured the best use of the existing photographs. Had the significance of fingerprints been understood at the time, perhaps this would have provided a solution. The existence of a single fingerprint, identical to a fingerprint of the Claimant, on something belonging to Roger Tichborne would have been sufficient to clinch the case.

Possibly the truth will never now be known but on the other hand it is not beyond all conjecture. Much of the evidence in the criminal trial was published. The summing up of the Judge ran to well over a quarter of a million words. Will modern

A BARONET FROM WAGGA WAGGA
The Tichborne Claimant

The most stupendous legal proceedings in history date from a day in 1865 when a stout, uncouth man emerged from his hut in Wagga Wagga, deep in the Australian bush, and announced he was the long lost Sir Roger Charles Tichborne, heir to fortunes in Hampshire, England.

The Tichborne Claimant, as he became known, set in motion a drama on which the dust has not finally settled. The trials ran for years, involved 36,000 cross examination questions and defence counsel speeches that lasted months. Even the sending of special commissions to Australia and Chile failed to prove to everyone's satisfaction whether the Tichborne Claimant was a long-lost son of the aristocracy or Arthur Orton, a butcher from Wapping, London.

Today, science has taken the fun out of questions of mistaken identity — the basic plot of most of Gilbert and Sullivan's operas. Our blood group, chromosomal arrangement, and fingerprints all tell tales to deny

Below: *A daguerrotype of Sir Riger Tichborne as a young man shows him to be a handsome specimen.*

Above: *The Tichborne Claimant during the trial.*
Below: *The Claimant's alleged home in Wagga Wagga.*

spoken or written words to the contrary. (Lie detectors and modern graphology will take care of those.) No longer will any human being be able to withstand the rigours of thorough scientific examination and claim he is someone he is not.

As it was, the Tichborne Claimant endured ten years of trial, ten years of penal servitude after, and 12 years of miserable obscurity before dying on All Fools' Day, 1898 with the name Sir Roger Doughty-Tichborne defiantly engraved on his coffin. The question remains, could any impostor have had such stamina?

The original Sir Roger was born in Paris in 1829 into a family that had been piling up its fortune in England since before the Conquest. When he vanished in 1854 he was a young man with a taste for too much alcohol and tobacco and a frustrated love for his wealthy cousin Katharine Doughty. He left England on a self-improvement trip abroad — 'specially in the drinking line'. After adventures in the Andes he went down in the shipwreck of the *Bella,* bound from Rio to New York.

Unless the *Bella* never went down, was renamed the *Osprey* and found her way to Australia, as would later be suggested.

The insurers paid out. Sir Roger's father and then his younger brother died, leaving the latter's infant son to dream of collecting the inheritance in due course. Only Roger's mother, the Dowager Lady Tichborne, refused to

believe her favourite son had departed this world. But then, everyone knew she had always been a curmudgeonly old trout. In 1865, 11 years after the event, she wrote to Mr Cubitt's Missing Friends Office in Australia seeking aid in her quest.

Cubitt's eyes lit up. Times were hard. There was no shortage of Missing Friends in Australia; most of them with every intention of staying missing. But it was difficult to see why any black sheep would not prefer to be grazing the ample home pastures of Tichborne. His enquiries led swiftly to a butcher contemplating bankruptcy in Wagga Wagga, who had mentioned to his lawyer that he had property in Hampshire.

Almost anyone else, on the face of it, would have been a more likely candidate than the butcher, He was living under the name of Thomas Castro and, after an initial show of reluctance at having his cover blown, was brought to Sydney for inspection. He impressed most who met him as being a slob of the first order. But 'notwithstanding his dirt, bad English and uncouth look, his manner is so utterly unlike that of an impostor that I am inclined to believe in him' reported one of the first to interview him.

Therein lay the roots of the vast appeal that the Claimant would have for the working classes, who in their confused way would see him as a symbol of their own struggle to relieve the landed classes of their wealth. The writer Karl Marx was expressing similar notions in a book called *Das Kapital* at about the time Sir Roger came back from the grave.

The Claimant liked Sydney, and his hotel — which he promptly bought for £10,000 — and wrote a letter to dear mother, after all this time, seeking expenses that would enable him to leave the colony. The first shock waves of trouble to come reached the trustees of the Tichborne Estate.

Even before leaving Sydney, Sir Roger (as he is now to be called) had acquired his first useful ally, Bogle, an elderly negro servant who had been with him in previous years. The recognition was mutual and joyful. Just as joyful, sceptics would say, was Old Bogle's delight at the prospect of a return fare to England.

It remained to face mother in Paris. Few would believe that a mother could not recognize her own flesh and blood, or that anyone would be so rash as to attempt such a deceit. "This is my son," she exclaimed, bending to kiss him in the darkened hotel room where he was lying muffled up and indisposed. The trustees of the Tichborne Estate reached for their sedatives.

Until her death 18 months later, Lady Tichborne never wavered in her support. Sir Roger, back on a £1000 allowance, got busy on the task of ousting the current tenant of Tichborne and prising the annual £25,000 rent roll out of the Trustees. It took him six years to bring the

case to court, and when the case opened on May 11 1871 the world was neatly divided into two camps. There were those who could report how, on meeting Sir Roger, they had been impressed by his knowledge of some intimate little detail that proved his authenticity.

On the other side were those who had noted some monumental gap in his memory that proved his falsehood. Whatever else one might lose in the Australian bush, for example, it was difficult to understand how one could misplace all knowledge of one's first language, French, or the tattoos off one's arms.

The tattoos were, however, but one of many demonstrations that no human being can reliably be counted on to remember a single coherent fact, and that most people are lying in their teeth most of the time. The evidence of those who swore Sir Roger was tattooed was balanced by those who swore he wasn't. As the dazed jurors watched the lawyers slugging it out and their own lives slipping away from them, some of them experimented with blue pencils to create tattoos that would be here on Monday and gone on Tuesday.

A curious aspect of the case was that, as it expanded to involve witnesses by the hundred, Sir Roger expanded with it. The man who had supposedly perished in the *Bella's* shipwreck had been 'of delicate constitution,

for perjury. Which meant a new trial.

Appetites thoroughly whetted, the public was agog for the rerun. Public subscription funded Sir Roger's release on bail and he stumped the country raising funds for his defence. Brass bands and firework displays marked his passage. A year dragged by while witnesses were winkled out of the distant Andes and Australia by the shipload (the defence would promise to call 253). The prosecution painstakingly prepared to demonstrate again that during Sir Roger's missing years a certain Arthur Orton, a far-flung butcher from Wapping, had been following the baronet's progress around the world with unfailing doggedness. Sir Roger admitted to knowing Orton. They confronted Orton's parents with him. The Ortons denied he was their son with the same conviction Lady Tichborne had announced he was hers.

By the time Sir Roger's defence counsel, Dr Kenealy, had wandered all through the evidence again Lord Chief Justice Cockburn had marked him down for personal retribution later. No witness was left unsavaged or unsmirched after Kenealy had done with him. Sir Roger was so grossly ignorant that he was unaware if Caesar figured in Greek or Latin events?. Well, everyone knew that the Jesuits at his public school were ignorant too, and come to that perverted.

It was February 28 1874 before Lord Chief Justice Cockburn finished a summing up that had itself gone on for a month and would make two fat volumes when printed. The jury was in no mind to notch up any more records for longevity. Some felt there was no need to retire from the dock at all, but it was thought better to make a token disappearance. As Sir Roger heard their feet pattering back up the stairs he gloomily gave his watch to Old Bogle's son as a parting gift. Outside the court, 600 police struggled to contain a boisterous crowd.

Sir Roger, declared the foreman, was not Sir Roger. He was Arthur Orton and guilty of perjury. The judges sent him down for 14 years penal servitude. 'Goodbye Sir Roger! I am sorry for you,' said his counsel as they took him away.

Curiously, in prison, his hair did not revert to the carrot red of Arthur Orton. Curiously, too, his letters to his supporters have the dignity and impeccable spelling of an educated man. But there is no end to the curiousities of the Tichborne case.

Released after ten years, he determindly went back on the campaign trail, which dwindled to signing autographs in public houses. Desperate for money, he allowed a ghosted 'confession' to be printed, then retracted it. He died on April 1 1898 in poverty, at the dawn of a new world of science that, had it risen earlier, would have spared him, one way or the other, his long ordeal.

rather tall and thin'. The figure that confronted the jurors with his favourite reply to any question, 'I don't remember,' now blocked out the light at a monumental 27 stone.

To defend this apparition it was necessary to demonstrate that if Sir Roger nowadays looked like a monster he had not been much better in his youth. Sir Roger's counsel flung cartloads of mud at the long-suffering Tichborne family, in the effort to show that with such a background a man could well slouch off to the back of beyond in shame. The *hoi polloi* in the gutter outside the court found this demolition job on the private lives of the upper classes much to their taste.

Cousin Katherine, the erstwhile beloved and now the eminently respectable Lady Radcliffe, was in court when Sir Roger finally went over the top. Sensationally, he announced that one reason he had left home was because he had feared with good reason he had got his cousin pregnant. He had written as much in the contents of a sealed package, which he presumed was lost. Unfortunately, it was not lost: it was produced in court and shown to contain nothing more than a promise to build his cousin a church.

That should have been the end of it. Sir Roger's civil case was dismissed. Next, of course, he had to be arrested methods of text analysis and statistics someday perhaps yield the solution? Will examination of photographs of the Claimant and those not only of Roger Tichborne but of Tichborne's relatives prove amenable to techniques such as those of the Swiss workers in disputed paternity mentioned earlier?

The Claimant claimed to be the eleventh baronet, Sir Roger Tichborne. About a hundred years later an obituary of the 14th baronet, Sir Anthony Tichborne, contained the following phrase 'He was largely built – with a disconcertingly striking resemblance to the Victorian Claimant...'! As one modern observer recently put it: 'The Claimant's story was incredible if it was true but even more incredible if it was false.'

The Anastasia case

The doubt which surrounded the Tichborne Claimant cannot however be said to surround the case of Madame Tchaikovsky who claimed to be the Grand Duchess Anastasia Nicolaievna, the youngest daughter of the Czar of Russia and the only survivor of the Russian Royal family who were murdered by the Bolsheviks at Ekaterinburg in July 1918. Madame Tchaikovsky claimed to have escaped the massacre with the help of a Russian soldier named Tchaikovsky whom she subsequently married. Madame Tchaikovsky was identified by several persons as the Grand Duchess Anastasia.

The most impressive of these witnesses was an old nurse of the Imperial family who identified her as Anastasia. The supporters and opponents of Madame Tchaikovsky were many and her ambiguous position, which she maintained for seven years, was finally determined in 1927 by Professor Mark Bischoff of the Institute of Police Science in the University of Lausanne in Switzerland. Bischoff examined photographs of Madame Tchaikovsky and of Duchess Anastasia. These were adjusted in size and superimposed in profile for comparison purposes. Similar procedures were used for comparing the right ears on photographs of Madame Tchaikovsky and the Duchess Anastasia. The differences were sufficient to prove that the photographs were of two different people.

If confirmation were needed it came the following year with the publication in American newspapers, of photographs purporting to be of the claimant, Madame Tchaikovsky. Professor Bischoff examined these by the methods outlined above and proved that they were in fact retouched copies of a genuine photograph of the Duchess.

The Dreyfus affair

Handwriting is often considered to be peculiar to the individual but it is a field of great difficulty and it requires great experience and many built-in controls to be both safe and effective. The famous Dreyfus affair resulted in the conviction of a French Army officer, Alfred Dreyfus, for spying. The affair shook and divided France in the same way the Tichborne Claimant case did England. Dreyfus' conviction rested largely on a handwriting comparison made by Bertillon who concluded that Dreyfus had written the note in question (the famous 'bordereau'). Bertillon applied his concepts from anthropometry in the examination. Subsequently Dreyfus was found to be innocent of the charge and released from prison. The affair cast a cloud over Bertillon's distinguished career and showed once again that one should apply with great caution identification methods produced for one field of study to another.

Left: *Alfred Dreyfus, the protagonist in one of the most famous French cases. He was convicted of being the author of a letter, known as the bordereau, which contained evidence of the betrayal of key military information to Germany. Dreyfus was trapped into penning a test letter (see right), and Bertillon was asked to compare the handwriting. Although he hadn't any expertise in this field, he concluded that Dreyfus had written the bordereau. Dreyfus was disgraced, deported for life. Not until 1906 was he declared innocent — 12 years after his trial.*

THE FORENSIC SCIENCE LABORATORY

The apocryphal story telling how Archimedes of Syracuse one day leapt from his bath crying, "eureka" is one of the earliest examples of science in support of law in the documented history of civilized man. Archimedes was faced with determining precisely the gold content of the metal used to make the king's ornate crown. The goldsmiths said it was of the highest purity but the king was suspicious and had charged Archimedes with devising a method whereby their honesty could be tested. He knew all about measurement of weight and the density of various metals. Yet until inspiration struck him that day as he lay contemplating the immersion of his limbs, and the proportional displacement of the bath water, the problem of how he could measure the volume of that irregularly shaped precious object had defeated him.

Nearer to the present day, in the latter half of the eighteenth century, a Swedish chemist named Scheele wrestled with a different but equally perplexing forensic problem – that of detecting arsenic in the bodies of poison victims. Arsenic (arsenious oxide) had been a widely used and favourite tool of the poisoner for centuries. It was not only devastatingly effective but the symptoms of arsenic poisoning were often mistaken for the symptoms of cholera and, until Scheele's discovery of an analytical method in 1775, it had been virtually undetectable in the body after death. Sheele's method was not the end of the story since it only detected arsenic present in large quantities, but his work did stimulate his contemporaries to pursue that elusive metal and, at the same time, caused would-be poisoners to begin to search elsewhere for the 'perfect' murder weapon.

There are many more accounts in this book of apparently isolated early triumphs of science against crime. Surprisingly then, as a discipline in its own right, forensic science got off to a late and shaky start, particularly in the United Kingdom.

Although by the late eighteenth and early nineteenth centuries scientists all over the world, and in a variety of fields, had contributed to the deliberations of criminal courts, it was left to a few visionaries of less than 100 years ago to point the way towards the establishment of forensic science as an integral part of any system of justice. Hans Gros, Professor of Criminal Law at the University of Graz in Austria, published his book, *Criminal Investigation* in 1892. Regularly revised and up-dated, this book is still consulted today and reveals its author as probably the first man fully to understand and appreciate the importance of scientific evidence. A few years later, in 1902, Professor R. A. Reiss set up a department at the Swiss University of Lausanne to teach forensic science. His department has since grown to the much acclaimed Lausanne Institute of Police Science.

Locard's exchange principle

At the University of Lyon in France in 1910, Edmund Locard formulated his exchange principle in which he postulated that the criminal always leaves something behind at the scene of his crime

Above: *A bayonet blade is examined for blood and other stains under ultra violet light.*

which was not there before and, similarly, carries away with him something which was not on him when he arrived. For example, a man who stabs another to death may very well carry away evidence of his deed as stains of the victim's blood upon his clothes. At the same time, in the struggle, minute cloth fibres from the killer's clothes might be left on the victim.

The principle works in non-violent crimes too. A house-breaker who cuts himself in the process of climbing through a window he has just smashed may leave behind evidence of his visit as stains of his own blood on the window sill. He may also carry away with him fragments of glass and paint from the point of entry lodged in his clothes.

Locard's principle is an important one. It is the embodiment of much of the thinking and practice upon which modern forensic science laboratories all over the world are operated. We shall return to the exchange principle later.

If we regard a crime as a complex event in history – for that is what it is, an interaction in time and space between people and things – we can see that each creates a unique set of problems. These problems do, nevertheless, have common themes and involve the posing of some basic general questions applicable to all crimes. It is within the framework of such questions that the forensic scientist begins his work providing information, in the first instance, to the investigating police officer.

"Has a crime been committed?"

The forensic scientist can often provide inceptive information to help the investigating officer make up his mind about a particular situation and decide whether a crime has been committed, or whether there is some other explanation.

During the early hours of one morning in a North of England town, a patrolling policeman chanced upon what looked like a spent .22 cartridge and a trail of bloodstains. A local hospital rightly confirmed that the stains were indeed bloodstains and as there had never been any doubt about the cartridge, the murder investigation machine swung into action. By mid-day no body had been found but a forensic scientist had been called in to help. Help he did: he showed that the blood was dog's blood! Eventually the true story unfolded. A stoker at a nearby mill, faced with his wife's ultimatum, "either that dog of yours goes, or I go" had shot his pet and disposed of its body in the furnace he looked after. Whether or not he made the right decision is immaterial but the incident underlines the fact that circumstances are not always what they seem. As Sherlock Holmes once remarked, "the temptation to form premature theories upon insufficient data is the bane of our profession".

Of the early requirements of the scientist in cases where blood has been spilt, one is to satisfy himself that the substance *is* blood and another to determine whether it is human or not. The first part he achieves by a quick and simple chemical test for the presence of a constituent of blood called peroxidase; the second by means of the precipitin test.

The precipitin test

The precipitin test is carried out routinely at forensic science laboratories all over the world and each year many thousands of such tests are performed using the process of electrophoresis. A small amount of a solution prepared from the suspect bloodstain is placed in a well cut into a thin film of jelly on a glass plate. A similarly small amount of biological reagent known as anti-serum is placed in another well close to the first. Electrodes are then applied to each side of the plate and an electric current passed through it. Under the influence of the electric field protein molecules in the bloodstain solution and in the anti-serum begin to migrate through the jelly but in opposite directions. The plate is so arranged that the migrating molecules meet and react together near the middle of the space between the wells.

There are many different sorts of anti-serum each quite specific for a particular animal. Human anti-serum reacts with extracts of human blood but, with the exception of blood from some other closely related primates, nothing else. Dog anti-serum reacts with extracts of dog's blood and so on. A range of anti-sera appropriate to the types of animals likely to be encountered is available at each forensic science laboratory. A typical stock list in a laboratory would include anti-human, cat, dog,

horse, sheep, cow, hen, rabbit and a few others besides. Electrophoresis can also be used, as we will see later, in blood grouping tests.

Investigating arson

It might be supposed that fire destroys so completely that only rarely can the causes be accurately determined. This is not the case. Specialist fire-scene examiners from the forensic science laboratories can often determine how and where the fire started – was it an accident due to a carelessly dropped cigarette-end, an electrical fault, or was it arson? One of the things that the fire scene examiner will be looking for is evidence of where the fire started – the seat of the fire. Two or more seats of fire might indicate arson but, on the other hand, hot gases from a well established fire can heat up materials in other parts of the building sufficiently to cause these materials themselves to burst into flames. Flashover, as it is called, apart from spreading the fire with terrifying speed, has been known to ignite the curtains in a room causing them to fall blazing to the floor, producing, in effect, two more seats of fire.

An arsonist, one who deliberately sets fire to property, is likely to select the most combustible materials he can find with which to start his fire. Petrol is sometimes used but as a number of arsonists discovered to their cost, its vapour is also highly explosive when mixed with air. Paraffin, paint-thinners, and fuel oils as well as lubricants come readily to hand and the scientist's examination of the fire-scene will include a search for traces of these volatile accelerants. Even following the enormous heat of a raging fire, tell-tale traces can still be found using a highly sensitive laboratory process known as gas chromatography (GC).

Gas chromatography

Chromatography is a means of separating and analysing mixtures of liquids or gases by passing them through a substance which has the effect of differentially slowing down the passage of the different constituents. In GC, the gases to be analysed are injected into the stream of an inert carrier-gas, e.g. nitrogen, and swept through a long, fine-bore tube packed with a special material. As the con-

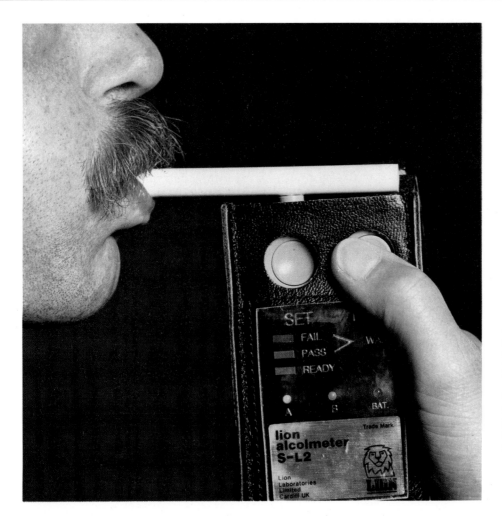

Above: *The Alcotest relies on discolouration of the crystals to indicate alcohol in blood.*
Left: *The Lion Alcometer SL2. This measures the amount of alcohol in the breath — the fuel cell generates an electric current proportional to the amount present. A series of lights indicate if the test is positive or not.*

stituents of the mixture come off the column at the far end, after different characteristic retention times, they pass through a detector which generates electronic pulses and drives a pen on a chart recorder. GC is also the technique used to determine whether or not a quite different type of offence has been committed, i.e. the driving of a motor vehicle by a person having more than a prescribed amount of alcohol in his blood. Only a drop of blood (or urine) is needed for analysis. After a carefully controlled, predetermined preparation procedure the sample is vapourized and the resulting gases injected into the carrier-gas stream. Within minutes the pen trace shows whether alcohol is present in the original sample and, if so, how much is present. The measurements are highly accurate.

Measuring blood alcohol levels

The prescribed blood alcohol level varies from country to country and in the United States of America, from State to State. In the United Kingdom the limit is 80mg of alcohol per 100ml of blood (107mg alcohol per 100ml urine). In Finland and some States of the United States of America the limit is as low as 50mg per 100ml of blood while in Maryland, USA it is as high as 150mg per 100ml. Machines designed to measure the amount of alcohol in breath have been devised and are in use in Canada and the USA. Police and forensic scientists are presently testing similar machines for use in the United Kingdom as well. Drinking and driving accidents are major problems, and police forces need a reliable and convenient method.

"Can you give me a lead?"

One of the most useful functions the forensic scientist can perform is to give the investigating police officer some piece of indicative information which will enable him to direct his available sources in the most advantageous way. It is probably the most difficult service to provide, but often the most spectacular when something is 'pulled out of the bag'.

In Britain during the 1970s, two little girls were found murdered near Sunderland. The police, the forensic pathologist and the scientists from the regional forensice science laboratory worked together looking for a clue to the killer's identity. The pathologist found some unusual bruises on the bodies, marks which could have been made by something incorporating a large diameter shaft containing a screw-thread. Tiny flakes of red paint were found on the bodies and in the grass nearby. It was likely that the two girls had been dumped from a car, and cars made by the then British Motor Corporation were equipped with red-painted car jacks, just the sort of object which, when used as a bludgeon, would produce those unusual marks, and the flakes of red paint. Analysis of the paint revealed that it was the same type as that used by BMC. The police concentrated their efforts towards the owners of BMC motorcars.

At the same time a quantity of sand found on the ligature used to strangle one of the little girls was analysed and found to be very like the sort of sand used by glass-makers. It did not occur in the area where the bodies were found.

The net closed tighter. During house-to-house enquiries, a routine police procedure in all major crime investigations, a man was located who owned a BMC motorcar and had been employed at a local firm of glass-makers. Everything fitted, and after questioning the suspect broke down and confessed.

Fibre traces

In another case, the forensic scientist investigating the death of a boy-scout in Yorkshire found some unusual fibres among the debris recovered from the boy's clothing. Careful analysis of these fragments revealed that they were a type of nylon fibre used to make carpets. With the help of fibre manufacturers, both in England and in France, the source of the fibres and the type of carpet was tracked down. The search had narrowed to a batch of carpets which, apart from off-cuts, had been used in contract work. Again, records detailing the disposal of the off-cuts were available to the police and these led to a number of cars fitted out with new carpets. Among the owners of these cars was one man whom the police were already interested in as a possible suspect. After questioning, the man admitted giving the boy a lift in his car, killing him and dumping his body in a roadside ditch.

These cases, both classics of their kind, feature the exchange of material from one person, thing or place, to another. They ably demonstrate the point that Locard made more than 80 years ago and at the same time reveal another important facet of the forensic scientist's mode of working. With each of the illustrated types of contact trace, as it is often called, the forensic scientist's approach was on two fronts. First, it was necessary to identify the material transferred, secondly it was necessary to compare this recovered crime material with samples from the suspect source (or, as in the case of volatiles at the fire-scene, with reference samples).

"Can the story be corroborated?"

While inceptive and indicative information are both principle concerns for the forensic scientist, the greatest amount of his time is spent in providing corroborative information. As well as perhaps confirming the views of the investigating officer that an arsonist has been at work or that a particular knife is the murder weapon, even where a suspect has made a full confession, independent corroborative evidence is usually required before he can be brought to trial. This is because scientific evidence is of a physical nature, it speaks to facts deduced from the physical residues of a criminal act whereas eye witness statements and even confessions themselves are types of personal evidence and open to error which may be the result of genuine mistake as well as fantasy or misdirected loyalty.

When independent physical evidence supports personal evidence, say the testimony of an eyewitness, then the courts tend to accept this combination as proof of an event. Identification and comparison procedures feature highly in this corrobora-

tive aspect of forensic science. In the last two cases we have seen the importance of at least two types of contact trace, paint and fibres. These were originally used indicatively but later went on to be used as corroborative evidence too.

The list of materials which could feature in criminal cases in this respect is probably limitless: soil, paint, glass, blood, hairs and textiles fibres are among the commonest but fish-scales, candlewax, shoe polish and flour have all featured at some time or another. To deal adequately with all the analytical and comparative aspects of any one of these would fill an entire book, but in order to provide the merest glimpse of just some of the techniques used by the forensic scientist, the essential features of three are described: blood, glass and fibres.

Above: *Technology has developed with swift, precise strides to provide the modern forensic science laboratory with advanced equipment. Here the operator is using a highly sophisticated electron-scanning photomicrograph which is equipped with a screen (VDU) for convenient viewing. The machine has a variety of uses.*

Blood

Blood is easily spilt as a result of bodily injury. Bloodstains often feature in crime investigation when they are of interest to the forensic scientist, both as a type of historical record of events and as a contact trace. From close examination of bloodstains left at the scene of the crime or carried away on the attacker's clothing, scientists can learn a great deal about the way in which the blood was shed and about the person who shed it.

In recent years Dr Herbert McDonnell at Corning in the United States has carried out detailed experiments in order to understand more fully what different shapes and patterns of blood-stains mean. Blood which, for example, is allowed to drip freely onto the ground gives rise to a characteristic pattern of spots and splashes quite different from that produced when a blow is struck against a bloody surface. Knowledge and understanding of the significance of the appearance and distribution of bloodstains is of enormous value in helping to reconstruct the sequence of events which occurred in a violent crime.

By any standards, blood is a very complex biochemical mixture in which are suspended red cells and white cells. The cells can be separated from the rest by centrification and this leaves a clear, straw-coloured fluid called serum (strictly speaking whole, fresh blood from which the cells have been removed is known as plasma, but the distinction need not concern us here).

The ABO bloodgroup system

During the early part of this century it was discovered that the serum of some people caused the red cells from others to form clumps. It was soon realised that in these cases, sites on the surface of the red cells (these sites we call antigens) were reacting with substances in the serum known as antibodies and that blood could be classified according to reactions which were observed. This is the basis of the ABO bloodgroup system in which there are essentially four bloodgroups: group A, group B, group O and group AB. Each of us belongs to just one of these groups, the group being decided at the moment of conception by factors inherited from each of our parents. Thus, one's blood group is fixed for life – it cannot change.

The names of the bloodgroups will probably be familiar to anyone who is a blood donor since these groups are of great importance in blood transfusions enabling hospitals to match blood for a particular patient correctly. The ABO system is also of interest to the forensic scientist because even in dried bloodstains the antigens can be detected and identified. If a person of group B is stabbed to death and a man whom the police suspect to be the killer is

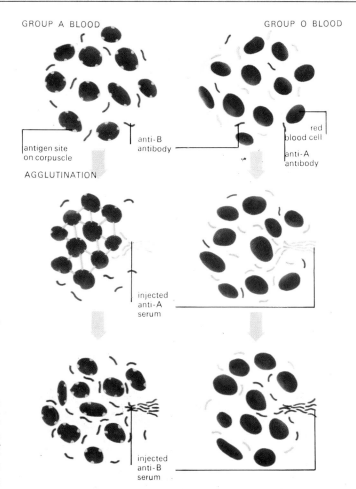

Above: *Blood can be 'typed' according to its ABO grouping by mixing it with anti-sera containing known antibodies, and the agglutination pattern identified from the reactions. Group O serum contains anti-A and anti-B antibodies and will agglutinate groups A, B, and AB. Serum from group A will agglutinate group B blood and vice versa. Both will agglutinate group AB. Group AB serum has no antibodies.*

found to have human blood of group B on his clothes, then this information is of considerable value to the investigating officer, particularly if the suspect's own blood belongs to a different group.

The four bloodgroups are not distributed equally through the population. Group O is the commonest, occurring in about 47% of the UK population. Group A is the next most common (42%), group B the next (8%) and group AB the least common (3%). Although the proportion of

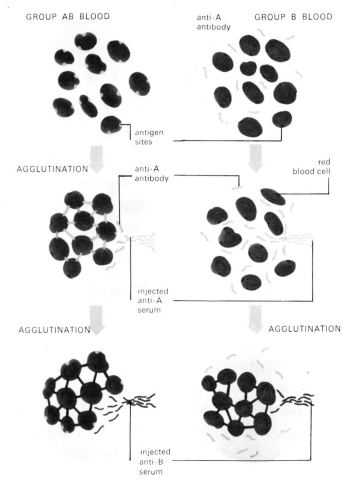

GROUP AB BLOOD

anti-A
antibody

GROUP B BLOOD

antigen
sites

AGGLUTINATION

anti-A
antibody

red
blood cell

injected
anti-A
serum

AGGLUTINATION

AGGLUTINATION

injected
anti-B
serum

people within these groups is fairly constant within a community, the percentages can vary widely in different countries. We can see the value of the information about the blood on a suspect's clothing is immediately increased by the knowledge that blood of that group (group B) is found in only 8% of the population at large.

Other grouping systems

During the years following the discovery of the ABO system other red cell antigens were found. Most of these were found to be next to useless to the forensic scientist because they were not stable in dried bloodstains. Other sets of antigens are stable, however, and more independent grouping systems like the Rhesus system joined the ABO system as

separate and independent methods of grouping blood. Among other things, blood contains an assortment of enzymes. These are complex proteins that control the variety of biochemical reactions taking place in our bodies. Some of these enzymes exist in different forms in different people: they are said to exhibit polymorphism.

Polymorphic forms of enzymes (isoenzymes) can be separated and identified using electrophoresis, the technique discussed earlier. Short lengths of bloodstained thread are moistened and pressed into a jelly-like coating on a glass plate. An electric current is passed through the plate and the proteins migrate through the jelly at speeds which vary according to their type. The net effect is the separation of proteins into a series of bands which can be made visible by applying specially prepared chemicals to the plate.

Different band patterns indicate different forms of the same enzyme, and these band patterns have been given names in order for the forensic scientist to describe the blood which contains them. Phosphoglucomutase (PGM for short) is one such polymorphic enzyme used to group blood and bloodstains in the forensic science laboratories. Originally, using starch based jelly, only three commonly occurring types of isoenzymes were known but a more advanced method of electrophoresis, called isoelectric focusing, improved matters considerably. These three common isoenzymes increased to ten with the use of the new technique.

As with the red cell antigens, distribution of the different isoenzymes is not equal and studies on the population of different countries has led to a knowledge of the frequency of occurrence of each pattern. One of the PGM isoenzymes, PGM 2 + 1 – occurs in approximately 5% of the United Kingdom population. Blood which also belongs to group B, therefore, occurs in only 2% (5% x 42%). We can see that the more grouping systems that can be applied to a spot of blood, the more the scientist can discriminate between that blood and blood from somebody else selected at random. Unfortunately, it is not yet possible to ascribe a sample of blood to a particular person, but some research workers in forensic science see this as a future possibility.

A VERY FISHY STORY
The Michael case

A case from a small English town which occurred in August 1980 epitomizes the work of the forensic science laboratory and highlights the various activities of most its departments. The laboratory used a wide range of expertise, from the most sophisticated machinery down to the simplest of detective procedures, namely close microscopic work.

Michael, a lonely, rather religious young man felt that life or God had failed him. One Sunday lunchtime, he bought a bottle of cider, a bottle of Martini, a bottle of wine, and a can of lager, and went to sit in the park. He started drinking, and gradually his depression took hold. He walked aimlessly for a while, and broke into the local church: "To get my own back on God" as he put it. He did not find anything worth taking, so he climbed back out of the broken window by which he had entered, and made his way to the local primary school. This was a jointed building, with an older structure and a new modern wing which in spite of conforming to various fire regulations was to prove easily inflammable. The flat roof was covered with bitumen, and contained a roof space below which would permit fire to sweep from one end of the building to the other.

Michael looked around the old section of the school again to see if there was anything worth taking, but found nothing to satisfy his angry mood. He got into the school office by smashing through a fibreboard partition and ransacking the room. Then he climbed back through the hole and made his way into the new wing. He broke a glass panelled door, entered the main hall, and set fire to the curtains. Before long, the entire wing was in flames — Michael ended by burning down the complete structure, and causing half a million pounds worth of damage.

A most interesting detail of human psychology now emerges in this case. The fire brigade were soon on the spot, as were two police officers who were on patrol in the area and saw large clouds of black smoke rising from the area of the school building. A crowd had gathered to watch the fire-fighting, a dramatic business as the steel girders which supported the flat roof, and which were covered with corrugated metal sheets, buckled due to the heat, and the whole new edifice soon collapsed.

On making enquiries in the crowd, the police officers discovered that neighbours with houses backing onto the school grounds had seen a man climb into the school buildings at the rear. A fairly clear description of him was obtained, and as in all cases where arson is suspected, the police officers looked carefully through the crowd to see if anyone fitted this description. It is known that people responsible for fires often remain or return to the scene of the crime to see the results of their work.

This case proved no exception. Michael was spotted standing in the crowd, wearing the same clothes that had been described to the policemen. He was in fact known to the police already, though not as an arsonist. But the combination of facts led to his arrest and detention, and his clothing was dispatched rapidly for forensic examination.

The question the police asked of the forensic science laboratory officers was: "Can the clothing be examined against the various controls submitted to try to establish his presence in the school?" His T shirt, blue cord jeans and tan leather boots

Right: The refractive index of glass can be of vital importance in a case. Here the technician is using a microscope equipped with a Mettler hot stage. Silicon oil is heated until the oil and the glass have the same refractive index.

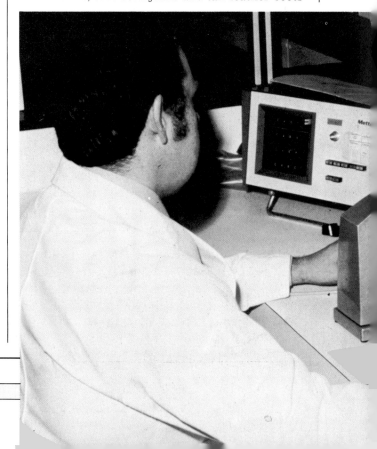

were sent in for examination, together with samples taken by the scene of crime officers: fibreboard from the damaged classroom wall in the old part of the school, glass from the broken window in the school hallway, and glass chips from the lower window of the classroom door, in the new building.

In the main hallway, police officers also noticed a broken fishtank. Pieces of glass from this tank were found on the floor, under debris from the collapsed roof. Significantly, this glass was not smoked, indicating that the tank might have been broken before the fire took place — in other words pointing to a break-in before the fire started, and suggesting that the fire had not ignited accidentally. Remnants of 'squashed fish' were seen on the floor of the hall; at the time officers jokingly remarked that perhaps samples of fishscales should also be sent to the lab for examination — a joke which was to prove more than amusing as the case unfolded.

While the chemists and biologists worked on the clothing, the arson experts visited the school premises and examined the damage. It was soon established that (as usual) there is a point at which the fire damage is more intense and complete: the seat of the fire. In this case, the middle set of curtains in the school hall were burned to such a degree that they were left in charred fragments on

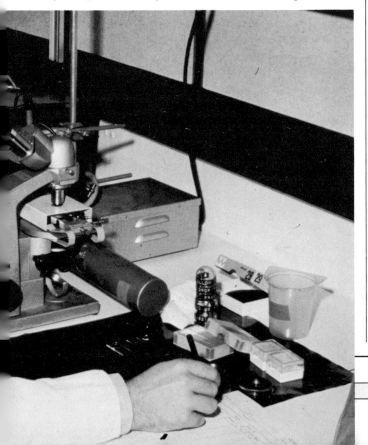

the floor. Curtains at either end of the room were burned but more so towards the top indicating that the fire had started with the middle set of curtains, shot up to the roof void, and spread laterally through the hall, dropping down from the ceiling. The curtain fabric was tested by the arson specialists in the Metropolitan Police Laboratory, London: the fabric proved difficult to light when a match was dropped on it or under it (this would have to be shown to the court in case the defendant tried to claim that the fire had been started unintentionally). When the flame was applied directly to the fabric, it burned very readily. From the fire specialists' point of view, arson was indicated.

The forensic chemists soon came up with other corroborative evidence that made the case stronger. A sample of light blue paint from the exterior of the classroom door was examined on the SEM (the scanning electron microscope). This revealed the various layers of paint colour: light blue topcoat over light grey, blue grey, and yellowish layers of paint. A sample of dark blue paint from the interior of the classroom door was also looked at, and revealed a combination of dark blue topcoat with a blue-grey undercoat. These were the 'controls' to be matched up with the samples of paint and painted glass chips or plain glass chips found on Michael's clothing.

In all, more than 250 glass fragments were found on the surface of the suspect's jeans. A normal level of discovery would perhaps find half a dozen chips on a clothing surface. This in itself placed the suspect more firmly on the scene of a break-in. Of six fragments examined for their refractive index, one had the same refractive index as the glass of the fish tank, and one had the same RI as the sheet glass from the lower window of the classroom door.

Furthermore, one non-matching sample of glass from the jeans was coated with paint — a dark blue topcoat over a blue-grey undercoat, which visually and chemically matched the layers of paint from the inside of the classroom door, as established by the examination of the control sample by the SEM. As if this were not proof enough, the chemist at the Metropolitan laboratory in London found that the glass of the fishtank had a most unusual refractive index — 7 in 4,500 samples recorded in the lab's glass index had that particular RI. In other words, there was a one in five hundred chance of finding that particular refractive index in fishtank glass. The links between the suspect and the scene of the crime were, to coin a phrase, watertight.

As for the fish: gold scales were found on the boot sole and trouser leg of Michael's clothes. These were dispatched to an officer in the biology division, for close examination and identification. She compared the scales with those in a well-known handbook, *Preliminary Key to Fishscales by Families* (Maitland, 1972), and surmised that they were goldfish scales. But as always, the evidence must be as exact and exclusive as possible. Unfortunately, it was not possible to go back to the school building to search for the body of the fish, as it had been entirely demolished. Instead the biologist went to the Natural History Museum in London, and checked through all records of similar scales kept there. She narrowed down the sample, microscopically, to three possibilities (the sample was 4mm square). Fish of this family kept in cold water aquaria and gold coloured were the *Crassius oratus* (goldfish) the *Crassius crassius* (crucian carp, a close relative) and the *Leuciscus idus* or gold orfe. But by examining the scales, the biologist was able to say that the shape and number of radii ruled out the carp and the orfe — the scale in question must have come from the classic goldfish, *Crassius oratus*. On checking with the school authorities, the type of fish kept was substantiated.

When all this evidence was presented by the prosecution to the court, Michael was found guilty and sentenced to a term of imprisonment for arson.

Below: *This tiny goldfish scale was one of the crucial pieces of evidence in the 'Michael' case.*

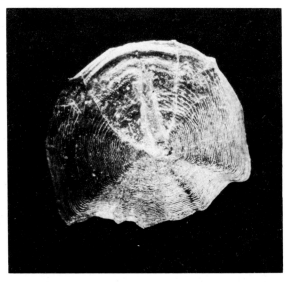

Male or female?

Recent work in the United Kingdom and the United States of America has produced promising results in determining the sexual origin of bloodstains. The method involves radioimmunoassay (RIA) a sophisticated process in daily use in many medical laboratories. Using RIA it is possible to detect various sex hormones in bloodstains and from measurements of how much of each is present it is possible to predict the sex of the person who shed the blood. While information about blood-group combinations and frequencies of occurrence is of enormous value, none of it can be used directly by the investigating officer unless and until he identifies a person from whom blood can be taken for comparison. Knowledge of the sex of a person is, on the other hand, commonplace information and immediately useful to him.

Glass

In the late 1960's Dr D.F. Nelson of the Government of New Zealand's Department of Science and Industrial Research showed by experiment that a man smashing a window was showered with glass fragments. Dr Nelson used high-speed photography to demonstrate that up to one third of the glass fragments produced travelled backwards to envelope the person who smashed the glass.

A significant proportion of breaking and entering offences involve the smashing of glass windows and microscopic fragments of glass which become lodged on the surface of clothing, in pockets and even in hair are a valuable source of evidence connecting the criminal to the scene of the crime.

Forensic scientists pay a great deal of attention to the microscopic bits and pieces of material that comprise the debris recovered from clothing, especially if it is known that the offence in question involved the breaking of glass. Much skill and patience is needed in order to recover the microscopic fragments which, with the aid of advanced instrumentation, will be analysed and compared with glass recovered from the suspect source.

Each recovered fragment of glass is carefully examined to see if any clue as to its source is evident. Curvature of one surface may indicate bottle or other container glass, while a flat face may

Above: *The Becke line (halo effect) on the glass fragment disappears when the refractive index of the glass and surrounding liquid are the same.*

indicate window glass. A flat face which exhibits fluorescence immediately suggests float-glass, manufactured not by rolling molten glass into a plate, but by floating it on a bed of molten tin. It almost goes without saying that coloured glass fragments, commonly greens and ambers, are rarely associated with windows but are more likely to have come from containers of various kinds.

The refractive index

Glass is refractile – it has the property of bending rays of light that pass through it. It does this because the light travels more slowly through the glass than through air (or more precisely, through a vacuum). The ratio of the speed of light in a vacuum to the speed of light through glass, or other transparent material, is known as the refractive index. Scientists measure the refractive index of glass fragments to a high degree of accuracy and use these measurements to compare glass from different sources. Refractive index determinations are carried out with a microscope fitted with a heated stage or sample carrier. The glass fragment is mounted in a drop of silicone oil.

The refractive index of the oil selected is known to change with temperature, and at the match point when the refractive index of the glass and that of the oil are the same, the glass fragment is no longer visible. On either side of the match point a halo, known as the Becke line, is visible at the edge of the glass fragment and, according to the appearance of the Becke line, the scientist knows whether the temperature of the oil has to be raised or lowered in order to achieve the match point. From a prepared calibration curve of the oil the match point temperature can be quickly converted into a refractive index value for the glass under examination.

In the United Kingdom, data on glass fragments examined by the forensic science laboratories has been collected and stored on computer files at the Home Office Central Research Establishment. Scientists in the operational laboratories can interrogate the computer through the terminals in each of their laboratories and obtain from the data files a measure of how common the glass of a particular refractive index has been found to be. This is a valuable aid to the scientist in assessing the significance of the glass evidence he has found.

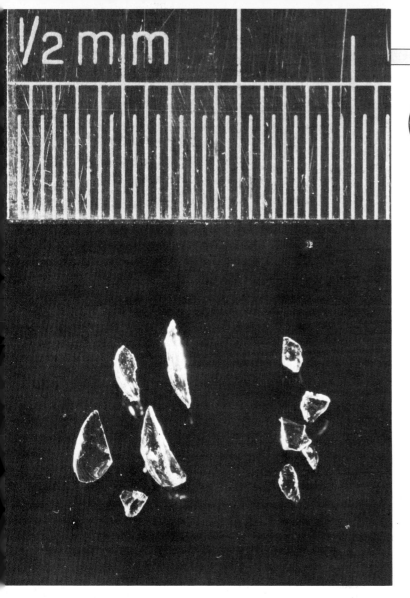

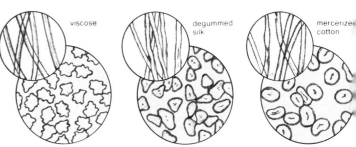

Above: *A tiny fragment of fibre left behind at the scene of a crime can be of vital importance in tracking down a suspect. Here is a selection of the most common fibres seen in cross section under a microscope. Notice the wide variation in structure.*

Above: *These fragments of broken glass were recovered from the suspect in the 'Michael' arson case.*

Fibres

Fabrics from which our clothes, carpets and soft furnishings are made are woven from different types and colours of yarn. The yarns used in weaving processes are made from naturally occurring fibres, such as wool, cotton, linen, or man-made fibres such as nylon, rayon, acrylic and polyester. All these fibre types can be dyed to produce a variety of colours as required.

It is a feature of many woven cloths that they shed tiny fragments of fibres. These fragments rest on the surface on the cloth and remain there until they are either brushed off or transferred to another cloth with which they come into contact.

The discovery by the scientist of fibre fragments on one set of clothing that match the fibres from another is evidence that the two sets have been in contact with each other. Such a find is of considerable importance in a rape case for example when a suspect denies any knowledge of, or contact with, the woman he is alleged to have attacked.

Microscopy birefingence and spectrometry

A high powered microscope is the first means of identifying and comparing the recovered fibres. Wool and cotton fibres, as well as most other natural fibres exhibit a very characteristic microscopic structure and rarely is any other identification technique necessary. But many man-made fibres present more difficult problems and other techniques are brought to bear, e.g. chemical solvent tests, birefingence determinations and infra-red spectrometry.

Birefingence is an optical property of most fibres and depends upon the way in which light passing through the fibre is slowed down differentially. Polarized light, i.e. light which vibrates in only one plane, when passed through a fibre emerges as two components – one in which the light vibrates parallel to the length of the fibre and the other in which the light vibrates at right angles to the length of the fibre. These two components travel at different speeds through the fibre and therefore out of phase when they emerge. Thus the

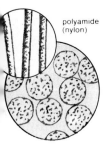
polyamide (nylon)

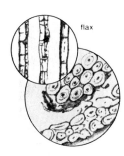
flax

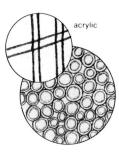
acrylic

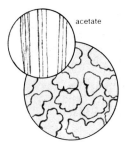
acetate

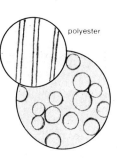
polyester

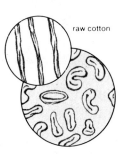
raw cotton

fibre has effectively two refractive indices. The difference between the refractive index of the fibre in one direction and that in the other is called the birefingence value. Birefingence values are different for different fibre types and they can be used as useful diagnostic features.

Spectrometry is a method of analysis whereby selective absorption of light passing through a transparent material is analysed and displayed graphically. The infrared spectrometer used in fibre identification produces a 'signature' of the fibre type which, when compared with a library of such 'signatures', enables the fibre to be identified. This mode of spectrometry is also used in the identification of oils, greases and waxes, plastics, and certain drug compounds.

Spectrometry in the visible and ultraviolet regions of the spectrum are used in both drug analysis and in the analysis of fibre dyestuffs. In the latter, the amount of dyestuff in the fibre fragment is very small and the method of analysis of visible spectrometry has been miniaturized using an instrument called a microspectrophotometer attached to a microscope.

Once the fibre type has been identified the scientist can get on with its comparison with fibres from a known source. Optical microscopy, using a comparison microscope fitted with white, blue fluorescent and ultraviolet light sources are employed here. Diameter, cross-sectional shape, longitudinal striations, inclusions and other internal features, as well as fibre colour, are compared by this means.

Examining dyestuffs

Dyestuffs can be compared using the data generated by the microspectrophotometer and, in addition, the dyestuffs can be extracted and analysed using thin-layer chromatography. In this form of chromatography liquid extracts are spotted onto the base of a specially coated plate, which is then dipped into a solvent. As the solvent climbs through the coating material, the various dyestuff components are dissolved and carried along with the advancing solvent front. As already described in gas chromatography, the compounds travel at different speeds and are consequently separated out along the length of the plate. Thin-layer chromatography patterns from recovered fibre dye-extracts can then be compared with patterns from dyes in fibres from the known source.

So far, only the role of the forensic scientist in relation to the investigating police officer has been discussed. However there is another very important role – as a servant of the courts. While on the one hand the scientist joins the investigating team in the hunt for a criminal, the guilt or innocence of the person charged with the offence is decided solely in the courtroom by a lay-jury presided over by a judge. It is here that the scientist finally presents his findings as evidence and it is for the judge and jury to decide what weight they will place upon them in the context of the other evidence.

The forensic scientist must be, and must be seen to be, impartial and unbiased in presenting his evidence. He is also required to communicate in lay terms the results of his using highly complex techniques and the interpretation he places upon them. He is in a unique position among witnesses being entitled to express opinions without waiting to be invited. His opinions must be soundly based, fully supported by scientific data and able, therefore, to pass muster in rigorous cross-examination in a court of law.

FORENSIC MEDICINE

Forensic medicine is an umbrella term covering the many areas where law and medicine come into contact. The older name was 'medical jurisprudence', and in both Europe and America the term 'legal medicine' is more often used.

The aspect which catches most public interest is *forensic pathology*, the application of pathological expertise to the investigation of criminal or suspicious deaths. However, for the sake of completeness, the other facets should be briefly mentioned. For instance, there is a huge field of activity which is concerned with the legal and ethical responsibilities of doctors, ranging from professional secrecy to the formalities of certifying births and deaths: from medical malpractice, such as surgical negligence, through to the problems of organ transplantation: and from therapeutic abortion to euthanasia.

The whole gamut of laws and regulations affecting doctors, such as the coroner and courts, poisons regulations, drinking drivers, drug addiction, mental offenders, child abuse, control of the medical profession, industrial injuries and diseases, disability and compensation – all come under this heading. The education of the medical student in these matters is the responsibility of forensic medicine specialists in universities. The forensic psychiatrist has his own sub-speciality within forensic medicine in dealing with the relationship of mental abnormality to crime. And last, but not least, the clinical forensic physician or 'police surgeon' has a wide responsibility in dealing with forensic medical problems in the living. The last two specialities will be discussed at the end of the chapter, while we begin by looking at the work of the forensic pathologist.

Forensic pathology

Forensic pathology was really the mother of forensic science – indeed, until the first quarter of this century, there was virtually no distinction between the two. The medical pioneers of the late nineteenth and twentieth centuries were their own forensic scientists. They practised and, in fact, discovered, many of the basic techniques used in blood grouping, hair and fibre examination, ballistics, toxicology and other procedures. This new offspring of pathology grew until it dwarfed its mother in the complexity and diversity of its technical methods and instrumentation. The sophisticated technology described in the rest of this book is now beyond the expertise of the forensic pathologist, but collaboration and mutual understanding of each other's needs are vital for the proper functioning of an integrated system of forensic investigation.

The antiquity of forensic pathology makes its historical pedigree impressive, though the nineteenth century was really the time when rapid development began. However, to find the beginnings of forensic pathology, we have to go back to the end of the thirteenth century, to the early Italian universities. At Bologna, law was the prime subject rather than medicine and doctors began performing autopsies in suspicious deaths to assist the lawyers in investigating their cases. In fact, this pre-dated any anatomical dissections, and there is good evidence to indicate that anatomical knowledge in the modern sense came about as a by-product of these forensic autopsies carried out seven hundred years ago.

The rise of modern forensic pathology, however, came with the recognition of the need for medical evidence contained within various legal codes in Europe in the sixteenth century. It was put on a scientific footing by the rapid advances in the nineteenth century. The great German pathologists like Virchow made pathology the basis of medical knowledge and it was then that the study of injured and diseased tissues was called 'morbid anatomy', a term which is still used today.

A succession of notorious murder cases in the few decades before and after the turn of this century established forensic pathology in the eyes of both the medical profession and the lay public, especially as the fascination of murder was an unfailing source of interest for the media. The first half of the twentieth century was the time of the great individualists in the subject – men like Sir Bernard Spilsbury, Sir Sydney Smith, John Glaister, Francis Camps and

Below: *Sir Bernard Spilsbury, a leading forensic pathologist, was well respected for his work between the two world wars.*

Keith Simpson became household names in Britain, as did Milton Helpern and Alan Moritz in the United States.

The work of the forensic pathologist

What then do forensic pathologists actually do? Fundamentally, they apply their expert knowledge of the pathology of injury and sudden death to fatalities which are either frankly criminal, suspicious or even merely unexpected.

Though the legal requirements and procedures vary widely from country to country, deaths generally fall into two broad groups – those which can be certified by the physician who attended during life, and those which must be reported for medico-legal investigation. Though post-mortem examinations ('autopsies') may be held on either group, in the cases where death is due to recognized natural causes, the autopsy is merely for medical interest and to increase knowledge and assist research. In the medico-legal cases, autopsies are intended to discover the cause of death and to obtain all possible information that might assist in the investigation of the reason for the death.

Though it is the criminally-produced deaths that get all the public interest, numerically they are the smallest part of this group. The ratio varies according to the national system – in England and Wales, there is a high autopsy rate because the coroner, the public official charged with investigating such deaths, tends to ask for post-mortems on the majority of cases reported to him. On the continent of Europe, in Scotland and many other parts of the world, this autopsy rate is lower, because the cases are more closely screened for potential criminality and many of the presumed sudden natural deaths, and even accidents and suicides, are dispensed with without autopsy.

However, in every jurisdiction, the obvious or suspected homicide is subjected to a post-mortem examination. These, and a large proportion of the remaining less sinister deaths, become the object of attention of the forensic pathologist.

The forensic autopsy

The object of the medico-legal autopsy is to determine the identity of the deceased, if this is uncertain; to determine the cause of his death; to list all the injuries or ailments present in the body; and often to determine when and sometimes where he died. When this has been done, the pathologist must draw inferences and conclusions from an expert interpretation of all the collected data, in order to assist the law enforcement authorities to reconstruct the events leading to the death on an objective, as opposed to a subjective basis. This is a tall order and often cannot be achieved, either wholly or even in part.

Identification

When a body is found, the first essential is to establish its identity. In the vast majority of cases, the circumstances make this self-evident, though where criminal proceedings follow, even this has to be strictly proved in court by a chain of identification. This can travel from a relative or neighbour, to a police officer, and eventually to the pathologist.

Where no visual identity can be established, then the pathologist may be at the start of one of the

Right: *Professor Keith Simpson, a well known British pathologist, at work in the City of London mortuary. Simpson provided forensic evidence in many famous cases.*
Below: *A blood test team examine the evidence in a murder case in New York City.*

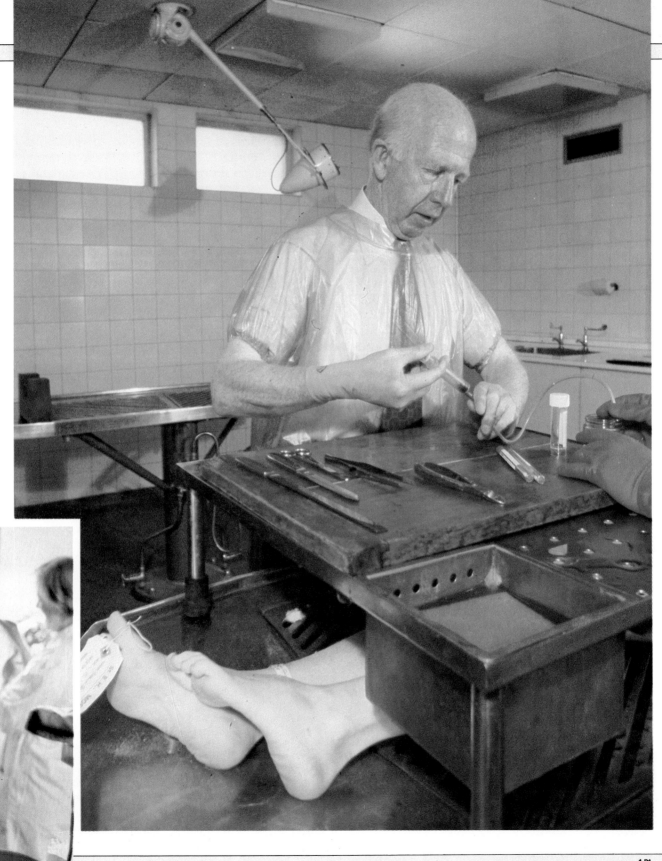

THE SYDNEY 'SHARK ARM' MURDER
The Patrick Brady case

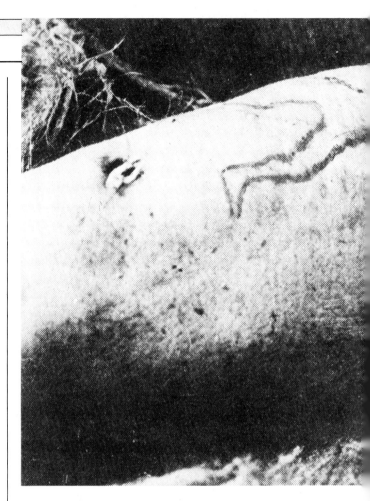

One of the most extraordinary cases in forensic pathology must surely be the Australian 'Shark Arm' murder. The chances of what took place actually happening in real life must be statistically astronomical, but happen it did, in the spring of 1935.

In the middle of April, two fishermen caught a 14 foot tiger shark off the beaches near Sydney, when it became entangled with their lines. Being somewhat at a loss to know what to do with the powerful, snapping monster, they gave it to Coogee Beach aquarium, who added it to their exhibition.

The shark never seemed very happy after being taken into captivity. It refused to eat and spent all its time swimming restlessly up and down the pool. About a week later, on 25 April in front of a crowd of people, it suddenly went crazy, thrashing about in a shower of spray, until it vomited up a huge mass of material.

The spectators, having paid good money to see the sleek, torpedo-like fish, were not amused to see amongst the disgusting refuse from its stomach a well-preserved and obviously human arm!

The police were called immediately and recovered the arm, the condition of which worried them from the moment they saw it. For it appeared to have been cut off at the shoulder – and even more sinister, it had a length of rope tied tightly around the wrist.

It was obviously European in origin and equally obviously a man's arm, rather than female, as it was muscular and brawny and had a striking tattoo on the outer side. This was a very unusual design, depicting two boxers in a sparring position. The police called in fishery experts, who were amazed that the very powerful digestive juices of the shark had not dissolved the limb. Normally, the flesh would have been destroyed in 36 hours, but the pundits suggested that the sudden change in the shark's environment when it was captured and placed in the aquarium, may have upset it so severely that its digestive system went on strike.

This indicated to the police, of course, that the fish must have swallowed the arm very shortly before being captured a week earlier. They were naturally anxious to know if any more of the victim was still inside the shark. Obligingly, the poor animal died at that point and the fisheries people carried out a post-mortem. However, there were no more bits of body left inside its stomach or intestines and the police had to make do with the remarkably well-preserved arm.

The skin on the fingers was still intact, but in a very fragile condition. It took weeks to remove it carefully in small flakes and re-assemble it, but eventually, the finger-print experts managed to get a set of faint but definite prints.

Before this was achieved, detectives were provided with a description of the arm and also photographs of the boxing tattoo. They began a largescale search of the Sydney area, on the presumption that the shark could not have swallowed the limb very far from the city beaches if it had been caught there so soon afterwards.

Several men with tattoos were on the missing-persons list and the search soon narrowed down to two possible candidates. Ones was James Smith, a man who worked as a marker in a local billiard hall. He was an ex-boxer, 40 years old, and his wife and brother positively identified the arm as belong-

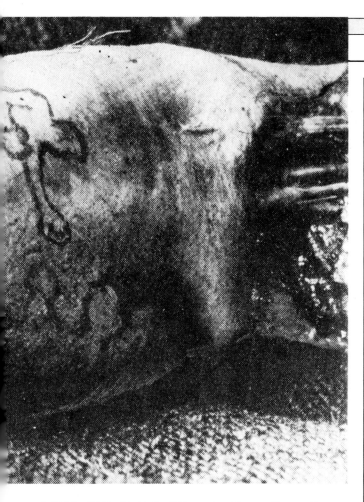

Left: *The arm of James Smith, disgorged by a captured shark. The tattoo was the only distinguishing feature, and enabled the police to identify the arm.*

and Air Force planes made low sorties along the beaches.

This was the point where the forensic pathologists came on the scene. The medico-legal expert in Sydney at that time was Dr Palmer and he was assisted in the examination by Dr Coppleson, an expert on shark bites. Chance – which played a major part in this macabre case – also brought the famous Professor Sir Sydney Smith into the forensic limelight again, as he and his wife were making a round-the-world trip to attend the meeting of the British Medical Association in Melbourne.

Though Sir Sydney, now in Edinburgh University, said that after many years in Egypt camel-bites were more in his line than sharks, he agreed to look at the famous arm and add his opinion.

The three doctors decided that there was no doubt that Smith's arm had been cut off the body with a sharp knife and that it had not been bitten off by a shark. It had been severed at the shoulder joint with a clean cut and the head of the upper arm bone pulled out of the socket, the rest of the muscles being cut free.

The amputation also seemed to have been carried out some considerable time after death. It was certainly not a surgical operation of any sort and it seemed highly unlikely that Smith could still be alive. At one stage, the police had considered suicide, mainly because of the rope around the wrist. It is well known that some swimmers who wish to kill themselves by drowning tie on a heavy weight to make sure of going to the bottom, but if the experts had decided that the arm had not been detached by a shark bite, the suicide theory would not stand up.

They next examined the seaside cottage and found that a tin trunk, a mattress, three mats and a length of rope were missing, according to the owner's inventory. The police and the pathologists built up a tentative reconstruction of the crime, in which they assumed that the man had been killed by some means yet unknown. He was then cut up on the mats in the cottage and most of the body squeezed into the tin trunk.

There was no room for some of the mutilated parts, so these were roped on to the outside, including the tattooed arm. The whole lot, including the mats and bloodstained mattress, were taken out to sea in a boat and dumped over the side. The arm

ing to him. As part of the coincidence, it was the only bit of James Smith that could have been identified in this way, as he had no other special marks. If the shark had swallowed the *other* arm, the case would nave ended there.

Smith had vanished from home two weeks before, on April 8, which was nine days before the shark was captured. He had told his wife that he was going to stay in a rented cottage on the coast for a fishing holiday, his companion being 42 year old Patrick Brady, who was well known to the police for forgery offences. They found and arrested Brady, who denied knowing anything about Smith's death, but he accused Smith's employer, a wealthy boat-builder named Reginald Holmes.

Meanwhile, the police were still trying to find the rest of the victim, as the finding of one arm did not conclusively prove that Smith was actually dead – as a lawyer was later to argue in court.

They searched all the beaches near where the shark had been caught. Even the armed forces joined in, as Navy divers explored the sea bottom must have worked loose and was soon swallowed by the unfortunate shark, to whom it gave fatal indigestion!

The rest of the story was equally bizarre. Three days after the arrest of Patrick Brady, the employer Reg Holmes (who denied being involved with Brady in forgery deals, or even knowing him at all) was chased by a police launch in Sydney Harbour, as he was steering so erratically. After a four-hour high speed chase, worthy of any modern television adventure drama, the police caught up with him and found his face and head covered in blood from a slight bullet wound.

They thought that he had tried to commit suicide, but he swore that someone had tried to kill him. They knew that he was involved with Smith in some way, apart from employing him, as Smith's widow said that Holmes owed her husband 60 pounds. Now he told the police that Brady, whom he had previously denied knowing, had killed James Smith and disposed of the body.

He was right in claiming that someone was trying to kill him, for shortly afterwards, on the very eve of the coroner's inquest into Smith's death at which Holmes was to be a vital witness, he was shot dead in his own car. It was parked late at night under the famous Sydney Harbour Bridge and the killer, who must have been a passenger in the vehicle, used the roar of traffic passing overhead to drown the noise of the shot.

It could not have been Brady, as he was in police custody. When the inquest began, almost 40 witnesses were heard before Brady's lawyers obtained a Supreme Court order to stop the proceedings on the grounds that one arm did not prove that the man really was dead!

Brady was released on bail and when his trial for murder came along in September, he was acquitted for lack of evidence. Two other men were tried for shooting Holmes, but after an abortive trial and a re-trial, they too were acquitted.

The whole episode was wrapped up in the Australian underworld of forgery, drug-trafficking and intimidation. Brady lived until 1965 and stoutly maintained his innocence to the end. He alleged that the arm in the shark should have contained bullet holes — though three expert doctors did not see them.

Probably no case ever held more unlikely events — that that particular arm, with its unique tattoo, should have been swallowed by that shark, that was to be immediately caught and delivered to an aquarium where it vomited it back — quite apart from all the gangster business that followed.

most arduous of all his tasks. Lack of an identity may be because the corpse is found at a place remote from his usual haunts. He may have got there because his killer dumped him or for a variety of less sinister reasons. In these cases, photography, clothing, fingerprints, a physical description of height, sex, race, weight, hair colour and eye colour may assist, together with details of teeth, scars, surgical operations, old injuries, congenital deformities, tattoos and occupational marks. For instance, a male body with numerous blue scars on the fingers narrows the search down to coal miners.

However, the pathologist's skills are called into greatest demand when the body is unrecognizable, either from decay or mutilation. Many murderers dispose of their victims in such a way that they hope that the long delay in discovery – if that ever occurs – will cause such gross putrefaction that the identity cannot be determined. Without proof of identity, a criminal charge can never be successfully prosecuted. In addition to reliance on natural decay, a murderer may mutilate the body, as in the Setty case in Britain, where a dismembered corpse was dropped in parcels from a light aircraft over the Essex marshes – or the more recent Lancashire drug gang murder, where a body sunk in a quarry lake had the hands chopped off to remove fingerprint evidence.

Many of the identity problems occur in bodies removed from water, as they are likely to remain hidden for longer, even though the decomposition is rather slower. Other identity problems involve only bones, for if the body is concealed for long enough – a couple of years in temperate climates – then it will be reduced to a skeleton. In such cases, the pathologist may have to call upon the resources of his specialist colleagues, such as anatomists, dentists, and radiologists – and even entomologists or botanists where the duration of the life cycles of various insects or plants may assist in determining the time since death.

What needs to be known, whether it be a heap of bones in a sand-pit or a bloated corpse from a canal, is this:

Is it human? Not infrequently, animal and human remains have been confused. Anatomical study may have to be supplemented by serological tests conducted by the forensic science laboratory. These depend on the fact that when animals such as rabbits are injected with small amounts of protein from different species of other animals, they produce anti-bodies which are specific to those species. When an extract of the unknown remains is mixed with blood serum from these rabbits, a reaction takes place only with the specific serum, indicating the animal of origin.

Is it male or female? Again anatomy provides a possible answer. If the whole body or skeleton is present, the answer can always be given, except in the very rare cases of intersex or hermaphroditism. The shape of the skull and pelvis is characteristically different in the two sexes, as long as they are past puberty. Where the body is grossly decom-

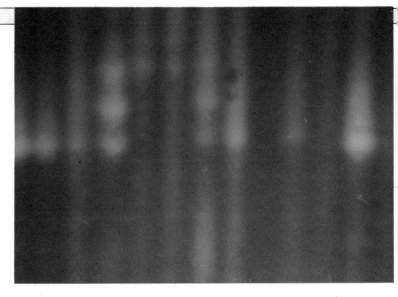

Above: *Electrophoresis is used to reveal patterns of proteins under ultra-violet light in order to identify blood.*
Below: *Agglutination: red blood cells remain separate* (top), *partly clump together* (centre), *and clump completely* (bottom).

Below: *An auto analyzer, which is used to determine the Rhesus grouping of dried blood stains.*

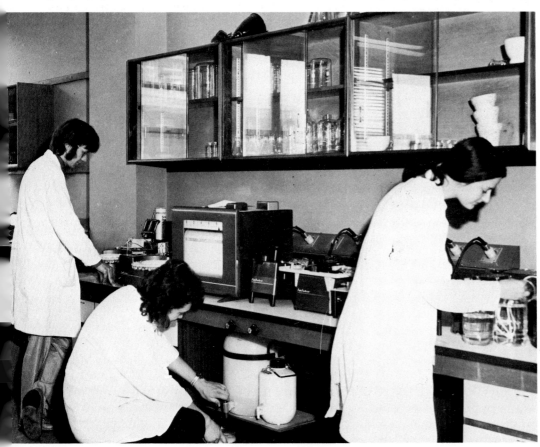

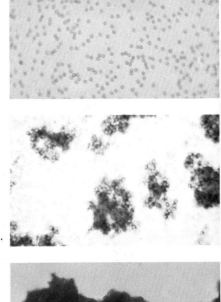

Above: *Age can be determined by the examination of the skull. The sutures on the skull of a young person are open and eventually close up. Thus it can be seen that the skull on the right belongs to a person over 30.*

posed, the female womb is often preserved longer than any other non-bony organ. Where only a few bones are present, then expert anatomical help may be needed. Methods have been developed for telling male from female by the chromosome substance in the cells of the skin, but this is impracticable where there is decomposition.

What is the height? Where the whole body or skeleton is available, then direct measurement gives an answer to within a couple of centimetres – the dead body is not exactly the same height as in life. Where only limb bones are present, then complicated anatomical measurements and the application of mathematical formulae give an approximate answer, but ethnic and nutritional factors may introduce errors.

What is the race? In these days of rapid air travel and great mixing of populations by immigration, the ethnic identity is quite important. Skin pigmentation, the type of hair and certain ethnic and religious markings and artefacts naturally assist. Anatomically, negroes tend to have limbs relatively longer than Caucasians and certain subtle differences in skull measurement may assist, though there is considerable degree of uncertainty. The teeth of Mongoloid people are a special shape.

What is the age? In infancy, the age can be estimated almost to the month and in childhood to the year, by the development of the bones. These grow from separate centres, which appear and fuse at fairly constant times, so that direct examination and X-ray can give accurate information up to about the age of 20. Together with the teeth, the dating of young persons is accurate, but after the third decade accuracy falls away rapidly. New techniques involving radiology and the minute examination of the pelvis offers hope of increased accuracy even in the older age groups.

What is the personal identity? Once the broad groupings already mentioned have been made, investigators need to put an actual name to the victim if possible. Dental identification may assist greatly and this is discussed in another chapter. As in the intact body, old injuries, disease and deformities may be a vital help, even where the remains are only a partial skeleton. One case seen by the author was identified after months of work because the bones showed evidence of a disease called 'acromegaly' and also the skull was perforated by a small hole sustained in a road accident seven years earlier. The air sinuses in the forehead can be crucial, as no two persons in the world have identically-shaped sinuses. If a hospital X-ray of the potential match is available, it can be superimposed upon post-mortem X-rays of the skull to see if the sinuses coincide. These sinuses survive even fierce fires and some military air-crew have their skull X-rays on file, so that they can be identified after a crash.

Once the body is identified the detective almost always poses another major problem for the pathologist.

When did he die? Because of potential alibis of suspects, the date and time of death can be a most vital issue in the homicide case. Unfortunately, it is also one where claims for accuracy are usually unfounded. The older practitioners of forensic medicine were often too optimistic in this, as in other aspects of their subject, tending to over-

interpret and be over-confident of their ability to deduce facts from insufficient data.

Of all the massive scientific literature in forensic medicine during the past century, nothing has stimulated more research and expenditure of printing ink than methods to determine the time of death. Though advances have been made, they have increased knowledge of how wide to set the limits of accuracy, rather than radically improving accuracy itself.

Post-mortem hypostasis

Certain changes after death are used to establish the time when life expired. When a person dies, the heart stops and naturally all circulation of blood ceases. The blood tends to settle in the lowest blood vessels under the influence of gravity and produces a reddish-purple discolouration of the skin on the back of the trunk and limbs. This is called 'post-mortem hypostasis' and though it has been used as a timing factor, it is far too variable to be of any use. However, it can be useful in that its colour can suggest certain conditions. For example, a cherry-pink colour is characteristic of carbon monoxide poisoning, such as that from car exhausts and faulty

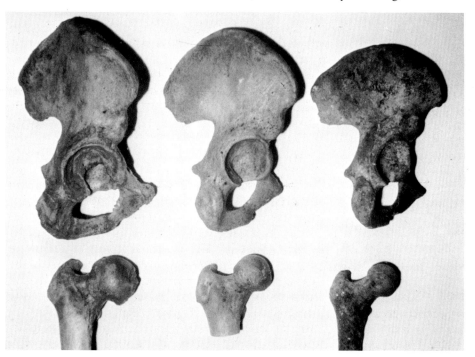

Left: *The pelvis can be used in sex identification. The pelvis on the left is of a known male, the one in the centre of a known female, and the one on the right is from a skeleton of a murder victim found 40 years after death. Note the wider notch on the left, the size of the cup for the head of the thigh bone and the direction it faces, and the shape of the upper blade of the pelvic brim.*

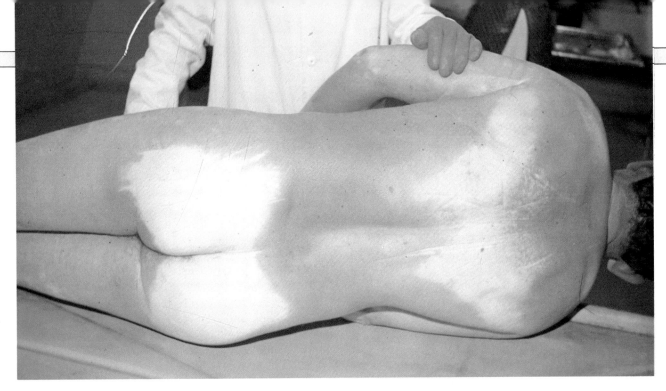

gas appliances. A bright red is often seen in exposure to cold and a deeper red can occur in cyanide poisoning. If a body is found with a hypostasis on the upper side, then it must obviously have been moved some time after death. A hanged body, if left long enough, will have the hypostasis in the legs and hands, not the back.

Rigor mortis

Another well known change is rigor mortis, the stiffening of the limbs due to chemical changes in the muscles after death. Though this can be a very rough guide to the time since death, the errors can be very large. Rigor usually comes on in the jaw in a few hours after death and spreads to all the limbs in 8-12 hours. It lasts about a day, then passes off, but the durations given are subject to very wide variations, often depending upon the temperature of the surroundings. In cold weather a body may still be limp after five days.

Body temperature

The best indicator of time since death is body temperature. If the temperature at death is assumed to be 37°C – not always a justifiable assumption – then soon after the metabolic processes cease, the temperature falls until it is slightly above that of the environment. It never reaches the latter unless

freezing conditions prevail. The temperature rises slightly after a few days, owing to putrefaction.

Theoretically, the graph of falling temperature against time should offer a method of back-calculation of the time since death, but so many variables exist that no accuracy is guaranteed. Fatness, thinness, clothing, wind, rain, draughts, external temperature, body posture, age and other factors form a permutation that makes an exact calculation impossible. During the first 24 hours after death, the use of the thermometer by the pathologist should give the time of death to within about two hours, but under actual working conditions, errors outside this are not uncommon.

Chemical methods

Many chemical methods have been devised, using body fluids, the contents of the eyeball, electrical responses in the muscle, the state of the digestion of the stomach contents – and many other techniques – but so far, no one has come up with a foolproof method that survives practical testing at a scene of crime. Instead of giving a precise time of death, the cautious pathologist will give a range of times to the detectives, within which he feels confident that the deceased died. The actual time of death, has, of course, been of great importance in many murder investigations, usually in relation to a suspect's alibi, but a pathologist who still tries to give a ludicrously 'accurate' answer – measured in fractions of an hour – does a disservice to the investigation by misleading the police with evidence that cannot be substantiated in the witness box when the case comes to trial.

Injuries and wounds

The prime function of the pathologist is to find the cause of death and where this is due to violence, to describe and interpret any wounds in terms of the method of infliction and the risk to life they presented.

Wounds are usually classified as abrasions, bruises and lacerations. Abrasions exist where only the skin surface is damaged. These 'grazes' may faithfully record the shape of the object which caused them, such as the pattern of a plaited whip, or the tread of a motor tyre on the skin in a road accident. The pathologist must carefully measure and describe them, usually with the aid of photography, as they may need to be matched against some object or potential weapon. They may even

be due to teeth in biting injuries, as will be described in the Dentistry chapter.

Probably the most striking pattern of abrasions is seen in the facial injuries from a broken car windscreen, where the fragments of shattered safety glass produce multiple marks of a characteristic shape.

Bruises

Bruises are the next type of injury, in which there is a haemorrhage beneath the intact skin. Black eyes, swollen lips and all kinds of skin bruises are well known to everyone, being caused by blood escaping into the deep tissues. Because of the overlying skin, the pattern of the weapon is not so well outlined. Fresh bruises are purple or blue and the pathologist has to recognize the spectrum of colour changes as the bruises get older, the tints passing through brown, green and yellow until they finally fade. This may be important, especially in the battered child, as it indicates that all the bruises were not inflicted simultaneously, but the abuse was spread over a period of time.

Above left: *Discolouration on the body caused by post mortem hypostasis. The pale areas on the shoulders and buttocks are due to pressure against the supporting surface. The redness is caused when the heart stops beating and the blood becomes subject to the effects of gravity. Post mortem hypostasis is normally complete within 8 to 10 hours of death, and taken together with the extent of rigor mortis and drop in body temperature, can help the pathologist estimate the time of death.*

Right: *A flow chart outlining the complex procedure which must take place after the discovery of a dead body in unusual circumstances.*

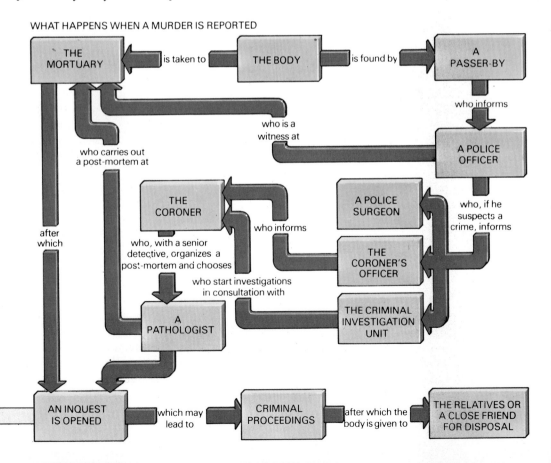

WHAT HAPPENS WHEN A MURDER IS REPORTED

THE MORTUARY — is taken to — THE BODY — is found by — A PASSER-BY

who informs

who is a witness at

A POLICE OFFICER

who carries out a post-mortem at

who, if he suspects a crime, informs

THE CORONER

A POLICE SURGEON

who informs

after which

who, with a senior detective, organizes a post-mortem and chooses

THE CORONER'S OFFICER

who start investigations in consultation with

THE CRIMINAL INVESTIGATION UNIT

A PATHOLOGIST

AN INQUEST IS OPENED — which may lead to — CRIMINAL PROCEEDINGS — after which the body is given to — THE RELATIVES OR A CLOSE FRIEND FOR DISPOSAL

THE VANISHING BRUISE
The Sydney Fox Case

Forensic experts often hold different opinions about the same set of facts, but a dispute about the actual facts themselves led to a confrontation between the famous pathologist Sir Bernard Spilsbury and several distinguished colleagues. The case was that of Sidney Fox.

Both Sidney and his mother Rosaline were far from being reputable people. Mrs Fox, who was 69 when she died, was a Suffolk country girl whose youngest son, Sidney, was illegitimate, homosexual and a professional petty criminal.

By 1929, when Sidney was 30, the pair of them eked out a precarious existence by shifting around the country from hotel to hotel, living on a small pension and dud cheques. Sidney supplemented this drab life by theft and blackmail and often saved on hotel bills during frequent episodes of prison hospitality.

The old lady, who had Parkinson's disease, aided and abetted him in his sordid occupation. In 1928, he served his last prison sentence for stealing jewellery from a Mrs Morse, whose husband was about to sue him for divorce. Though a homosexual, Fox could force himself into seduction if it was in the course of business, but with this particular woman, there was a strong suspicion that he tried to kill her by gas after insuring her life in his favour. This was a telling point in what was soon to happen to his mother.

In October 1929, they arrived at the Hotel Metropole in Margate, almost penniless and without a scrap of luggage. A few days later, Sidney scraped together a single fare to London (he borrowed the money to come back) and went to an insurance office to arrange for two accident policies on his mother's life to be extended until midnight the following day, 23 October.

The value of the insurances was £3000, a considerable sum in those days. The very curious act of extending them by a bare 36 hours became highly suspicious later, when it was learned that old Mrs Fox died accidentally only a few minutes before the policies finally expired!

On the following evening, at about 11.35 pm, Sidney Fox, clad only in his shirt, ran down the staircase at the Hotel Metropole, yelling "Fire, Fire!" Another guest went to help him, dragging his mother's body from a smoke-filled room, the door of which Fox admitted closing as he left "so that the smoke would not escape into the hotel".

Inset: *Sidney Fox, who was convicted of his mother's murder by evidence which was largely circumstantial.*

Above: *The room at the Hotel Metropole in Margate where Fox was accused of murdering his mother.*

A doctor was called who certified death as due to shock and suffocation. An inquest was held and a verdict of accidental death recorded. Sidney obtained a death certificate and a few days later, Rosaline Fox was buried in her native village in Suffolk.

On the morning of the funeral, her son was claiming the insurance payment, but a suspicious agent sent a telegram to his Head Office, saying "Extremely muddy water in this business".

Scotland Yard were informed, and 11 days after the funeral Mrs Fox's body was exhumed from that country churchyard and a post-mortem was carried out by Sir Bernard Spilsbury, the Home Office pathologist. Now the controversy began in earnest.

Spilsbury found no external sign of injury and no burns. There were no finger marks on the neck, no bruises, no bleeding into the tissues beneath the skin, no fracture of the delicate cartilages of the larynx (the 'Adam's apple') and no signs of asphyxia in the face or elsewhere.

Yet he firmly gave the cause of death as 'manual strangulation'. It later transpired that this was based on the alleged discovery of bruises at the back of the larynx, on the epiglottis (the flap which separates the windpipe from the gullet) and on the thyroid gland in the neck.

When Sidney Fox was arrested and charged with murder, his lawyers wanted second opinions on these medical aspects. They engaged two well-known experts, Professor (later Sir) Sydney Smith from Edinburgh University and Dr Robert Bronte, who had been the State Pathologist for Ireland.

The prosecution, to even up the score, asked Dr Henry Weir, a heart pathologist, to give a second opinion for them. All four pathologists met at Spilsbury's laboratory in University College Hospital, to examine the tissues from the neck, which Spilsbury had preserved in formaldehyde after the exhumation.

He stood impassively while Professor Smith and Dr Bronte looked at Mrs Fox's larynx. They stared at it for a long time, turning it this way, then that. Finally, Sydney looked up at Spilsbury. "I can't see anything," he said. Bronte also shook his head in mystification. "There's no bruise there," he declared, pointing to the back of the larynx.

Spilsbury was unmoved. A stern, humourless man, he would not unbend, even for old colleagues. "It must have faded," he replied, "It was there when I made my examination."

Nothing would make him modify his opinion, even though the other doctors pointed out that the only thing to be seen was the putrefaction of the graveyard. He had not taken a microscopic sample of this bruise, which might have settled the dispute.

The bruise was alleged to be the size of a large coin, a sizeable injury, which could hardly have vanished if it was a true bruise, which is formed by blood escaping from the small blood-vessels into the tissues.

But Bernard Spilsbury had a reputation for never admitting that he might be in error. Many years later, two South African forensic patholog-ists, Prinsloo and Gordon, wrote an article drawing attention to the frequency of false post-mortem haemorrhages in this very spot. They showed that they appeared a considerable time following death, due to blood settling under the force of gravity, which took the blood cells down to rest between the larynx and the front of the spine. Where post-mortems are carried out soon after death, they are rarely seen.

When Sydney Smith and Bronte looked for the other signs that Spilsbury used to substantiate his cause of death, all they could see were a few insignificant pin-pricks of blood on the epiglottis, which can be found in almost any post-mortem. There was a bruise at the side of the tongue which was likely to have been caused by her badly-fitting false teeth.

As to the bruise alleged to be on the surface of the thyroid gland, it was too faint to be mentioned. Smith and Bronte protested at Spilsbury's reliance on this and even Dr Weir declared it to be spurious. Spilsbury still claimed it was a bruise, but said that he would not press the point.

When the case came to trial at Lewes Assizes, the prosecution was led by the Attorney-General, Sir William Jowitt, who seemed determined to get a conviction.

When Bernard Spilsbury gave evidence, he calmly and evenly described the invisible bruise at the back of the larynx as being "about the size of half a crown". When defence counsel cross-examined him about it, he would not even consider the views of other eminent pathologists. "It was a bruise and nothing else," he exclaimed brusquely, "There are no two opinions about it."

Smith and Bronte believed that death was due, not to strangulation, but to heart failure precipi-tated by the smoke and fire — and even Spilsbury's ally, Dr Weir, agreed with them, and he was a pathologist at the National Heart Hospital. But nothing would move Spilsbury. He stuck implac-ably to his first opinion — based on virtually no evidence at all — that Rosaline Fox had been throttled by hand.

When Sydney Smith entered the box to give evidence for the defence, the Attorney-General tried to give him a rough ride, but the canny and experienced Scottish professor was a match for him. They soon got on to the vanishing bruise.

"Sir Bernard says there can be no two opinions about it," snapped Sir William Jowitt.

"It is very obvious that there can," replied Sydney Smith.

"But you are bound to accept the evidence of the man who saw the bruise?"

"I do not think so."

"How can you say that there was no bruise there?"

"Because if it was there, it should be there now. It should be there for ever. The larynx is there to be examined by anybody."

In spite of this battle royal between the witnes-ses, Spilsbury's reputation at that time was such that everyone tended to accept everything he said as Gospel truth.

The defence counsel, J.D. Cassels QC (also later to become a judge), said that "It will be a sorry day for the administration of justice in this land if we are to be thrust into such a position that because Sir Bernard Spilsbury expressed an opinion, it is of such weight that it is impossible to question it."

In another well-known case in Edinburgh, a barrister went so far as to address Spilsbury as 'Saint Bernard' instead of 'Sir Bernard'!

When Sidney Fox himself gave evidence, he made such a poor showing, especially over the matter of shutting the door on his mother in the burning room, that he literally made a rope for his own neck.

The judge summed up largely in favour of Fox, as far as the forensic evidence went. His actual words were: "There were no external signs of asphyxia, there were no marks on the throat. Sir Bernard Spilsbury has said it was quite possible there would be none, but you and I might find that hard to believe. As regards the brittle bone in the throat known as the hyoid, it is a very curious coincidence that it was not broken in this case. That is a very strong point in favour of the accused . . ."

But not strong enough for the jury. After just an hour, they filed back, not looking at the man in the dock, which is always a tell-tale sign. When the verdict was given, Sidney whispered "My Lord, I did not murder my mother."

Sir Sydney Smith says in his memoirs that he believed him, but the circumstantial evidence against him was very strong, and he went to the gallows at Maidstone Jail early on the morning of 8 April 1930.

Lacerations

The third category of injuries is the laceration, where the skin is breached. All grades exist, from a small cut to complete mangling of a limb. If a sharp instrument is used, the laceration is called an 'incised wound' of which there are two main types. If a laceration is long and shallow, it may be called a 'slash', such as may be seen in many a knife fight. When the knife is driven in deeply, so that the wound is deeper than it is long, then it is naturally known as a 'stab' wound. Stabbing is the most common method of homicide in Britain, being much more frequent than strangling or blunt injury.

The pathologist has to categorize and describe all those injuries and try to say how they were caused. A finely patterned abrasion may be from a blow from a fist within a knitted driving glove. Four small bruises in a line may be from a set of knuckles; and in a stab wound, the depth of penetration, the direction and angle and the probable degree of force used could all be vital to the investigation of the incident. As the patient is dead and the culprit unlikely to tell the truth, it is left to the pathologist to interpret what happened to the best of his ability, though again it must be said that in former years, this ability was pushed to unwarranted lengths, almost to the point of sheer speculation.

Gun-shot wounds

Another form of injury, which in some parts of the world is far more common than stabbing deaths or throttling, is the fatal gunshot wound. The science of firearms examination and ballistics is part of forensic science, though it originally grew from forensic pathology. The pathologist, however, still has a prime role to play in the examination of shooting deaths.

Firstly, he has to recover samples for the forensic science laboratory, which includes the bullet or shot, which may be identifiable both as to manufacturer and origin and also, in the case of a rifle bullet, to a match from a suspect weapon. Skin

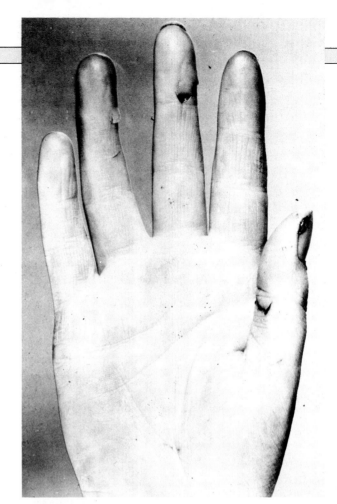

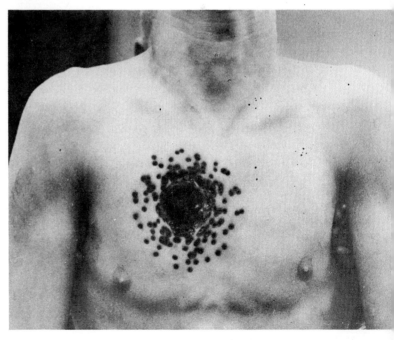

Above right: *The hand of a murder victim, showing evidence of attempts to fend off or grab the knife.*
Right: *The effect of a 12-bore shotgun blast on the chest of a victim when fired from a range of about 5 metres. The pattern made by the pellets is very characteristic.*

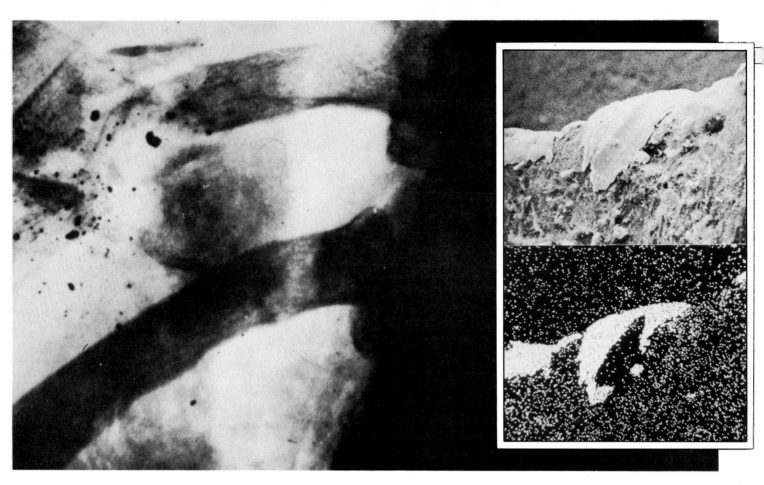

Above left: An X-ray of a murder victim's ribs shows the path along which the bullet passed.
Inset: Using a scanning electron micrograph, it is possible to show a smear of metal left around the point of entry by a bullet which passed through the victim's skull.

from around the wound may also offer unburnt powder flakes and other foreign material which may assist in the laboratory identification of a suspect.

Apart from this aspect, it is the pathologist who has to estimate such factors as the range and the direction of the fatal shot. Where a high-velocity rifle bullet is involved he must determine which were the entrance and the exit wounds, which would indicate the direction from which the gun was fired. The entrance wound is usually inverted and may have a ring of grease, dirt and abrasion around it. If the discharge was within a short distance, then burning and powder staining may be present, though the latter is now uncommon with modern propellants. The exit wound is often everted and ragged, though there are exceptions.

Range is very difficult to estimate with a rifled weapon, beyond the short distance where scorching and soiling occur. With a shotgun, which fires a large number of pellets, there is rarely an exit wound. The distance can be determined with more accuracy, as the shot spreads out in a narrow cone – the larger the wound, the greater the distance. A very rough rule of thumb is that the spread of the pellet pattern in inches equals the range in metres. The angle of shot can often be determined by the geometry of the wound. A circular pellet pattern means a discharge at right angles to the body, while a shot from the side makes an elliptical wound.

Asphyxial deaths

A significant part of criminal forensic pathology involves asphyxial deaths, where the fatality results from obstruction of the air passages and associated damage. Modern ideas on asphyxia have changed and it is now known that many deaths that were formerly blamed on asphyxia, i.e. lack of oxygen, are caused or contributed to by other factors, especially sudden stoppage of the heart. A prime example is strangulation, where the neck is squeezed either by a hand (throttling) or with a ligature (garrotting). About half such deaths occur very rapidly and even instantaneously, before any oxygen deprivation can develop. These deaths are due to pressure on the nerves and arteries in the neck and are the basis of the fatal blows delivered in 'commando punches' and various oriental martial arts. The distinction may be legally important, as those sudden deaths due to pressure on the neck may be inadvertent. They may have occurred during horse-play, or where no real intent to kill existed. The point is often argued in criminal courts, where the defence may plead for a reduction of a murder charge to manslaughter in the circumstances.

The scene of the death

The pathologist, in his role of expert adviser to coroners and detectives, often visits a body at the scene of the death, rather than waiting for it in his mortuary. Where a death is obviously criminal or even merely suspicious, the scene will be preserved intact by the investigating officers until the forensic team arrives. This consists of photographers, scenes of crime officers, the pathologist, finger-print experts and the forensic scientists. The pathologist will usually make the first examination after photographs have been taken and has to assess the general appearance of the scene. He will look for obvious wounds upon the body, for bruises, especially around the neck, and for anything inconsistent with a natural, suicidal or accidental death. He may take the temperature of the body at the scene to try to establish the time of death or leave this until he has the better facilities of the mortuary available.

If there are wounds, then any bleeding or blood splashes on surrounding objects will be evaluated. If there has been a long post-mortem interval, he may assess the degree of decomposition and possibly infestation with maggots and other predators, to try to estimate the time or even date upon which death occurred. The pathologist is responsible for seeing that the corpse is carefully transported to the mortuary for the post-mortem examination. For this, it is wrapped in a large clean polythene sheet, so that any trace evidence such as hairs, fibres, dust etc. is not lost to the forensic scientists during transit.

Below: *The spiral pattern of the cord is clearly visible on this strangulation victim's neck.*

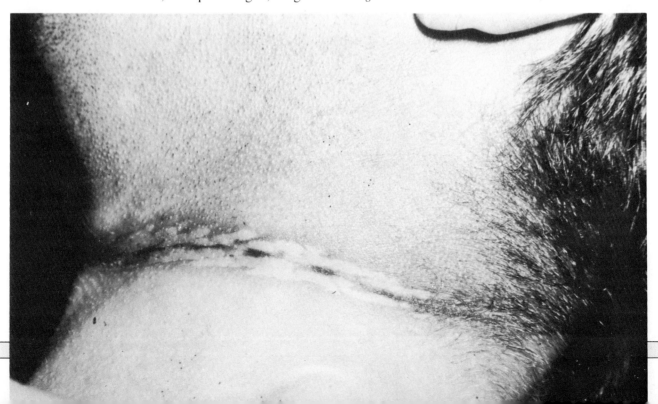

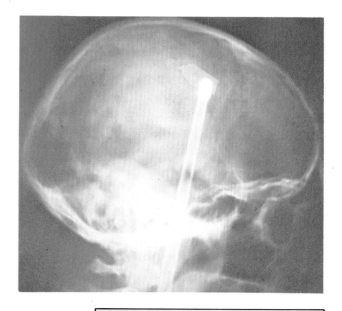

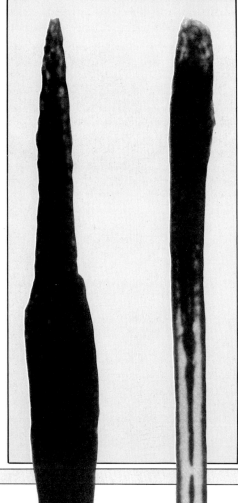

The autopsy is often carried out immediately, even if it is in the small hours of the morning. Good facilities are needed and if no modern public mortuary is available, then the examination is usually carried out in the autopsy room of a local hospital, where the instruments, X-ray equipment and assistants are available. A full autopsy is carried out and the immediate conclusions given to the senior detectives, who are usually present at the examination. This is followed up by a detailed written report, often amplified during the next few days by the results of special examinations such as microscopic examination of the tissues, analyses for toxic substances, alcohol and any other ancillary investigations that may be needed.

Pathological evidence

Eventually, where a suspect is charged with the crime, the case comes to trial and the pathologist gives his evidence. Not only are the bare factual findings of the autopsy offered, but his opinions are given on any medical aspect which might assist the court, such as calculations of the time since death, interpretations of the nature of the injuries and many other factors which might include the contribution to the death of any natural disease that may have been present.

In many murder cases, the opinion of the pathologist is challenged by the lawyers conducting the defence of the accused man. Increasingly often these days, the defence lawyers retain another pathologist to conduct a second autopsy on their behalf or request him to examine critically the report of the first doctor. At trial, both these pathologists may give evidence and when one is giving his testimony from the witness box, the other listens carefully to what he has to say. He may then indicate, to the counsel conducting cross-examination, pertinent questions which may expose some weakness in the deductions of the other doctor. There is rarely much dispute about the facts revealed in the autopsy, but two equally expert

Top left: *This X-ray photograph reveals a crossbow bolt deeply embedded in the victim's skull.*
Left: *The hair on the left, when compared with the normal hair on the right, shows characteristic distortion symptomatic of thallium poisoning.*

doctors may have quite different ways of interpreting those facts and it is up to the jury to decide which argument is the most persuasive.

Accident, suicide or murder?

Much of the work of the forensic pathologist deals with deaths other than homicide and one of his more important tasks is to differentiate between these types of fatality.

If a man is found with his throat cut, is it murder or suicide? If another is found shot in a field with a gun alongside him, is it murder, suicide or accident?

Many such problems arise and only experience can help the doctor to the right conclusion – though sometimes there are insufficient data to arrive at such an answer and the result may be an 'open verdict' by the coroner.

There are some pointers and short-cuts which are used, though they are not infallible. For instance, there is a supposition in Britain that 'a shot woman is a murdered woman', as UK females rarely use a gun for suicide and rarely handle guns so as to risk an accidental death. In the case of a cut throat, the presence of a number of 'tentative' trial cuts, usually trivial in nature, indicates a suicide, as the person often makes a few hesitant cuts before he summons up enough courage for the final act.

A suicide who uses a gun will shoot himself in one of a few 'selected sites', such as the forehead, the mouth or the chest – but almost never in the stomach, eye or back or back of the neck, all of which strongly suggest homicide. Similarly, a suicide will use a knife on his wrists, neck or over the heart, but rarely elsewhere.

Multiple injuries by no means rule out suicide. A person intent on self-destruction may stab himself deeply in the chest seven or eight times, even though each wound may look fatal. Again, he might

Below: *The presence of microscopic diatoms in the bone marrow or blood of a victim indicates that death was probably caused by drowning. Very few or no diatoms indicate that death must have taken place outside the water.*

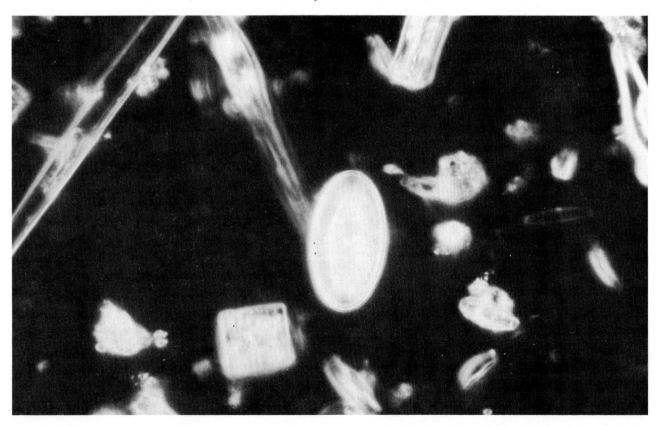

PATHOLOGISTS GALORE
The Steven Truscott case

The ever-important issue of "When did death occur?" was the focal point of the very controversial Canadian case of Steven Truscott, which smouldered on for over seven years. It was notable not only for the fact that a 14 year old boy had been sentenced to be hanged for raping and murdering a young girl, but that no less than seven pathologists from three countries gave evidence on the time of death.

The affair began in June 1959, at Goderich near Clinton, Ontario, where there was a Royal Canadian Air Force base. A 12 year old girl, Lynne Harper, the daughter of a Flying Officer, had her evening meal at 5.30, then went out into the hot summer's evening to join her friends.

At seven o'clock, she was seen chatting with a class-mate from school, Steven Truscott, whose father was a Warrant Officer at the base. He had a green racing bicycle and with Lynne sitting across the bar, they set out for a ride up a country road out of the village.

There were other children about and one of them, cycling in the opposite direction, passed them opposite a small wood called Lawson's Bush. Yet a few moments later, another boy came along and saw no sign of them on the road.

Steven Truscott returned alone and later said that he had dropped Lynne off at the main highway, where he saw her get a lift in a grey Chevrolet with yellow United States numberplates.

When Lynne failed to return home that night, a search was mounted and next day both police and Air Force men combed the district. Nothing was found and the next day, a tight cordon of men beat their way through the fields and woods. In the afternoon, Lynne's body, already starting to decompose in the very hot weather, was found in Lawson's Bush, partly concealed by branches.

She was lying on her back, almost naked, with part of her torn blouse tightly wound around her neck. Her legs were apart and between her feet, two small mounds of soft earth had been pushed up, bearing the imprints of crepe-soled shoes. The situation suggested rape, but due to the condition of the body, this could not immediately be confirmed.

The police called their forensic pathologist, Dr John Penistan, who had trained in Oxford before emigrating to Canada. He carried out a post-mortem that evening and confirmed that Lynne had been strangled and that there was semen in her vagina. The crucial matter was the time of death and from an examination of the amount and state of digestion of the stomach contents, Dr Penistan concluded that she must have died within two hours of her last meal — that is, not later than about half-past seven. The composition of the meal, which was turkey, cranberries and vegetables, confirmed that it was indeed the meal taken on Tuesday evening.

Steven Truscott was interviewed and when medically examined, found to have graze marks on each side of his penis, though he maintained that he had had a rash there for several weeks.

He was subsequently sent for trial and found guilty, being sentenced to death by hanging.

Though no one believed for a moment that this would ever be carried out in Canada on a 14 year old boy, the case shocked the country. There was an appeal, which was dismissed, and as expected, his death sentence was commuted to life imprisonment. He was too young to go to jail and went to the Ontario Training School for Boys.

But the story was far from over. A number of years later, in 1966, a journalist, Isabel LeBourdais, published a book in England about the alleged injustice that had been perpetrated. It was very emotive, but contained a number of inaccuracies, especially about the medical aspects of the case. However, it re-awakened the interest of the Canadian public and there was an outcry for a new trial.

It was not legally possible to appeal from Ontario to the Ottawa courts, but special legislation was passed and in October 1966, the matter was considered by the Supreme Court of Canada.

In the run-up to this appeal, a number of forensic pathologists had become involved. In Britain, the two best-known professors, Keith Simpson and Francis Camps, were reading the LeBourdais book. Camps went so far as to write to the Lord Chancellor of England, expressing his disquiet at the medical evidence and offering his services on behalf of Truscott.

Professor Simpson was more circumspect, confining himself to a review of the book in a medical journal. He was of the opinion that Dr Penistan was quite correct in his conclusions, saying that many of the author's criticisms were ill-founded and based on outdated textbooks.

The Canadian government took the matter very seriously and their Director of Public Prosecutions and a leading barrister flew to London to confer with Keith Simpson; he in turn consulted a professor at Guy's Hospital who was a world authority on digestion and stomach emptying.

Eventually, a panel of eleven judges assembled at the Supreme Court in Ottawa, over seven years after the death of Lynne Harper.

Steven Truscott, who had not given evidence at his first trial or the appeal, was there to speak, but it was the doctors who held the centre of the stage in a hearing which had world-wide publicity.

For the Canadian Government, the medical advisors were Professor Keith Simpson, Professor Milton Helpern, the venerable doyen of forensic medicine from New York City, Dr Samuel Gerber, coroner from Ohio and Dr Jaffe, forensic pathologist from Toronto, as well as Dr John Penistan.

For Truscott, the defence had Francis Camps and Dr Charles Petty, a well-known pathologist from Baltimore. These seven pathologists were all there to debate one issue, the time of death. This was vital to Truscott's alibi, since he was back with the other children soon after the crucial time of seven-thirty that night.

The whole issue was very difficult and in spite of the firm opinions voiced by so many eminent medical men on both sides, the truth is still difficult to decide. No doubt the balance of probabilities came down on the correct side and together with the considerable amount of circumstantial evidence, it seems certain that no miscarriage of justice took place.

Both Milton Helpern and Keith Simpson have devoted a lot of space to the Truscott case in their respective autobiographies.

The basic point of controversy was how much reliance could be placed on the state of digestion of the stomach contents as an indicator of the time since death.

When a meal is eaten, there is considerable variation in the rate of digestion and speed of emptying of the stomach. The type of food makes a difference, fatty meals slowing the process down. Some people digest faster than others and even the same person may have different rates at different times, depending on the state of health and emotional factors.

When some disturbance occurs, such as fear, fright, injury, pain or any strong emotional upset, then either digestion can stop or, sometimes, emptying can be hastened. For example, after severe head injuries, food may stay in the stomach for several days, looking as fresh at the end as when it was swallowed. However, as a general rule, the average meal stays in the stomach for a couple of hours or so.

Applying this to the Truscott case, Dr Penistan carefully measured the amount and examined the state of Lynne's stomach contents and concluded that, as the circumstances suggested, she was her usual state of health and mind until 7.25 that evening; nothing had occurred to change the normal digestion rate until the final quick rape and strangulation, which could not have taken more than a few minutes.

He therefore came to the conclusion that from the considerable volume and only partial digestion of the food, it could not have been longer than two hours since she had eaten it, which was at 5.30 pm.

At the Ottawa court, argument waxed long and strong over these issues. Francis Camps maintained that no conclusions at all could be drawn and that death could have taken place at any time between one and ten hours after eating.

This would give plenty of time for the girl to have been taken away, raped and murdered in the grey Chevrolet — the existence of which was never demonstrated. But as Professors Helpern and Simpson pointed out, it was an odd murderer who would bring the body back and scatter the shoes about the scene. In any case, everything pointed to the crime having been committed in Lawson's Bush.

Other matters reinforced the case against Truscott. Two doctors who examined him when he was arrested said that the marks on his penis were consistent with forcible intercourse, even if he also had a skin ailment. He had a cut on his leg of about two-days duration and also his trousers (which he had since washed) had a corresponding tear in the leg.

It was suggested that this was due to the barbed wire around the wood. There were also grass stains on the knees of the trousers. His crepe-soled shoes, which he was known to own, were never found. Most damning of all was the evidence heard at Ottawa, that when he applied to the Parole Board for release, he had written for "a chance to prove that one dreadful mistake would not lead to another".

In spite of great publicity during the hearing, with Isobel LeBourdais giving a nightly commentary on television, the Supreme Court held that there was no justification for a new trial and the sentence was re-affirmed.

In 1969, Steven Truscott was released from prison and is now living under a new name in another part of Canada. His part in the sad affair is almost forgotten, but the forensic controversy and the acute differences between more than half a dozen forensic pathologists are firmly established in the annals of legal medicine.

discharge two or three bullets into his brain, even though the first one might be thought to be instantly fatal.

Bodies recovered from the water present the pathologist with the problem as to whether they drowned or were thrown in already dead, after being murdered. The state of decomposition or damage from the body swirling in the tide or river may make physical detection of injuries impossible, but there is a technique which may help to decide whether drowning occurred or not.

When a live body falls into water, the drowning process causes fluid to be sucked into the lungs and much of this will enter the blood stream. Many natural waters, such as the sea, rivers, ponds and canals, contain myriads of microscopic algae called 'diatoms'. These have tough shells made of silica, which are resistant to acids. If a sample of tissue such as bone-marrow or kidney is taken at post-mortem and dissolved in acid, any diatoms will be left behind and can be seen under the microscope. If they are present in those tissues, they can only have got there from the lungs via the circulating blood stream, so the person must have been alive in the water. There are technical snags in the procedure, but it can be very useful: the type of diatom can be recognized by an expert botanist and this may even help to establish where the person drowned, either in fresh water or the sea – and even sometimes, which part of the coast. This again emphasizes the multi-disciplinary nature of forensic science, where any sort of expert, even on the most obscure subjects, may need to be called in.

Forensic psychiatry

In many criminal cases, the mental state of the accused is a vital issue and certain doctors become involved in the examination in order to assist the courts in assessing the psychological factors involved. These specialists form an increasingly important sub-section of legal medicine called 'forensic psychiatry'. They are primarily psychiatrists, and many are hospital specialists, who have a particular interest in the mentally abnormal offender. There are a few forensic psychiatrists who practise this speciality as a full-time occupation, most of them working in special institutions. Others combine this interest with duties as clinical psychiatrists or as prison medical officers.

The main issues which face them include the ability of an accused man to plead in court. If a defendant is so mentally disturbed that he cannot appreciate the significance of his trial – or even understand that he is on trial – then obviously he must be detained in a place of safety without any judicial decision being made about his culpability.

Where the accused does stand trial, very complex issues of his criminal responsibility must be explored by the forensic psychiatrist. The famous M'Naghten Rules were founded in Britain – so-called because an insane assassin once shot Daniel M'Naghten, the secretary to Sir Robert Peel, founder of the police force. Under these a person could be found guilty but insane if he was sufficiently mentally unbalanced either not to know what he was doing at the time of the crime, or, if he did, not to know that it was wrong.

In recent years, the concept of 'diminished responsibility' has been developed in English law and other Western legal systems, though it existed in Scots law for a long time. This is a much lesser degree of mental abnormality than needs to be proved under the M'Naghten Rules. The use of these concepts in murder cases was originally to avoid the death sentence where mental abnormality was present. Where the death sentence has been abolished, the disposal of a convicted man to either a specialist prison or to other types of psychiatric care depends largely upon the opinions of the forensic psychiatrist. There is little doubt that forensic psychiatry is becoming an increasingly important (and controversial) area of forensic medicine.

The police surgeon

Whereas the forensic pathologist deals exclusively with the legal aspects of death, the police surgeons deal with the clinical side of legal medicine, since their patients are usually alive. The word 'police surgeon' is something of a misnomer, but survives from the time when certain doctors treated all the illnesses of police officers and their families. These days they are general practitioners who have a part-time contract with the police forces, being called out to any incident where medical knowledge is necessary.

Apart from routine duties such as examining police recruits and attending to injuries sustained by police officers during riots and other duties, police surgeons have two major tasks. Firstly, they are responsible for examining persons thought to have been drinking and driving. The breath tests are carried out by police officers and those found positive on two tests are brought to a police station where the police surgeon examines them. In Britain, the law no longer accuses drivers of having their driving ability impaired by alcohol (though this is still invoked if drugs are involved), but of having more than a certain level of alcohol in their blood or urine. The doctor has two duties – firstly, to examine them to make sure their symptoms are not due to disease or injury and to decide if they are safe to be released to drive afterwards. Secondly, he takes a blood sample, which is sent to the forensic science laboratory for analysis. If the blood contains more than a certain volume of alcohol conviction is automatic.

The other major duty of the police surgeon is the examination of the alleged victims of rape and other sexual offences. A full clinical and gynaecological examination is carried out and again close liaison with the forensic scientist is necessary, as samples of blood, hair, genital swabs and fluids etc., need to be sent to the laboratory for meticulous examination for any evidence of sexual interference.

The police surgeon also becomes involved in attending scenes of death to certify that the victim is dead – and if the arrival of the pathologist is likely to be delayed, he may commence the medical examination at the scene. He may also see and report on non-fatal injuries from assaults, child abuse and many other events where a medical report is needed for the due processes of law.

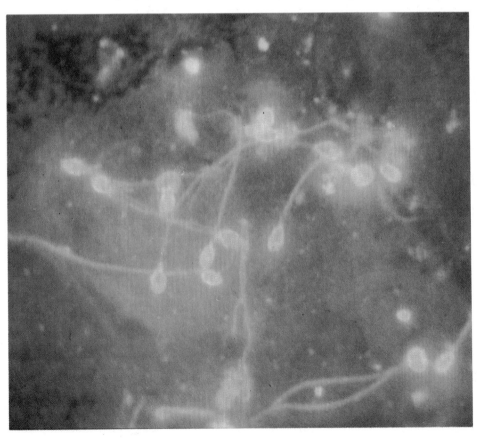

Left: *In rape cases, or in other offences of a sexual nature, the sperm in semen samples examined under a microscope can help identify the guilty person.*

TOXICOLOGY

Any casual student of criminology could be forgiven for thinking that homicidal poisoning was the favourite pastime of middle-class Victorian England. Jack the Ripper and Charlie Peace apart, it was the poison trials which caused the greatest sensations and sold most newspapers to the 'man on the Clapham omnibus.'

Above: *The trial of the Victorian poisoner, William Palmer, in the Central Criminal Court. Palmer, a doctor practising in the north of England, was constantly in debt, and it was suggested that he poisoned several people as a short term solution to his financial problems. Much of the evidence against him was circumstantial, and medical opinion was divided. Nevertheless, he was found guilty, and hanged at Stafford gaol.*

'Poisoner!' hissed the crowd outside Stafford gaol when Dr William Palmer was publicly hanged there in 1856 for murdering 14 people with antimony. The same cry followed Florence Bravo and her companion Jane Cox in 1876, when they were released due to insufficient evidence, though a coroner had found that Florence's husband Charles had been 'wilfully murdered' at their sedate Balham home.

Three years earlier, nurse Mary Ann Cotton had been strangled slowly to death when the hangman bungled his job at Durham Prison. This time the crowd outside approved, for Mary Ann had killed between 15 and 20 people – husbands, lovers, and children – with arsenic, becoming Britain's greatest ever mass murderer. Across the Atlantic, an aristocratic American, Florence Maybrick, gained grudging sympathy when she was sentenced to life for using arsenic to kill her unfaithful husband in 1889. To end the century, another American, Dr Thomas Neill Cream, the 'Lambeth Poisoner', killed at least five prostitutes with strychnine before going to the gallows in 1892, equalling the Ripper's record and, in fact, falsely claiming to be him on the scaffold.

The art of the Victorian poisoner did not, however, end with the death of the old Queen. In 1907 Richard Brinkley went to the gallows for killing his elderly, well to do woman friend by pouring prussic acid into her bottle of stout – a classic Victorian touch – while in 1916 Frederick Henry Seddon, who had murdered his lodger with arsenic in a particularly squalid fashion for her money, appealed to the judge from the dock of the Old Bailey as a 'fellow Freemason'. The judge wept, but sentenced him to death. Only two years before, Dr Hawley Harvey Crippen, perhaps the best known poisoner of modern times, had died on the scaffold for the murder of his promiscuous wife with the vegetable drug hyoscine – then used in small doses for the treatment of sexually unbalanced mental patients.

A personal affair

All these people had something in common besides poison: they killed for love and money – or greed and lust – which are very personal motives. The

poisoner has to have close contact with his victim, and it is this which usually causes his downfall. As crime writer Colin Wilson puts it: 'In real life – as in fiction – it is always easier to identify and bring a poisoner to trial than it is to get the bandit before the jury for the dollars stolen from a bank. Poisoning is usually a personal affair, with a motive like a shining beacon. This is why the clear up rate for poisoners . . . is far higher than any type of crime.'

The determined poisoner has a vast range of materials to hand, but in fact few poisons are as obviously toxic as arsenic, strychnine, or cyanide. Any bright schoolboy with a slight knowledge of organic chemistry could pick a dozen or more lethal substances from the average hedgerow on a nature walk, and in fact any chemical is poisonous if taken in quantity or by the wrong person. Conversely, some substances which appear to be deadly may not kill at all.

In the spring of 1978 a German laboratory technician was convicted of attempting to murder his wife by administering cancer cells to her. He had smuggled a cancer culture from the research laboratory in which he worked and mixed it into her

Above: The notorious doctor Crippen being escorted off the Montrose by Inspector Drew. After poisoning his wife, he tried to escape by sea with his mistress, who was disguised as a boy. This ship was alerted by radio — the first time it was ever used in crime detection.

food. Although she became ill, she did not die for the culture was not in itself dangerous in that form. Similarly the scare which followed the news, in the late 1970s, that a large consignment of Israeli oranges had been injected with mercury was without foundation, although the fruit was withdrawn from the market in the face of public alarm. Mercury in a metallic state is fairly innocuous – indeed it was taken orally as a treatment for syphilis in the eighteenth century – and it is only when injected or inhaled as dust or vapour that it becomes toxic.

The Rasputin case

Frequently, the body may manufacture its own antidote, as Professor Keith Simpson, the eminent British pathologist, has pointed out could well have been the case with Rasputin, the monk who dominated the Russian Imperial family immediately before the Revolution. In December, 1916,

Rasputin was lured to the house of Prince Felix Yussopov with the promise of an orgy. Yussopov and three friends had, in fact, determined to kill the powerful peasant, and had prepared wine and chocolate cake laced with what Yussopov described as 'enough potassium cyanide to kill a monastery of monks'.

Rasputin ate and drank vast quantities without any apparent effect, and in the end Yussopov shot him in the back at point blank range. Two hours later the monk revived and vigorously attacked the Prince. He was then beaten about the head with a heavy instrument, and thrown into the River Neva. Two days later his body was washed up; there were signs that he had regained consciousness again.

Rasputin, a man of giant stature and constitution, might well have survived the bullet and the battering and even the icy water failed to drown him immediately. But what about the cyanide? Professor Simpson pointed out that cyanide is more or less harmless until it comes into contact with the gastric juices, so that its action of the body may be delayed by 'dyspepsia'. 'Should the victim suffer from chronic gastritis as Rasputin probably did,' he wrote, 'he may swallow many times the fatal dose and escape the fate an ordinary subject would quickly meet.'

The toxicologist's role in crime

Forensic toxicologists are called upon to prove or disprove conjectures such as the one quoted above practically every day of their working lives: not as dramatic, perhaps, but usually much more important to the cause of justice. In the United States they usually operate as part of the Coroner's Department alongside the Medical Examiner; in Britain and the Continent they either work full time in the Government forensic laboratories or from the clinical chemistry departments of the great teaching hospitals.

Toxicology means the study of substances such as chemicals and bacteria which are harmful to human beings, although in practice bacteriologists usually handle cases in their own field. The average

Right: *The graph illustrates the changing trends in poison abuse over a 45 year period.*

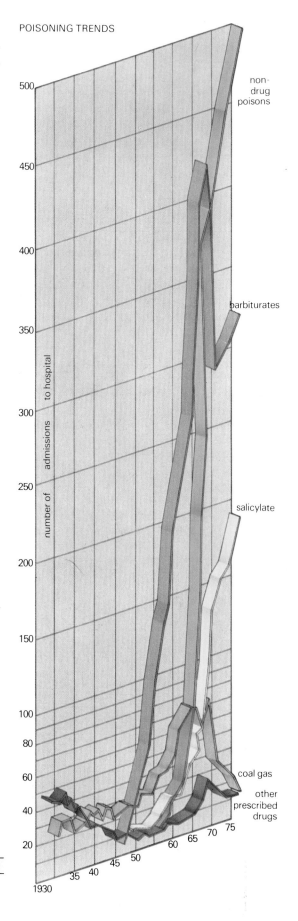

forensic toxicologist is a doctor of science who has specialist qualifications in analytical or clinical chemistry, or in clinical pharmacology. In cooperation with the forensic pathologist who performs post-mortem work he will examine and identify suspected poisons and illicit drugs in body tissues and fluids, and perform examinations and conduct tests in serious drink and driving cases – although the more routine cases are handled by assistants. In recent years, the toxicologist is frequently asked to make similar tests and examinations upon athletes suspected of using stimulants and other drugs.

Toxicology is one of the busier branches of forensic science, playing a major part in many kinds of homicide investigations, and it is perhaps no accident that the Home Office Central Research Establishment of the Forensic Science Service was originally headed by Dr Alan Curry. Dr Curry and Dr Irving Sunshine of the County Coroner's Office in Cleveland, Ohio, are generally considered the two supreme criminal toxicologists in the world.

Much of the work they and their colleagues do is concerned with 'routine' poisoning cases. Every year in Britain alone, 100,000 people are admitted to hospital with suspected poisoning, and a further 4,000 die from poisoning of all kinds. Most of the latter are never admitted to hospital, being 'successful' suicides.

Cries for help

After working as a forensic toxicologist for almost 25 years the writer is very aware that careful distinction must be made between 'genuine' attempted suicides and those which are merely 'cries for help' which go too far. As very few deaths occur in the group that reaches hospital, it would appear that many of these cases are not 'genuine'. Sometimes they are kept in hospital merely so that they can be seen and helped by a psychiatrist. They represent a very much younger age group than those found dead at home.

One group certainly not intending to kill themselves, though their life style may represent a form of death wish, are the drug addicts; one rarely finds the death of a so called addict much above the age of 30. I have known people of this group who have injected themselves with narcotics or taken a

Above: *A standard method of measuring cyanide levels in the blood. This picture illustrates a unique case of cyanide tolerance described on page 82.*

large quantity of barbiturates, just to cure themselves of a hangover.

Some actually inject barbiturates into themselves to make the dose more potent, or make up 'cocktails' of drugs, but, even with the more bizarre preparations, few of them intend to kill themselves.

Another group who do not intend to kill themselves are the ones who take what can be described as a moderate dose of paracetamol, a common analgesic which can be bought without prescription. A massive dose of this is usually fatal and is fairly obviously genuine. But many of the 'moderate' overdose group, who take maybe five or six tablets to knock themselves out and attract attention, begin to recover only to succumb to the incredibly toxic effect of compounds – metabolites – which destroy the liver several days later.

Murder by poison

Although suicide and 'accidental' suicides of the type quoted make up the bulk of the toxicological work carried on in the West, murder by poison did not by any means die out with the Palmers, Maybricks and Crippens. As an officer of London's Metropolitan Police Forensic Science Laboratory points out, of the annual number of people who die or are admitted to hospital suffering from poisoning, perhaps 99% are suicidal or accidental. That still leaves 40 deaths and 1,000 non-fatal poisonings which may be criminal. Without suspicion there is no investigation, and therefore no analysis.

Normally if a person dies under suspicious or dubious circumstances, the pathologist passes on samples of the major organs for further analysis in the laboratory. But 'suspicion' becomes the key word in hunting down deliberate poisoners. As Professor Alexandre Lacassagne, founder of the Department of Forensic Science at Lyons University impressed on the nineteenth century toxicologists under his guidance: 'One must know how to doubt.'

The scene of the crime

Often, the first suspicion must be voiced by the police officer called to a scene of sudden death, and detectives are given careful schooling in what to watch for. Poison should always be considered, they are told, if death or illness occurs rapidly, without

warning in young children, alcoholics, the insane, the senile, and the chronically sick. All these people can be described as 'classic' potential victims. For one thing they are more vulnerable than healthy adults, and for another they can be a nuisance: they tend to be in someone's way.

It is far more difficult to dope the healthy adult in reality than it is in fiction. The single sleeping tablet in the security guard's cup of tea will not cause him to suddenly fall asleep. Most of the sedative or narcotic pharmaceuticals do not dissolve completely in drinks and they usually taste very bitter. Anybody taking the old fashioned 'Micky Finn' would be possessed of neither taste nor smell!

Right: An American explorer, Charles Francis Hall, who died in suspicious circumstances at the North Pole in 1871. As he was buried there, his body was well preserved. Nearly a century later, scientists found a lethal dose of arsenic in his body tissues.

When in doubt, therefore, the officer specially trained to work at the scene of a crime is very careful indeed. Tablets, capsules and medicines found near the victim are sent off with their containers carefully labelled and with a note of the position in which they were found. Similarly, cups, glasses and bottles are taken for examination, their contents drained into test tubes, along with any other odd tubes, packets, or bottles which lie in the house unlabelled.

Anything which has a warning label on it is noted, though not submitted unless it seems to have been used recently, or unless it is in an unusual place.

Obviously, the police are interested if they find

Above: *Graham Young, the mass poisoner. His trial shocked the British public in the 1970s, when it was revealed that at 14 he had already tried to poison several people. He was then sent to a special prison for mentally disturbed criminals, and had been released as "cured".*

anti-freeze in the lounge, ant powder in the bathroom, or even cleaner in the bedroom. They also examine sugar basins, tea caddies, coffee jars – 'do they appear to be contaminated?'

The police officer with little or no knowledge of chemistry is asked to smell cautiously at strange substances, but, of course, never to taste. Any unusual odours are important, and officers are required to make a note of them, trying to relate them to something they are familiar with – for instance fruit, fish, bad eggs, sour milk, nail varnish.

In a full scale investigation, perhaps in the hunt for a multiple poisoner, a much more thorough search will be instigated. Dustbins will be emptied and rummaged through, sink traps and lavatory pans will be drained, and stains of vomit or urine will be gathered, as well as quantities of the liquid – up to eight pints – used to wash out the stomach of any survivors in hospital.

Above: *Examining a liquid chromatograph chart.*
Below: *Rapid screening tests for drugs can be made automatically on this EMIT (enzyme multiplied immuno-assay technique) device. EMIT is used to detect a wide range of drugs, including opiates, cocaine, barbiturates and amphetamines, and is of immeasurable help to the toxicologist.*

Above right: *Radioimmunoassay. Samples of test solution are incubated with a series of radioactively labelled antibodies. If a drug is present, it will combine with its specific antibody. Amounts are estimated by measuring the radioactivity.*
Below: *Thin layer chromatogram. This technique can analyse about 90% of common poisons.*

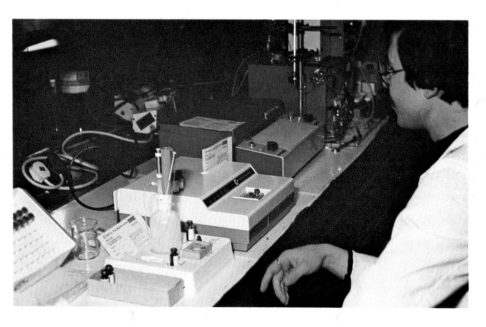

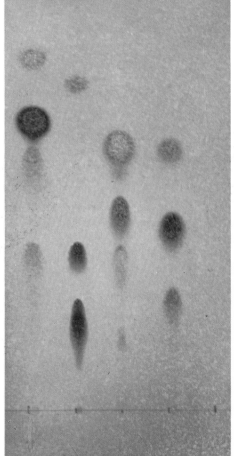

Taking samples

If a toxicologist is unable to perform or attend at the post mortem, the scene of crime officer will watch it and take notes from the pathologist. Eventually he will leave with a container of sealed jars destined for the laboratory. In every case of poisoning these will contain the stomach and its contents, at least one third of the liver, a minimum of 25 milligrams of blood from both chambers of the heart and various other sites in the body, and urine from the bladder. If a volatile toxic is suspected – one that evaporates quickly – the brain and lungs will be taken, while if death is due to cyanide the spleen will be removed. Signs of vomiting and diarrhoea might mean that a closer examination of a kidney is called for, while portions of hair, nails, and a segment of bone, preferably from the femur, will tell the toxicologist if arsenical poisoning caused death. Even when the body is putrid or badly crushed, vitreous humour from the eyeball may have been invaded by the poison, and will reveal its nature under analysis.

Although there are very few homicides in relation to the number of suspected suicides examined, the amount of extra work that is entailed in a full scale murder investigation is often out of all proportion to its scientific requirement, though not, of course, to the requirements of the courts. Every angle has to be scrutinized.

Changes in toxicology

It was Mathieu Joseph Bonaventure Orfila, born in Minorca in 1787, who is generally recognized as the father of modern toxicology. In the early nineteenth century at the University of Paris, he began the monumental task of cataloguing poisons and their effects. He received fortuitous assistance from a contemporary and colleague, Marie Guillaume Alphonse Devergie, the man who first brought the microscope to bear on practical forensic pathology and published the results in 1835 in his classic *Médecine légale, théorique et pratique.*

In the 150 years since then, the practical application of the principles laid down by both men has come on apace. In a modern laboratory, the two pioneers would recognize items such as test tubes, conical flasks, and jars, and Devergie might just discern the vague outline of his early instrument in the shape of its modern successor, but little else except the poisons and the human tissue itself would be familiar.

Lab technology

Today's toxicologist is largely dependent on a battery of analytical techniques using various forms of chromatography – a method of separating, measuring and analysing chemical mixtures. The machines used are complex, but in basic terms chemicals are fed into an electronic machine which the toxicologist adjusts to his requirements; the amounts of each substance present emerge in the form of either a graph or, in ultra modern instruments, a computer print out.

There are several methods for different jobs: gas chromatography, paper and thin layer chromatography, and most recently high pressure liquid chromatography. This can detect tiny traces of such formerly 'difficult' substances as LSD in the urine, and monitor the strength present by a process known as radioimmunoassay. Thus in a sample of blood, urine or other liquid the measurement of drugs or poison present using these methods need be no more than .000000001 grams. No toxicology laboratory can now do an up-to-date and thorough job without at least two of these appliances.

When the Seddons poisoned their victim with arsenic and Crippen used rather more than a therapeutic dose of hyoscine to remove his spouse for ever, they used compounds which would not normally be found in such quantities in the body. In fact at the trial of the Seddons, for example, it was stated that the differential diagnosis between gastroenteritis and arsenical poisoning was the finding of the arsenic itself.

Today, however, we can detect 'normal' amounts of arsenic in living people, and follow the ingestion of perfectly normal foodstuffs that contain more arsenic than others. Arsenic has always been present in the body and in certain foods we eat without doing harm. After death, however, chemical changes in the body might possibly make a heavy meal of fish, say, eaten some time prior to death look like an arsenic poisoning case. Such a mistake could not be made today since technology has advanced so rapidly and precisely.

THE BLACK WIDOW
OF LOUDUN
Marie Besnard

At first glance, Marie Besnard, called the 'Black Widow of Loudun' by the popular press, seemed an unlikely candidate for the guillotine. Small, prim and rather dumpy, she was the very epitome of French peasant respectability as she stood in the dock of Poitiers courthouse, accused of multiple poisoning. Was she a hapless victim of a jealous neighbour's malicious gossip, or a cruel ruthless mass murderer? The question vexed French lawyers for 12 years, and her ordeal was to become a classic in the annals of French forensic toxicology.

The accusations first came to light in July 1949. Marie Besnard had just buried her second husband, Léon, a rope-maker in the small town of Loudun (famed, in an earlier age, as the centre of a French witchcraft cult) – he had died, so the doctor said, of a heart attack. But not according to a poison-pen letter received by the authorities. It alleged that Léon Besnard, just before his death, had complained to the writer (who, of course, preferred to remain anonymous) of having been served 'tainted soup' by his wife. The letter suggested, in fact, that just knowing Madame Besnard could be a hazardous business, and went on to name some 12 other possible victims of the famous soup, including a first husband, her parents, a father-in-law and a Loudun pâtissier.

Mass exhumation of the possible victims was ordered, and the retrieved organs were sent to Marseilles to the laboratory of one of France's leading toxicologists, Dr. Béroud. He found evidence that the bodies did indeed contain abnormal quantities of arsenic, of a level, he felt, that could quite feasibly have found its way into plates of soup. Marie Besnard was arrested and a date for her trial set.

From the first it was a struggle of experts: Dr Béroud for the prosecution dominated the court. He was, he said firmly and unequivocally, absolutely convinced that Léon Besnard, and the others, had succumbed to a fatal dose of arsenic.

The defence showed interest in the details. Dr Béroud explained that the organs had been packed into separate jars and sent to Marseilles for analysis. Such was the meticulous attention to detail that particulars of each jar (and each victim), and the total quantity of jars sent, were logged both in Loudun and at Marseilles. Records were carefully compared and, the defence pointed out, did not tally: somewhere on that macabre journey the number of jars increased – and what's more, jars of intestines appeared in Marseilles (and were quoted in the trial as having been found to contain arsenic), whereas only jars

Above: *Marie Besnard's defense counsel, Maître Hayot, displays some grisly evidence to the court.*

of muscle were logged as having left Loudun! Since it seemed unlikely that the intestines could have joined the procession of their own volition en route, the defence suggested that perhaps the Loudun consignment had become mixed up with other specimens at the laboratory. Dr Béroud protested but could offer no explanation. It seemed as if the case of the excess organs was becoming a classic mystery in its own right.

The defence tried again. To underline his authority and experience, the doctor had claimed to the president of the court that he could recognize arsenic rings in a test tube with the naked eye. Defence counsel, with a flourish, produced six test tubes for him to pronounce upon. After some deliberation the doctor returned three, which he said contained arsenic and which were promptly admitted as evidence. Defence counsel informed him (and waved a laboratory certificate to prove it) that none of the test tubes contained arsenic, that the rings he had 'recognized' were, in fact, antimony rings.

With Dr Béroud's testimony discredited, the defence then called its expert witness, Professor Perperot. Dig anywhere in the Loudun area, he said, investigate any number of buried bodies, and you would find fairly abnormal quantities of arsenic in them – because it came from the soil. The court pronounced itself baffled, ordered another round of expert witnesses to be appointed to clarify and solve the problem, and adjourned the trial.

If the first trial ended on a technical note, the second one, which was moved to Bordeaux and did not take place until 1954, seemed to start on a note of high farce. The originator of the 'tainted soup' letter was produced in court, one Madame Pintou, a lady who claimed to be a friend of both the Besnards. Some skilful defence questioning elicited the rather confusing testimony that although she had reported Léon Besnard's statement to the authorities, her behaviour to Madame Besnard after his death was effusively friendly – even noble, the defence suggested. Was this the reaction of someone who believed that her neighbour had killed her husband? Madame

Above: *Madame Besnard with Maître Jacqueline Favreau-Columbier during the final trial.*

Pintou admitted that it was not. Did she believe then that Madame Besnard was a poisoner? No, she did not, she sheepishly replied. Nor did she now, she confessed eventually under steady defence questioning. Exit the prosecution's star witness in the second trial.

Once more the stage was set for a confrontation of 'experts'. One prosecution witness claimed to have detected arsenic in the by-now famous organs by geiger counter — but when his figures were sent to the British Atomic Authorities for verification, they were found to have an 80 percent error rate in them. Retorted the expert witness: 'The English don't know how to use an atomic pile!' A second defence witness was produced to confirm that the arsenic found in the bodies could have been caused by the presence of arsenic in the soil. So the second trial, too, finished in a stand-off between the experts, which would normally have led to the accused's aquittal. But not this time. The president of the court ruled that since he and the jury did not have sufficient evidence with

which to judge the case, three more investigating scientists would be appointed, and a third trial date would be set.

Marie Besnard, this time, was allowed to return to Loudun to await trial on bail (ironically partly furnished by relatives — second cousins, who presumably donated generously in gratitude at having survived the family purge). Her twilight life continued here, with postponement after postponement of the trial until 1961, when she again appeared before the Bordeaux courts. This final trial followed what had become the usual pattern of experts wrangling over whether the bodies were poisoned by soup or soil, and again it resulted in their agreeing to disagree. This time, however, the case went to the jury. Eleven times it was asked if 'Marie Davaillaud, the widow Besnard, deliberately administered a poisonous substance likely to cause a more or less rapid death'. Eleven times came back the reply: 'No.'

Marie Besnard was free at last. After 12 years and three trials for multiple murder, at the age of 65 she was able to pick up the pieces and remake what was left of her life.

The Bradford insulin murder

This murder took place in 1957, and was investigated by a team led by Dr Alan S. Curry. The case changed the whole pattern of toxicological examination. The Curry team, assisted by scientists from Boots' chemists, established that though certain chemicals might be 'normally' in the body, they could be criminally boosted to toxic levels.

The case began in May 1957, when a 38 year old male nurse named Kenneth Barlow called a doctor to his Bradford home one night with the report that he had found his wife Elizabeth dead in the bath. Barlow, still in his pyjamas, said that she had been unwell all evening, had vomited in bed, and had gone to take a hot bath. Barlow had dozed off and had awoken to find her under the water. He had been unable to lift her out, and so had pulled the plug and tried artificial respiration, all to no avail.

The police, including a sharp eyed detective sergeant named Naylor, were called to the scene and became immediately suspicious. Mrs Barlow's 'hot bath' had given off very little steam, for the walls of the bathroom were dry. Nor had Kenneth Barlow made much of an effort to pull his wife from the tub, for his pyjamas were equally dry. When the doctor noticed that the crooks of Mrs Barlow's elbows were also dry – an odd circumstance given an otherwise wet body which had allegedly been subject to artificial respiration – Sergeant Naylor made his arrest. A search of the house revealed two hypodermic needles, which Barlow explained by saying that he was treating his own carbuncle with penicillin taken from Bradford Royal Infirmary, where he worked. Inquiries there showed that he had access to insulin, and that he had boasted that a large dose of the substance could be used to commit the perfect murder.

On examination, one of the syringes was found to contain traces of insulin, while the other was empty. Mrs Barlow's eyes were dilated, which suggested poisoning, but after a complete series of tests Dr Curry was able to exclude all the common poisons. These completely negative findings, plus the circumstances, suggested that drowning may have been the result of insulin poisoning.

A minute examination of Mrs Barlow's heavily freckled body revealed two skin punctures beneath

Above: *Kenneth Barlow, a male nurse, murdered his wife by injecting her with a fatal dose of insulin.*

the buttocks, one a few days old, but the other very recent. In a long and unique series of experiments, Dr Curry's team were able to demonstrate that although insulin is normally present in the body the amount of insulin in this case was vastly in excess of the normal amount. Insulin is a large protein molecule, and the technological achievement lay in identifying this molecule for the first time in a case of murder.

At Mrs Barlow's trial the only medical defence put forward was that she had slipped under the water and, in a moment of fear, her body had reacted by injecting a massive dose of insulin into her bloodstream, causing coma and death. Insulin rapidly disappears from the body, but Dr Curry had discovered a total of 240 units of it, a fact, he pointed out to the court, that meant her natural insulin secretion would have had to reach an impossible 15,000 units. Barlow was sentenced to life imprisonment.

The question of tolerance

Often, toxicologists are faced with the question of tolerance, particularly where a chronic drug addict is concerned. In one recent case, they examined material from the body of a drug addict who had been injected by a colleague with two tablets of the narcotic analgesic Palfium. The colleague told police that his friend was used to taking this amount.

His body also contained measurable amounts of another narcotic analgesic named Diconal. By measuring a cross section of the blood levels of patients who had been taking the drugs therapeutically, it was shown that in every case the blood level of

the drugs was less than a quarter of the level of that found in the addict (EA) (see illustrations below). The injection had therefore constituted an overdose. As a result of these findings the police pressed a charge of manslaughter on the addict's colleague.

In another case, exactly the opposite occurred. A laboratory put forward the theory that a number of deaths had been caused by the compound dihydrocodeine, taken in overdose. A comparison with the level of dihydrocodeine in the blood of patients who had been prescribed the drug showed that their levels were considerably higher than those in the suspect bodies – though the patients were, of course, alive and well.

TABLE 1

No.	Case	Age	Wt/kg	Sex	Plasma Level mg/ml	Clinical Comments
1	KJ	32	52	F	0.023	Receiving 15mg per day. Sarcoma Alternates Pethidine
2	PM	47	73	M	0.056	Receiving 15mg per day. Leukaemia Sometimes 30mg
3	IR	62	71	M	0.031	Receiving 10mg per day sometimes 20mg Page's Disease
4	PL	31	65	M	0.012	Receiving 10mg per day. Leukaemia Alternates Pethidine
5	JB	58	48	F	0.019	Receiving 10mg per day. Therapy 2 weeks Fractured Wrist
6	JS	64	49	F	0.052	Receiving 15-25mg per day. Carcinoma
7	BK	41	73	M	0.042	Receiving 15mg per day. Carcinoma Stomach
8	AR	73	69	M	0.060	Receiving 40mg per day. Carcinoma Lung

Left: This is a collection of cases whose therapeutic treatment with Palfium and Diconal has been carefully measured and monitored. This provides the toxicologist with a range of blood levels when the intake is under normal conditions.

TABLE 2

No.	Case	Blood Level	Other Drugs	Comment
1	KD	not determined	none detected	Large amount 42.5mg present in stomach contents. Not determined in urine.
2	JB	0.24mg/ml	Dalame 0.3mg/ml Alcohol = 90	Dalmane also taken in overdose quantity but Dextromoramide far more important
3	JW	0.27mg/ml	Cyclizine 1.1 C and DP in urine	Alcohol – nil Dextromoramide and Diconal combination
4	EA	0.22mg/ml	Cyclizine 1.1 Dipipanone 0.6	Alcohol – nil Current Case
5	KM	0.2mg/ml	Cyclizine 0.14 Methaqualone 2.6	Traces Morphine and Diphenhydramine present
6	HL	0.5mg/ml	Diazepam 0.13mg/ml	Liver level 0.9mg/ml

Left: This table (which includes EA's case) is a collection of post-mortem cases where death has been caused by overdoses of Palfium. The chart shows that EA's blood levels are commensurate with known death by overdose, rather than with regular therapeutic use.

FROM RUSSIA WITH LOVE?
The Markov murder

The slaying of Georgi Markov will remain one of the most chilling demonstrations of science and technology harnessed to murderous ends.

By September 1978 Markov, a healthy six foot tall Bulgarian of 49 years, working in London for the BBC World Service, was a thorn in the side of the regime that ran his native country. There was every reason for Bulgaria's government to wish his courageous, provocative broadcasts could suddenly cease.

On September 7, Markov was waiting for his evening bus home on Waterloo Bridge when a jab in his right thigh caused him to turn in surprise. The man behind him dropped the offending furled umbrella, muttered an apology, and hastened to hail a taxi. His problem in explaining his destination suggested, later, that he was probably a foreigner. Bemused but little concerned, Markov went home to his wife.

That night he slept in his study. He was due on early shift next day and did not wish to disturb the family. But they were disturbed. In the small hours Markov began running a temperature of 104° and vomiting.

"I have a horrible suspicion" he confided to his wife, "that it might be connected with something that happened today." They examined the mysterious puncture. It looked as if someone had jabbed him with a ball point pen. There were a few drops of blood on his jeans.

Next morning, Markov seemed well enough to be left, but his wife arranged for the family doctor to call, before departing for work. The doctor was alarmed enough to have Georgi hospitalized immediately. His decline thereafter was swift. A circular area of inflammation now surrounded the original puncture. His temperature and blood pressure fell rapidly. Septicemia was diagnosed. Over the weekend the patient became violent and confused. He died on Monday morning. To their astonishment, the hospital found that Markov's white blood count had risen to 33,000 per cubic millimetre—a normal count is between five and ten thousand.

The death was sufficiently mysterious to provoke a high level investigation that reached from London's Metropolitan Police Laboratory to the governmental microbiological research institute at Porton Down. Here, pathologist Rufus Crompton examined the section of flesh excised from the dead Bulgarian's thigh. One inch from the puncture, and just below the skin, he felt a small hard object that he first guessed was a pinhead. On removal it turned out to be a minute metal ball. Crompton, bemused, put it in a paper bag, and turned it over to Dr Ray Williams at the Metropolitan Police Laboratory.

Electron microscopy revealed an impressive piece of precision engineering. The pellet, a mere 1.52mm in diameter, had two holes bored through it, crossing at the centre. In composition, the pellet proved to be an alloy, 90% platinum and 10% iridium. To drill holes .35mm wide in such a notably hard substance plainly involved someone with access to highly specialized equipment.

The position of the pellet in the body suggested that the mysterious assailant's umbrella had been equally specialized. Everything indicated a firing device in the ferrule, silently powered by a gas cylinder. The whereabouts of the umbrella remained a mystery. So, for the moment, did the identity of a poison sufficiently lethal to be effective in the minute quantity the pellet was able to hold.

Tests ruled out a radioactive source. The only other known candidates in the toxicologist's book were derivatives from two widespread – and at first acquaintance innocent-seeming – plants. One, the so called Rosary Bean, was already familiar as the world's commonest lethal source of vegetable poison. The beans, widely used to make simple rosaries, yield a toxin called abrin. Chemically, this is close to the residue of another bean, fruit of the castor oil plant: and castor oil plants are commonly cultivated in the countries where Markov's enemies could reasonably be expected to lurk.

Ricin, or ricinine, is not present in castor oil itself (despite the testimony of generations of children that castor oil is pure poison). It remains in the bean once the oil is extracted – anyone unwise enough to chew a bean thoroughly has a one in 20 chance of dying. Efficiently extracted however, ricin is twice as deadly as cobra venom. An albumen, it causes red blood cells to agglutinate; then it goes on to attack other body cells with devastating effect. High temperature, vomiting, disorientation and diarrhea are among the immediate host of effects. Significantly, the toxin is most effective at an astonishing dilution of one part in a million. For some years, cancer specialists had been experimenting with both ricin and abrin as a weapon against rogue cells.

At Porton Down, the pathologists experimentally injected a pig with the amount of ricin the Markov pellet could have contained. It died within

24 hours. The evidence was hardening but still circumstantial — for no trace of ricin itself had been found in Markov's corpse.

Yet that fact was only another indicator that ricin was the likely agent. One property of the toxin that makes it elegantly suitable as a murder agent is that the body's natural protein-making cells break ricin down so that, having done its damage, it disappears from the body.

The clinching conclusion to the investigation lay not in the laboratory but walking in the streets of Paris. In an incident outside a metro station the previous year another Bulgarian emigré had been mysteriously jabbed, fallen sick, but recovered. After some persuasion, he was now visited by a surgeon, who extracted a small metallic object from his flesh. It was brought by police escort to the lab in London, eagerly awaited by Dr Ray Williams and his assistant. There, an electron microscope revealed a pellet identical to the one that killed Markov.

What the investigation failed to reveal was the hand behind the umbrella. The implications, however, were sombre. How many other dissidents, emigrés, opponents of Warsaw pact regimes had lately died in apparently innocent circumstances?

The list drawn up by Markov's BBC colleagues for a special TV programme was a long one . . .

Above: *The ill-fated Georgi Markov.*
Below: *A microscope picture of the tiny pellet in Markov's body, photographed alongside a pinhead.*

The cyanide case

One of the oddest cases concerning the build up of a 'tolerance' – in this instance to a large dose of cyanide – concerned a heavy drinker who had smoked 60 cigarettes a day for over 25 years. While he was a patient in hospital, a routine blood sample was taken and found to contain a considerable quantity of cyanide. In fact, had it been taken in acute form – all at once, it could have been fatal. The illustration on page 71 shows one of the very sensitive standard methods whereby toxicologists measure cyanide in the blood. Cyanide gas eliminated from the whole blood-acid mixture at the bottom of the flask is trapped in the dye-forming process in the cup suspended from the stopper. The quantity of cyanide in the blood is directly related to the purple colour developing in the cup.

The amount of cyanide seen here is just the sort of picture that would result from a death by cyanide ingestion, or from breathing cyanide fumes from burning polyurethane plastics. Alternatively, it could be the result of the burning of a great deal of protein. Cyanide vapour is produced when protein is burned, and cigarettes contain protein. Calculations showed that over the years he had inhaled minute quantities of cyanide vapour with each cigarette; normally the liver dissipates the substance in a short time, but the patient's liver was not in very good condition after his drinking and the poison had stayed. However, the process had taken so long that his body had built up a truly amazing resistance to one of the most agonizing and deadly poisons known.

Below: *Samples of cyanide taken from the stomach (40), liver (41), brain (42) and stomach in a picric acid test (43) of a New York man in 1931. The man's car was in flames, and his body slumped over the front mudguard. At first it was thought that he had burned to death accidentally. However these lab samples helped prove that he had taken a fatal dose of cyanide.*

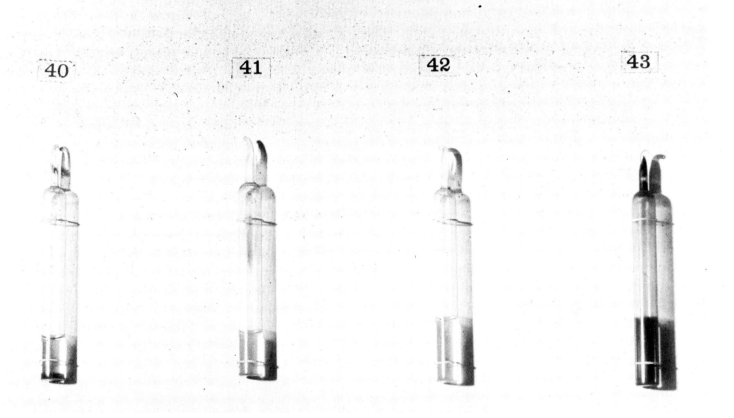

The Brixton tablets

The illustration above showing an X-ray picture of tablets is another of the more interesting cases from today's workload. The tablets are saccharin coated with LSD, and were found in the stomach of a remand prisoner shortly after receiving a visitor. The wrapping around the tablets had burst, and the prisoner died from a massive overdose of the drug (the first recorded death from an overdose of LSD). These 'deaths-on-crossing-a-boundary' are those of a new era. Drug smugglers make the headlines bringing heroin into Europe, or attempting to smuggle cocaine into North America.

Smugglers arriving in Miami have dropped dead – literally – in the customs hall, as a wrapped sample of cocaine swallowed inside a balloon or sometimes a contraceptive sheath bursts in the stomach.

Above: The first recorded death from an overdose of LSD. These saccharin tablets coated with the drug were smuggled to a prisoner in London's Brixton prison. The packet opened in his stomach, releasing a massive dose.

Obviously, some drugs are safely transported like this, but there are few available official figures.

To the layman, toxicology must be the most bafflingly complex of all branches of forensic science, but this is because, along with the related disciplines of biochemistry and serology, it has advanced with swift but precise strides during the last two or three decades. Its empirical techniques become exact science almost before the toxicologists themselves can keep pace. It all adds up to the fact that, although we cannot yet stop latter-day Crippens from poisoning their wives, we can at least prevent them from getting away with it.

FORENSIC DENTISTRY

It is a popularly held belief that forensic odontology is a newcomer to scientific investigations in the field of criminal law, but even a cursory search in history will provide examples in which dental evidence has provided a positive means of identification where other methods would have proved unsuccessful. Forensic odontology, forensic dentistry or even forensic odontostomatology are the terms used for that branch of forensic medicine which, in the interests of justice, deals with the proper handling and examination of dental evidence and with the proper evaluation and presentation of that evidence. It requires a dental expert to handle and examine the dental evidence with the degree of accuracy that the legal profession expects. Forensic dental work requires further training to the accepted and conventional dental education in which additional knowledge and experience serves to qualify the dental expert as a valued member of an investigating team.

Perhaps one of the earliest references to a form of dental identification in 2500 BC concerned the finding of two molar teeth linked together by gold wire in a tomb at Giza. One of the most popular identification cases occurred much later in AD 66 when Sabina, who was Nero's mistress, and Agrippina, his mother, decided that Lollia Paulina, the rich divorcee, constituted a threat to their security. Agrippina's soldiers were sent to kill Lollia Paulina with instructions to bring back her head when the deed was done. This was common practice at that time, to prove that the required death had occurred, but in this case Agrippina was unable to recognize the distorted features of her victim. She then parted the lips of the severed head and examined the front teeth to satisfy herself of the presence of the discoloured front tooth that confirmed the identity of Lollia Paulina. It is said that only then was she willing to pay the assassination fee.

In 1477 the disfigured body of Charles the Bold was identified after the Battle of Nancy by the absence of teeth from his jaws as a result of an accident that had occurred during his life.

Paul Revere

It is well known that in 1775 Paul Revere made his famous ride to warn the countryside that 'the English are coming' but it is not always related that he was a skilled coppersmith, silversmith, and engraver. He had been taught the art of dentistry by John Baker, an English surgeon-dentist, and he practised as a dental surgeon from 1768 to 1788. He was the first dentist of note to record personally a case of dental identification. Early in 1775 he constructed a silver wire and ivory bridge (the ivory from a hippopotamus tusk) for his close friend Dr Joseph Warren. This latter gentleman was known for his progressive views on smallpox inoculations and opposition to the practice of 'bleeding' ill patients, and also to the founding of a society for the study of anatomy from victims of 'body-snatching'. He had participated with Paul Revere in the incident of the Boston Tea Party, and as a member of the Sons of Liberty was one of the leaders in the outbreak of the American revolution.

When war broke out Warren was elected to the rank of Major-General in the Massachusetts

Above: The famous American trial of John Webster in the 1840s relied upon important dental evidence.

militia, having refused the appointment of surgeon-in-chief to the colonial army. During the Battle of Bunker Hill he was killed by a bullet in the brain and was buried in an unmarked grave, perhaps to prevent the plundering of his teeth as a source of teeth for dentures. (Battlefields in former times provided an abundance of front teeth for dental production which the normal demand could not supply. Young men and women short of money were often forced to sell their healthy teeth. The women also sold their hair for wigs.) However, Joseph Warren was dug up on the following day by the British and exhibited as a warning to the populace of what would happen to all revolutionaries.

In 1776, ten months after Warren's death, his brothers, Paul Revere and friends again disinterred the body to confirm the presence of the silver wire and ivory bridge replacing the upper left canine and first premolar tooth, which positively identified Joseph Warren. In all, the body was reburied five times, before being left in peace in the family plot in Forest Hill cemetery. His place in history therefore is assured as the first identification by a dentist and the most reburied of American heroes.

The Webster-Parkman case

The first American crime of national interest involving dental identification was the Webster-Parkman case in 1849. Dr John Webster was Professor of chemistry and mineralogy at Harvard and although said to be a good father and husband was somewhat irascible in disposition and unable to live on his salary of $1,200 a year. Each time he found himself unable to manage he borrowed from Dr George Parkman who had given up the practise of medicine for the practise of real estate.

For security, Professor Webster had mortgaged his home and goods together with his valuable mineral collection. Dr Parkman became annoyed when he found by chance that the Professor had already borrowed money on the mineral collection and had given a bill of sale on it elsewhere. Parkman then pressed for the return of his loan and began to make a nuisance of himself by insulting the Professor at his lectures and making disparaging remarks about them. One day Dr Parkman visited the Professor's laboratory again to demand the return of his money and in the ensuing argument was either struck on the head and killed, or stabbed by the Professor. Professor Webster dismembered the body, putting the head and some organs into the furnace. Other parts were placed in the dissection vault and the blood carefully washed away. Over a period of time he disposed of these parts in the furnace and maintained a jaunty manner which did not impress the college janitor. When the janitor received a Thanksgiving turkey as a gift his suspicions were further aroused.

He carried out his own investigation, looking through keyholes, under doors, and finally digging under the exterior wall to get to the dissection vault. When he found a pelvis and two pieces of leg he immediately informed the college authorities. At the subsequent official investigation Professor Webster denied that any of the remains belonged to Dr Parkman, but portions of charred teeth fused to gold were recovered and identified by Dr Nathan Cooley Keep, who had constructed the denture for Dr Parkman.

Dr Lester Noble, who was Dr Keep's assistant, was able to testify that the study models of Dr Parkman's teeth had been marked by him with the date 'Oct., 1846' and the recovered portion of porcelain denture fitted accurately the model of the lower jaw. This case marks the first time that evidence of dental identification was presented in an American court and such was the interest generated in Boston at the time that spectators in the court gallery were only allowed to remain for ten minutes before relinquishing their places to those waiting outside. Although the defence sought to discredit the evidence the jury were convinced that the dental evidence positively established the identity of the deceased. Professor Webster was found guilty of murder and hanged on August 30th 1850.

The Bazaar de la Charité fire

In 1897 a tragic fire occurred at the Bazaar de la Charité in Paris that took 126 lives in the short space of a few minutes. This bazaar was held annually by the wealthy women of Paris to raise funds for the poor. The bodies recovered from the fire were badly burned and mutilated and visual identification was difficult but some identifications resulted from the recognition of clothing and personal effects. Thirty victims remained unidentified until the Paraguayan consul made the suggestion that dentists of the known missing persons be requested to chart the teeth of these victims and compare the post-mortem findings with their own dentistry. Later that year, a paper, 'The role of dentists in the identification of the victims of the catastrophe of the Bazaar de la Charité, 4 May 1897', was presented by Dr Oscar Amöedo, Professor of the Paris dental school, at the International Medical Congress of Moscow.

This paper recorded the procedures and observations of the dentists engaged in the identification work and his conclusions concerning the need for the adoption of a uniform system of charting internationally. Amöedo has been called the 'father of forensic odontology' as he enlarged his ideas of dental identification in the text of L'Art dentaire en médecine légale, published in 1898 in French and in 1899 in German. There were more than six hundred pages with chapters covering all aspects of dental identification and dental jurisprudence. This classic text-book has remained a standard for all forensic odontologists to emulate in the subsequent years.

The Dobkin case

In recent times one of the most famous cases involving dental identification occurred in 1942 when a workman was helping to demolish the bombed premises of a baptist church in south London. He lifted a stone slab set into the cellar floor under the vestry and found a skeleton which he assumed was just another victim of the blitz. The head remained in situ after he lifted the skeleton and when the police arrived the remains were wrapped in a paper parcel and taken to Southwark public mortuary.

The following morning the remains were examined by a young pathologist named Dr Keith Simpson. There was still some flesh adhering to the bones including a dried up womb, with yellowish deposit on the head and neck and blackening by fire on parts of the skull and lower limbs. The neat burial under a slab did not suggest a bomb victim and

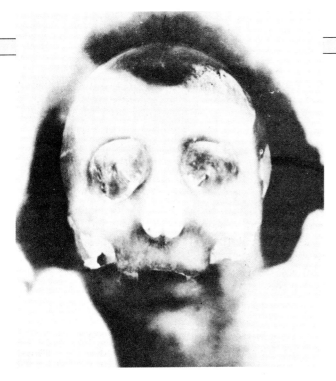

The dental evidence

The lower jaw was missing but the upper jaw presented extensive dental treatment including fillings and marks of denture clasps. The police searched through the lists of missing persons and discovered that Mrs Rachel Dobkin, the wife of a fire-watcher at the church, had been reported missing 15 months earlier. Her height was similar, she had sought advice concerning fibroid growths of the uterus, and her dental surgeon was a Mr Barnett Kopkin. He had kept precise records of Mrs Dobkin's treatment from 1934 to 1940 and was able to sketch a picture of the lady's upper jaw. When confronted by the skull of the deceased he was in no doubt that he was looking at his dental work on the jaws of the skull of his former patient. Further police investigation resulted in the arrest and subsequent trial of Harry Dobkin, her husband, who paid the final penalty for murder in Wandsworth prison.

Above: *A photograph of Rachel Dobkin's skull superimposed on a snapshot reveals a perfect match for identification.*
Below top: *The remains, covered in dust and cobwebs. The upper jaw teeth were intact and identified by her dentist.*
Below bottom: *The chapel cellar where the body was found. The sticks by the fireplace mark the corpse's position.*

certainly there was no evidence of a bomb crater. It was also confirmed that this was not the site of an old cemetery.

The pathologist was of the opinion that the skeleton had been on site from 12 to 18 months and it was known that the church had been blitzed two years previously. On full examination it was found that the head had been severed as were both arms at the elbow and both legs at the knee. Some portions of the limbs were missing but nothing further of human origin was recovered from the site. There were yellowish deposits on the earth and a wooden chest less than five feet in length.

On analysis the yellowish deposit on the head and on the earth proved to be slaked lime. After assembling the body the calculated height was 5 feet $\frac{1}{2}$ inch with due allowance for the missing parts and soft tissues. An age estimation on cranial suture closure revealed an age between 40 and 50 years. There were no means of visual identification and the enlarged womb revealed no foetal bones of pregnancy.

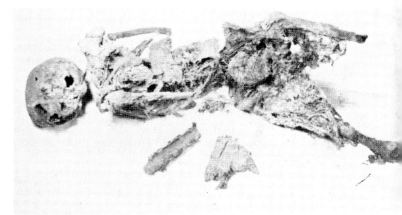

10 Rillington Place

The final example in this brief survey of cases where dental evidence was absolutely crucial is the Christie case. In 1953, when a Jamaican tenant of 10 Rillington Place, London, removed wallpaper from what he considered to be a sound wall, he found a cupboard which contained the bodies of three women. On further searching by the police, bodies were found under the floorboards and the remains of skeletons in the garden until at least six women victims had been accounted for. It was then remembered that two other bodies had been discovered in 1949 on the same premises. They were Mrs Beryl Evans and her baby Geraldine. As both had been strangled it was assumed at that time that Timothy Evans, husband and father, was responsible. He stood trial and was found guilty and hanged.

It was as a result of forensic teamwork that the identifications on all the victims were carried out, but the one identification of forensic dental interest was of Ruth Fuerst, an Austrian girl. Her skull had been fragmented and burned. Reconstruction of the portions resulted in almost a complete skull being assembled with the upper jaw containing a molar tooth with a full white metal crown. This was an unusual form of dental treatment in the United Kingdom and on analysis the crown proved to be of alloys used in central Europe.

From this information the investigation finally positively identified Ruth Fuerst. John Reginald Halliday Christie, the former tenant, was tried only for the murder of his wife, whose body was one of those under the floorboards, and his defence of insanity was rejected by the jury. He was sentenced to death and executed on July 15th 1953.

Developments in forensic odontology

Over the past 40 years the scope of forensic odontology has expanded considerably due to a greater intensity of international traffic with an ever increasing number of transportation disasters, and with the increase in international crime. It is often only the teeth and dental restorations that remain

Right: John Reginald Christie, mass murderer. Dental evidence helped to convict him.

to confirm the identity of each individual. The subject of forensic odontology can be divided into three main divisions of activity – civil or non-criminal, criminal, and training and research.

The civil division includes the identification of victims of major incidents and mass disasters resulting from natural catastrophes and transporta-

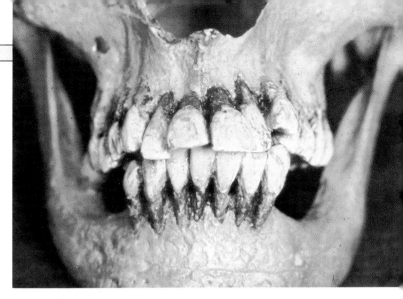

tion accidents. It also includes those identifications of human remains where death is not due to suspicious circumstances and of living persons when loss of memory or coma are concerned. Malpractice and neglect are also included in this division but are usually undertaken by those experts who remain more consistently with clinical practice.

The criminal division is concerned with the identification of the victims of murder, and the identification of the perpetrators of bite-marks on both the living and the dead. Bite-marks also occur extensively in non-accidental injury to children and in foodstuffs and materials left at scenes of crime.

The third division of training and research includes academic training of both undergraduates and postgraduates in medicine and dentistry and the courses given to police officers to demonstrate the aid that can be given to an investigating officer if dental evidence is required. In the increasing number of forensic dental cases all over the world the scope for research is unlimited.

The international picture

Forensic odontology has been recognized as a speciality for many years in Scandinavia and in most parts of Europe, as well as Japan, and due to the efforts of the experts in those countries has aroused ever increasing interest in the United States, the United Kingdom and the rest of the world. Such names as Gustafson, Strøm, Keiser-Nielsen, and Suzuki are 'household' names in the subject, having advanced the science by their contributions to the literature, and by their enthusiasm in supporting their forensic dental colleagues in other countries.

Attributing identity

Identification is based on two aspects of a person – the physical attributes and the personal. The physical attributes are relatively stable and concern the height, weight, sex, race, colour of eyes and hair, fingerprints, etc. whilst the personal attributes are variable and often misleading. But even if a body has been reduced by fire to a spinal column to the top end of which is attached the remains of jaws, there is still the possibility of positively identifying the deceased by dental means either by reconstructive or comparative methods.

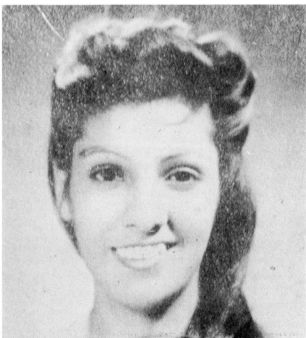

Top: *Forensic dentistry experts were called in to match the tooth arrangement of this skull found in a grave in Singapore with that of the photograph* (bottom). *The murderer had confessed to killing and burying his wife.*

The teeth and jaws can withstand a great deal more wear and tear than the rest of the body. Sometimes little reliance can be placed on clothing, documents, and jewellery, as there may be none of these articles present or none of the articles may belong to the particular body. In air disasters it is not unusual to find bodies completely stripped of clothing, or possessing documents relating to other persons and even jewellery belonging to other persons.

It is one of the golden rules to use as many methods of identification as possible to obtain identification. Unless an agreed number of methods are in concordance, the body is not positively identified until further information is obtained.

Relatives' identification

Visual recognition is the most usual means of identification, but it has been found that relatives are sometimes unable to recognize a familiar person after his death. Often, in a mass disaster, the emotional stress on relatives is such that they can consistently misidentify bodies on separate occasions if allowed to view the victims. It is considered the best policy to keep relatives at some distance from the scene of activity, but request their help in supplying a physical description of the person and relevant data on dental treatment and by whom it might have been provided. The acquisition of dental records of known victims, together with dental radiographs, will be of prime importance in the comparative method of identification.

The ante-mortem records of treatment, charting, and dental radiographs can then be compared with the post-mortem dental findings. At best a positive identification can be made and at worst the elimination of a number of possible identities can be achieved. It is quite often helpful in any investigation to be able to say who the body is not rather than who it is. Therefore dental means of identification are most useful when there is doubt in visual recognition and certainly when there is disfigurement by decomposition, fire, or mutilation.

Problems of mass disasters

In mass disasters there is usually severe trauma or fire which renders identification difficult. Disasters can be natural in origin, such as earthquake or flood, or caused by explosions and fires, and by transportation accidents of which air disasters form a high proportion. Identification is legally required for death certification and disposal of estates and insurance claims in transportation accidents.

Identification procedures require an integrated team of experts working on clothing, documents, jewellery, as well as forensic pathology and forensic odontology. Air disasters require teams to be on constant standby to travel anywhere in the world when such a disaster occurs, and take with them all the equipment and apparatus necessary to complete an investigation on site.

The Moorgate disaster

A tragic transportation accident occurred in London at Moorgate just before nine o'clock on the last day of February, 1975. The underground train failed to stop at the platform but continued on at high speed through the sand drag to crash into the wall of a blind tunnel. The rescue operations immediately put into effect were to remove casualties to those hospitals which were designated in area health authority plans and then to remove the dead victims for identification.

Of the many difficulties encountered, that of high temperature at the site was the greatest. The London underground system is normally ventilated by the passage of trains through the tunnel and when the accident occurred the electric current was cut off and ventilation ceased. When trains on an adjacent line began to run the temperature did not fall appreciably. Oxyacetylene cutting apparatus and any other heat producing equipment had to be removed. Even the body heat of the rescuers had to be taken into consideration.

In spite of all the measures taken to regain a lower temperature, it did not fall appreciably below 84°F for the whole time of the rescue operation. Under these conditions it was assumed that decomposition would be well advanced in those bodies not recovered for some days. The City of London coroner decided that dental identification should take preference over visual and other methods, rather than depend on the evidence of distressed or deeply shocked relatives.

Standardized procedure

The majority of patients in the United Kingdom receive their treatment from dental practitioners in the National Health Service. In the regulations it is required of the dentist to chart for each patient the teeth present, the teeth missing, and those teeth the dentist proposes to treat. It is not necessarily a full mouth charting, as an undergraduate is taught to do in dental school, but does provide in many cases enough information to compare with post-mortem findings. On many occasions it is necessary to augment the comparisons by the use of dental radiographs which one hopes will be part of the ante-mortem records. It is of some concern that all dental practitioners should carry out a full dental charting for each of their patients, not for the purpose of identifying dead bodies, but to keep proper records in case of possible future litigation resulting from claims of malpractice or neglect.

Below: In air crashes and other mass disasters, teeth can provide valuable clues. Heavily calcified teeth (below right) *can indicate the age of a person. This marked denture was found on a victim of the Moorgate disaster.*

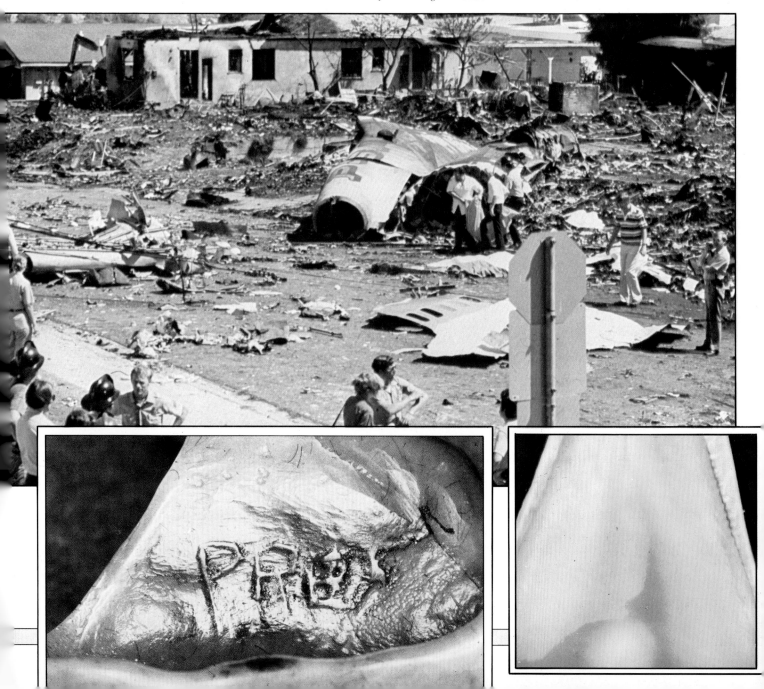

The method of charting is by standard symbols on a dental grid or odontogram which represents the five surfaces of the 32 adult teeth and on modification the 20 deciduous teeth. The standard symbols are taught to undergraduates in all dental schools in the United Kingdom, and therefore dental practitioners conform to a system which is readily understood in the UK and many other parts of the world.

It has been calculated that there are between 130 and 200 different methods of charting throughout the world, but most can be translated once given the key.

In the UK the teeth are enumerated from 1 to 8 beginning in the midline and extending in each quadrant of the jaws. In the United States, the method of charting is called the universal system, in which each tooth has its own number in the series of 1 – 32. An attempt has been made by the Fédération Dentaire Internationale to produce an internationally acceptable form of charting and it has been incorporated for many years in the disaster victim identification form used by Interpol. However, the form of the ondontogram has been found to be unacceptable under working conditions in mass disasters in the past and discussions are now proceeding to provide an odontogram that would be universally acceptable by Interpol countries.

.The procedure of the examination of the mouth of the dead body does not differ appreciably from the examination of the living patient in dental practice, providing the mouth can be opened. If this is impossible, because of rigor mortis or in a badly burned fire victim, then an X-ray method of examination has to be carried out.

Portable X-ray units

Such examinations may have to take place at the scene of a crime, and therefore a portable X-ray unit is vital to the procedure. There is a miniature apparatus which uses radioactive iodine-125 as the X-ray source which has been found particularly useful in the investigation of a large number of bodies. The radioactive nucleide is deposited at the end of a silver wire 0.5 mm in diameter and is shielded in a chamber. The iodine-125 is advanced from the chamber to produce the X-ray exposure in

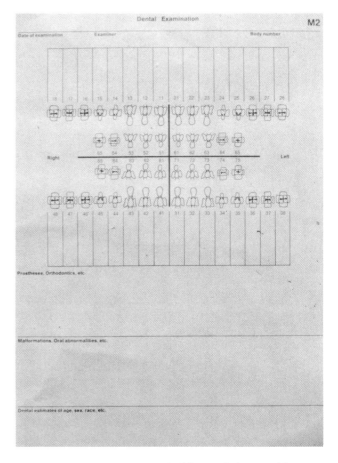

Above: *A mock-up of the standard Interpol chart used by forensic dentists for identification purposes.*

a flexible apparatus similar to a photographic release cable.

The head of the apparatus is small and flexible and can be passed even through the smallest apertures. Depending on the age of the iodine-125, the exposure to the X-ray film will be three to six minutes. (The half life of iodine-125 is sixty days.) Therefore a full panoramic view of the teeth and jaws can be obtained, or a selective field if normal periapical films are used. However some authorities will not allow the use of this apparatus as it contains a potentially dangerous radioactive material and is so small and light in size that it could easily be misplaced.

Another portable X-ray unit has been developed called the 'Bendix-ray Model 105' which has controls and weighs less than 7 kg. It is a 'cold cathode' pulsed X-ray unit operating on the principle of field emission. It can be operated from a battery, or from 110 or 220 kV electrical sources of 50 – 400 Hz. Because of its small size, battery capabilities, and low emission of harmful radiation it is one of the most versatile X-ray units available. It is simple to use and can make use of all existing X-ray and polaroid-land films.

Comparative radiographs

If human remains can be removed to properly equipped mortuaries or suitable forensic departments, then conventional X-ray units are employed in the radiographic investigation of the teeth and jaws. The two following cases illustrate the prime importance of the comparison of post-mortem radiographs of the teeth of an unknown body with the radiographs of a known person obtained during the police investigation.

The first case refers to the recovery of the body of a young man recovered from the river Thames. He had not been immersed for more than a few days, and his features were 'puffy' but perhaps recognizable visually. It is routine procedure for the police to take polaroid photographs of the face of such a victim, before decomposition prevents the possibility of visual recognition.

Under normal conditions in a mortuary the body will be placed in the refrigerator at 4 degrees or in the deep freeze. If some time elapses before prospective relatives are found the body will not be in a fit state to be viewed. Decomposition is only retarded by refrigeration and not prevented entirely, and so dental methods will provide a positive identification without the relatives having to view the body.

The first procedure entailed the comparison of the dental radiograph of the person known to be missing with the radiographs of the teeth of the body recovered from the river. Even though the radiographs were not taken at exactly the same angle it was not difficult to find the similarities in form of teeth, and presence and form of fillings in the posterior teeth. These radiographs are termed bite-wing views.

The positive identification of the young man was completed by comparison of ante-mortem views with post-mortem views of a particular upper front tooth. The ante-mortem periapical picture was taken by a dental surgeon to ascertain if he had correctly root-filled the front tooth of his patient before putting in a gold post and porcelain crown. Near the apex of the root is a lateral root canal, something that has occurred as a developmental anomaly. The post-mortem periapical radiograph presents the gold post and crown *in situ* but the same lateral root canal is clearly visible as seen in the illustrations at the bottom of the page.

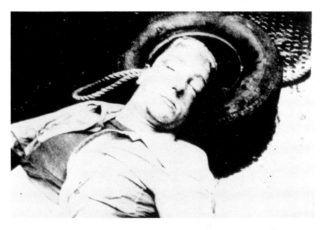

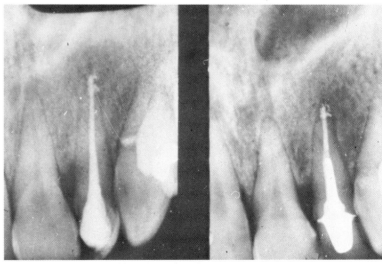

Top: *A man's body after recovery from the Thames.*
Below: *Forensic dentists compare his ante-mortem* (left) *and post-mortem* (right) *radiographs.*

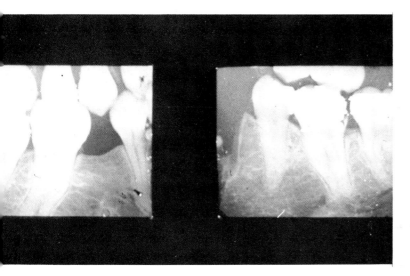

Identifying a murder victim

The second case presents the bite-wing radiographs of a murder victim whose face has been destroyed by fire in an attempt by the murderer to prevent or delay identification. Comparison of ante-mortem radiographs with the post-mortem views resulted in a positive identification, but the interesting feature here is the presence of radio-opaque artefacts.

When a dental surgeon prepares a silver filling, he has to mix the silver/tin alloy with mercury to obtain a plastic material to compress into the prepared tooth cavity. Before he fills the cavity he squeezes the excess of mercury out of the silver amalgam. When the silver filling sets in the tooth cavity there is always mercury present as an intermetallic compound.

On the application of heat, however, this mercury is set free as mercury vapour. The murderer set fire to his dead victim using perfumes and toiletries containing spirits; the intense heat has set free the mercury in the silver fillings of the deceased and this mercury vapour has then condensed on the surface of the tongue, cheeks and gums as globules of quicksilver, and so became apparent on the bite-wing radiographs.

Reconstruction techniques

Reconstructive methods are necessary when skeletal remains are found. There will be the possibility that the bones will be of archaeological origin, or buried long ago and not the result of recent criminal activity. Perhaps the collection of bones may reveal the presence of more than one person or animals. These general questions will have to be answered before individual data are assessed concerning the height of the individual, or the sex, or race.

The teeth associated with such remains may be complete in the jaws of a skull and show no signs of dental treatment, or the jaws may be missing teeth. In these cases the assessment of age becomes an important factor in the identification process.

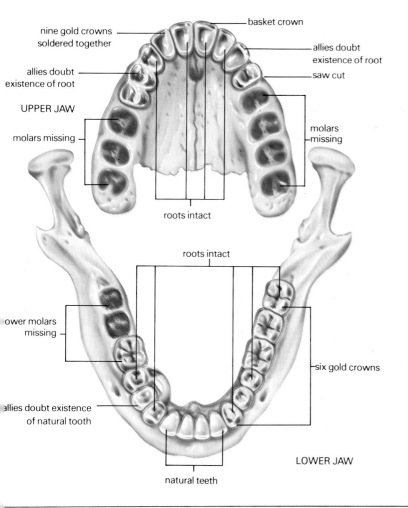

nine gold crowns soldered together

basket crown

allies doubt existence of root

allies doubt existence of root

saw cut

UPPER JAW

molars missing

molars missing

roots intact

roots intact

ower molars missing

six gold crowns

llies doubt existence of natural tooth

natural teeth

LOWER JAW

Top: Bite-wing radiographs of a murder victim (ante-mortem left, post-mordem right). Notice the artefacts of free mercury produced by the intense heat of the flames.
Left: Allied scientists used Hitler's dental records to help in identifying his corpse long after his death.

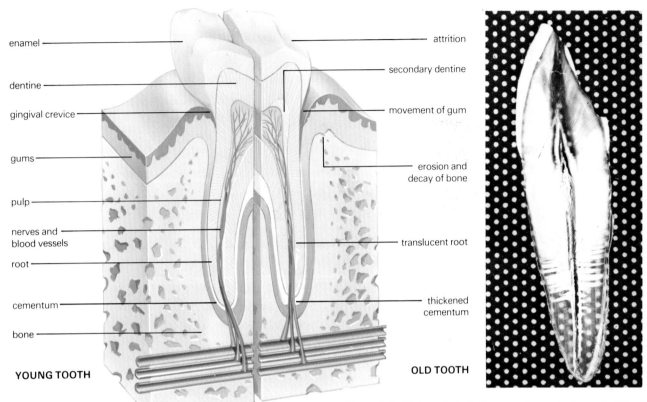

enamel

dentine

gingival crevice

gums

pulp

nerves and
blood vessels

root

cementum

bone

YOUNG TOOTH

attrition

secondary dentine

movement of gum

erosion and
decay of bone

translucent root

thickened
cementum

OLD TOOTH

*Above left: This analytical diagram of a tooth shows details of
the effects of ageing on the structure and surface.*
*Above right: After 25 years, the top of a tooth's root becomes
translucent, as in this longitudinal section.*

There are a number of methods available according to the provisional chronological age of the specimens recovered.

In the young the assessment is based on the incremental pattern of the enamel and dentine of the teeth. Mineralization of the deciduous teeth begins at about 20 weeks of intra-uterine life and one of the cusps of the first permanent molar mineralizes a week or two before birth. This tooth is an important landmark in age assessment of young human remains. Radiographs will demonstrate the mineralized tip of this tooth in the jaws of the dead body, and when recovered by dissection, the small piece of hard dental tissue can be sectioned and the fine lines of development can be counted.

The enamel and dentine tissues exhibit a series of incremental striations which are on average four microns apart. This is the daily growth of the dental tissues and the accuracy of this method can be 20 days either side of the true age, according to experimental error. In the living person, when

young, an age assessment can be based on the radiographic appearance of the development of the teeth in the jaws and the eruption of the teeth into the mouth. This method has wider variations related to diet, environment, and race, and becomes inaccurate after 14 years of age.

In the older person after 25 years there are senile changes associated with the teeth. There is wear on the biting surfaces, the gum level recedes (a person is said to be long in the tooth), the pulp chamber becomes smaller, the root resorbs and the tip of the root becomes translucent. These senile changes were made use of by Gösta Gustafson in his method of age assessment and he could be approximately three and a half years either side of the true age of an individual in accuracy. A. E. W. Miles used root translucency alone in his method of age assessment and can claim a similar accuracy.

THE ACID TEST
The John George Haigh case

The quiet art of the dentist may seem rather low-keyed when compared with the flamboyant court appearances of such great personalities of forensic science as pathologist Professor Keith Simpson. However, one of the most sensational murder trials in England was provided with dental evidence which was damningly conclusive.

It was John George Haigh's delusion — and many other people's before and since — that there can be no conviction without a corpse. As he put it to the British police in 1949, with the cheerful candour of the psychopath: "Mrs Durand Deacon no longer exists. She has disappeared completely and no trace of her can ever be found again. I have destroyed her with acid. You will find the sludge that remains at Leopold Road. Every trace has gone. How can you prove murder if there is no body?"

If spice was needed to the dish that the neat-faced ex-chorister had served to an avid public, he added that another eight victims had gone the same way, and that he had drunk their blood. The editor of the *Daily Mirror* newspaper, in a premature fit of enthusiasm to tell his readers the vampire had been caught, himself vanished for three months in jail for contempt of court. Meanwhile, stars of the legal profession clustered to the case like hornets. Sir Hartley Shawcross, Attorney General, would face his ex-colleague of Nuremberg trial days, Maxwell Fyfe. "I'm very glad to see we have got old Foxy," noted Haigh.

Behind the scenes the forensic experts, led by the formidable Professor Simpson, had the task of proving that, even after a long bath in neat sulphuric acid, enough of a human body will survive to tell the tale.

There was no shortage of supportive evidence. Apart from the frank confession, the trail that led the elderly Mrs Deacon to dissolution was littered with paperwork. There were receipts for her pathetic possessions that Haigh had sold to relieve his overdraft — and his debt to the hotel where both were residents. There were receipts for the metal drums, the sulphuric acid and the stirrup pump. But of Mrs Deacon, as Haigh had explained, there was very little indeed.

From the yard in Crawley, Sussex, where Mrs Deacon's last moments had been spent (Haigh, meanwhile, had been seen eating egg on toast in the nearby Ye Olde Ancient Priors Restaurant),

Professor Simpson removed the top three inches of soil over some 47 yards and had it packed in five stout wooden boxes. Back at the laboratory, Simpson spread out 457 pounds of greasy, oily residue on steel trays and began a three day study of the results.

Experiments with dead animals and amputated human limbs had already demonstrated to the experts that Haigh's claim was highly feasible. Interaction of the acid and the water in body tissues, they noted, created much heat. They observed how body fat rose to form a thick scum on the brew. And from the steel trays on their bench they were able to isolate some 28lbs of yellow fat.

More helpful, however, was a little group of items that had obstinately refused to go the way of all flesh. Out of their trays, the experts plucked three curiously faceted stones. Analysis proved them to be gall stones, and, more precisely, human gall stones. Other stubborn survivors of the bath were the handle of a red plastic bag and a lipstick container. But the two objects that were eventually

Above: *Mrs Olive Durand Deacon. Haigh tried to destroy her body with acid. Her acrylic dentures survived and were conclusively identified by her dentist.*
Above left: *Police searching for clues.*
Below: *Haigh, with characteristic smiling aplomb, is led into the court, handcuffed to a police officer.*

brought to court as exhibits one and two respectively were enough to clinch the case! Mrs Durand Deacon's new acrylic resin dentures had come through their ordeal in sparkling form. Her dentist was on hand to identify them. Haigh was hanged.

Had he taken the care to remove the dentures, or left his client a little longer in soak, there is no doubt that the forensic task would have been more difficult, though an eroded fragment of bone was sufficient to prove that it was female and elderly. Certainly no trace was found of Haigh's other claimed victims — some of whom may have been figments of imagination proffered, like the claim to have drunk his victims' blood, in the hope of a verdict of guilty but insane.

The jury did not forget that one of Haigh's first questions to the police was whether or not anyone had ever been released from Broadmoor. And as they decided that Haigh would not have a chance to find out, Mrs Durand Deacon's dentures were removed to take their place in the history of forensic science.

Tetracycline effects

In recent years the use of tetracycline for the treatment of infections in children has been discontinued, because the medication becomes incorporated in the mineralization of teeth and bone. Sometimes this attachment is clearly evident by the discolouration of front teeth of some children who received tetracycline when their front teeth were forming. In sections of teeth illuminated with ultra-violet light under the microscope, the tetracycline can be seen in the incremental pattern of the dentine as yellow fluorescent bands. The width of the bands therefore can indicate how many days that person received their medication and the intervals between the bands indicate the period of days between treatments.

In the early 1970s the bodies of two provisionally identified children were found in a wood several miles from their home. They had both been missing for three months and the bodies were in an advanced state of decomposition. Dental records, although available, were of no use for comparison purposes. The boy was 12 years and the girl was eleven and a half years of age. According to normal dental development, the teeth of the girl should have been at the same stage of development as those of the boy. However, her teeth appeared to be two and a half years in advance, and therefore the age of the male body matched that of the missing boy but the female body was at least two and a half years older than the known missing girl.

Sections of her teeth were examined but the fine striations of the incremental pattern were not visible over a large enough area to make assessment possible by this method.

The missing girl's medical history became available, and showed that she had had previous treatment with tetracycline when she was nine months old for an abscess on her neck, and subsequently for recurrent attacks of bronchitis and pneumonia. When the teeth sections were examined under ultra-violet light eight fluorescent

Scanning electron microscopes are used to compare growth lines in separate pieces of tooth (above and below left) *while stereometric plotting can show imprints of pipe stems on teeth* (centre). *These, along with tetracycline growth lines in teeth* (below right) *can all help forensic scientists to identify a body.*

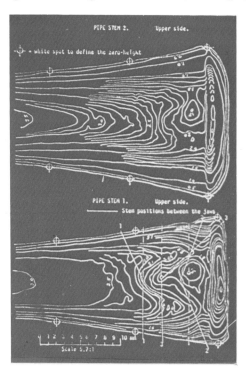

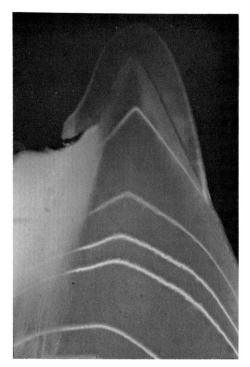

bands of tetracycline became visible, four of which could be related to times of treatment.

Bite-marks

It is more than 100 years since the first scientific paper on bite-marks was published and the number of reported cases increases each year. It is not so very long ago that some authorities stated that bite-mark cases were rare, but experts now are finding increasing experience in all types of bite-marks. Such marks can be produced by human, animal, or mechanical origin, in human skin and body tissues, foodstuffs, and other materials.

Human bite-marks occur in murder cases, sexual assaults and rape and non-accidental injury to children, while animal bites on humans can include those made by mammals, reptiles, and fish. The mechanical means of producing bite-marks include injuries by denture teeth, or objects with a 'tooth-like' edge, such as saws and sharpened combs (although the latter group should be correctly referred to as 'tooth marks'). Perhaps one of the best classifications of bite-marks on human skin is to be found in the Kama Sutra of Vatsyayana written 17 centuries ago.

In an ideal situation the dental expert should be able to recognize and prove the agent which produced a mark, but the common factor in all bite-mark cases is difficulty in interpretation. Some authorities hold the view that it is impossible to be certain that the teeth of a particular person could be responsible for marks or injuries on the body of a victim of crime unless there are significant features which are not present in any other person. They maintain that it is more reliable to exclude those suspects who could not possibly have made such a mark, rather than positively identify a perpetrator.

Bite-mark evidence

Comparison therefore relies on the similarities between the teeth of the alleged perpetrator with

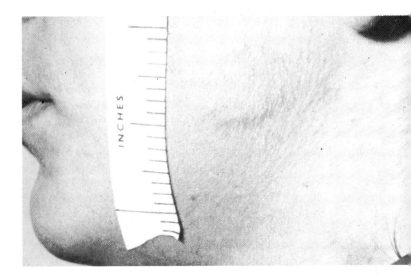

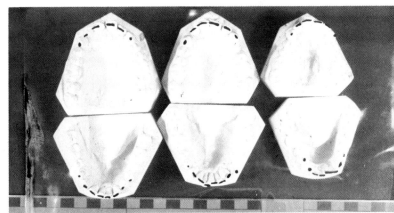

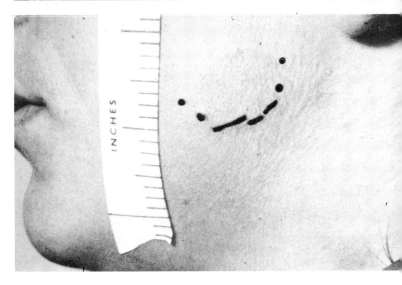

Above top: *In this rape case, a bite mark was left on the victim's cheek by the assailant.*
Above centre: *An acetate sheet is prepared for the comparison of the teeth of three suspects.*
Right: *The arrangement of the rapist's teeth is shown in direct comparison with the marks on the girl's cheek.*

the marks on the body of a victim. Many experts have had to devise methods of demonstrating these similarities, and significant features in a particular case for presentation as court evidence. In human cases the bite-mark can be on almost any part of the body but the site can suggest a relationship to the type of offence committed. In 'battered babies' bite-marks are frequently found all over the body including the genitalia.

In sexual crimes, rape or homosexual attack the bites may be numerous, slowly given and well-defined, whilst in non-accidental injury to children there may be only diffuse bruising with little definition present. In sexual assaults on women the site of biting may be the neck and breasts, and abdomen and thighs, although this does not exclude the possibility of 'erotic biting' on previous occasions, leaving marks which are present at the time of the examination.

Position of the body
When an injury has been recognized as a bite-mark it is important to appreciate whether the victim is in the same position as when he or she received the bite. Changes of position of the body can alter the shape of a mark depending on its site. Examination with ultra-violet light may elicit the slight fluorescence of saliva · on the surface of the bite-marks. The examiner can then take a swab of the area of the saliva and ascertain the secretor status of the perpetrator. It may be possible to identify the blood group of the individual by tests carried out by a forensic serologist. The ultra-violet light may also make visible previous injuries to the skin which are not visible to the naked eye. In the skin pigment cells or melanocytes migrate to the margins of wounds and after healing remain in proximity to the margins of the wounds. They absorb the radiation from a U-V lamp and show up densely black, clearly delineating the shape of old injuries to the skin.

Using photography
Photographs are then taken of the bite-mark on the skin, including a scale either in centimetres or inches, in close proximity to the mark providing it does not interfere with the outline of the mark in

Below: *These photographs show characteristic upper teeth marks in an apple left at the scene of a crime.*

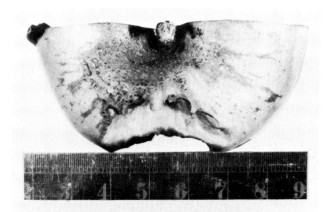

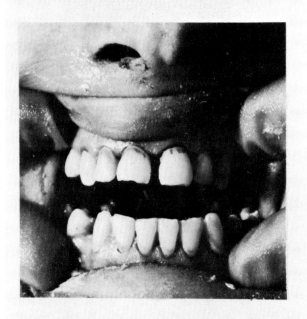

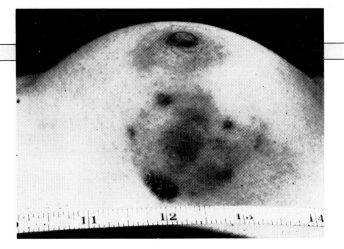

Above: *Evidence from the Biggar case, described by one of the investigating officers as "a triumph for forensic odontology". The matching of the marks on the victim's breast* (top) *and the attacker's tooth* (above) *had to be conclusive, since it was the only proof of the identity of the murderer — one of 29 suspects.*

dental stone or plastic. This basic procedure of photography and impressions is equally applicable to the living or dead subject or to the recording of bite-marks in foodstuffs. Nowadays there is a wide choice of modern dental materials for impressions and study models which reproduce details with considerable accuracy.

The next step in the procedure requires impressions of the teeth of a suspect or suspects, if apprehended, having first gained their consent to do so. The study models of the teeth of the suspects can then be compared with the photographs of the bite-marks on the victim as a 1:1 comparison. Many experts will make use of intermediate transparencies to assess similarities or dissimilarities. Similarities or even concordance of the teeth of a suspect with the bite-marks on the photograph may be revealed which will confirm the suspect as the perpetrator, or there may be no correspondence between them, thus clearing the suspect.

The expert will then be expected to present this evidence in court at some future time, ensuring that his statements are completely accurate since he will be cross-examined on this evidence. Precision is important, since inaccuracies reflect on the scientist's personal reputation. It is only in recent years that such dental evidence has assumed the role of the main evidence rather than supporting evidence, notably as a result of the Biggar case tried in Scotland in 1968.

Training for the future

Forensic odontology has now been accepted as an integral part of the forensic sciences and dental participation is a routine procedure in identification cases involving crime, mass disaster, missing persons and accidents. There are still too few dental surgeons with practical experience in forensic odontology partly due to the lack of training at post-graduate level, and also because the subject does not feature extensively in the curricula of many dental schools. However, there is a general increase in the interest shown by members of the dental, medical and the legal professions and with the enthusiasm and hard work of those dedicated to the subject, there will definitely be more formal recognition of forensic odontology.

any way. There are differences of opinion amongst experts whether the scale should be a rigid one or flexible conforming to the curvature of the bite-mark site. The presence of the scale will indicate the approximate proportions of the mark but is primarily to allow the photographer to reproduce subsequent photographic enlargements to life-size. The use of colour film or black and white film to record the mark will depend on the choice of the examining expert as to which details he wishes to demonstrate.

The majority of bite-marks present as bruising but on some occasions there may be indentations in the skin produced by the teeth of the assailant and the expert will take impressions of these indentations to reproduce them later as study models in

FORENSIC PHOTOGRAPHY

Just before Christmas, 1980, a security van carrying £800,000 was stopped in the genteel London suburb of Dulwich by a gang of armed men, who sandwiched the van between a builder's lorry and a heavy mobile crane. As the security guards were forced from their vehicle at pistol point, the gang's leader, 29 year old William Tobin, rammed the jib of the huge crane into the van's rear doors, forcing them inwards. But unfortunately for Tobin, one of his accomplices had tipped off Scotland Yard about the impending raid, and just as the crane forced a clear route through to the money, 40 armed detectives emerged from hiding. After a scattered exchange of shots, the gang were arrested.

Detective Superintendent David Little, head of the Yard's Central Robbery Squad, had a particular interest in Tobin, and had been investigating him thoroughly. In five years Tobin had amassed enough money from crime to own a Rolls Royce. On five separate occasions during that time he had been charged with armed robbery – including a case which involved the murder of a security guard – but on five occasions juries had acquitted him through lack of evidence. So alongside Superintendent Little's AFO's – approved firearms officers – lying in ambush at Dulwich were a team of 'scene of crime' officers manning a videotape camera and sound system, and the whole episode was filmed as it happened.

Videotape recording court evidence
The videotape recording was shown to a jury at the Old Bailey in September 1981.

Council for the prosecution Kenneth Richardson summed up tersely: 'If you can't convict on that evidence, the police might as well give up.' The jury took his point, and Mr Justice John Leonard accordingly sentenced Tobin to 16 years for attempted robbery and possession of firearms.

Senior police officers throughout the English speaking world must have echoed Superintendent Little's sentiments outside court, when he told reporters of his 'satisfaction' with the result, for although the Tobin case broke no new ground it provided another solid precedent for the use of video film as identification evidence in court.

History of forensic photography
Organized police work and successful photography date from roughly the same time; as early as 1848, Birmingham City Police were employing a photographer to take pictures of accused and convicted persons, beautifully posed examples of the Victorian portrait photographer's art. During the next 20 or 30 years every major police force in Europe and the United States had begun to build up 'rogues' galleries', gradually settling on the full-face, profile, and full figure shots familiar today. Simultaneously, the need for an accurate record of murder and other serious crime scenes produced the deliberately unemotional yet detailed photo-

graphs vital to successful reconstruction of events in the mind of the forensic examiner. Their style is already apparent in, for instance, the Metropolitan Police photographs of Jack the Ripper's victims in 1888; only the – perhaps mercifully – blurred focus shows their age.

Despite the obvious usefulness of photography in criminal investigation, however, the law wisely refuses to accept at face value the adage that the camera cannot lie.

Rules of photographic evidence
Photographic evidence in court has always had to be backed up by strongly corroborative evidence, and decisions made by the Courts of Appeal over the years have resulted in a series of rigid rules governing the use of photographs in identifying suspects. These, to be fair, concern themselves mainly with avoiding prejudice. For instance, it is not deemed acceptable for photographs of persons about to be put up for physical identification, to be shown previously to potential witnesses. If a suspect is not under arrest, and therefore physical identification is not possible, the police may show 'a series' of photographs to the witness but they should not appear to be prison photographs, and the subsequent evidence of the witness should be taken 'subject to the fact that he has previously seen a photograph.'

Below: *Early criminal photography. Here, the bank robber George Mason seems reluctant to face the camera.*

In the classic case of Rex v. Dwyer and Ferguson, 1924, in which two manifestly guilty housebreakers appealed successfully against sentences of hard labour, the Lord Chief Justice ruled that the trial had been 'perfectly satisfactory' except for two respects. In the first, witnesses had been shown clear photographs of the prisoners in prison uniform before being asked to identify them, and in the second these pictures had been produced in court and shown to the jury.

'In this matter,' ran the summing up, 'as in all matters, it is the duty of the police to behave with exemplary fairness, remembering always that the Crown has no interest in securing conviction, but has only an interest in convicting the right person.'

And this, despite occasional Press suggestions to the contrary, is what the scores of crime officers who man modern police photographic laboratories do. Most of them carry a police warrant card, although many in the United States and an increasing number in major British police forces are civilians. The majority – both police officers and civilians – are also trained in fingerprint work, with the principal fingerprint officer of a force often playing a double role as head of the photographic department.

Nowadays, photography has become such an integral part of every branch of modern police work that its exclusion would be almost totally impracticable, as a brief survey of the four main categories into which police photography falls – identification, scenes of crime, fingerprints, and laboratory work – makes obvious.

The practice of photographing convicted criminals for future reference is, as we have seen, well established and was standardized by the Committee on Crime Detection in its 1938 report, which set out rules for such matters as the size and quality of photographic prints, the equipment and even the lighting methods to be used. As a result the portrait section of the typical police laboratory is one of the

Opposite: The Photofit system compiles facial segments jigsaw style, until a recognizable image is achieved. This group, issued in 1980, concerns two suspects in a UK silver bullion robbery. The disguises are included too — the man (top left) disguised himself as a policeman (below left) wearing a moustache (below right).

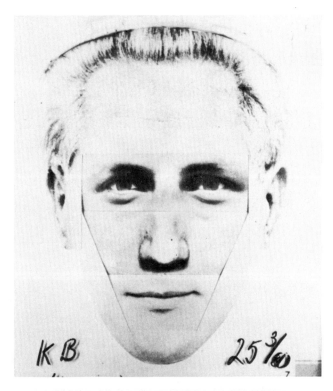

busiest, turning out black and white and colour prints of every serious offender for the Criminal Records Office at Scotland Yard, as well as the Regional Clearing Houses and the local files. The police are often photographed: for warrant cards mainly, but also for police newspapers and journals and, where necessary, the Press.

Mass photography investigations

Experience gained in taking photographs quickly and efficiently has come in useful on several occasions where mass photography has played an active part in crime detection. In the late 1960s in Britain, two 12 year old girls were going home from school in the Gateshead area of County Durham when they were attacked by a young man. One girl got away, but her companion was murdered.

A team of detectives was put to the laborious task of compiling a list of all males between the ages of 16 and 25 in the townships of Dunston, Swalwell, the Teams area of Gateshead, and the murdered girl's home town of Whickham, a total of 4,500 names. They were followed by ten police photographers armed with Polaroid 'Swinger' cameras, working allotted areas, and taking a single, instant print of each suspect. At the end of each day the pictures were shown to the surviving girl. Exactly 30 days and 3,017 photographs later, she was able to identify an 18 year old youth, who was later convicted of the crime. The youth was a soldier on leave at the time of the offence, and was safely back at camp when the operation was mounted.

The success of such operations depends, of course, on the cooperation of the public and the firm undertaking that the pictures will be used only in connexion with the particular inquiry in progress and afterwards destroyed. In the Durham case, only 18 people refused to be photographed, all for what the police regarded as 'acceptable reasons'.

Other systems

Such cooperation is not always forthcoming, and during the past two decades detectives have relied on the Indentikit system and its successor the Penry Facial Identification Technique, commonly known as 'Photofit'. Invented in Britain by Jacques Penry in 1971, the Photofit system makes use of hundreds

These photographs all show incidents in which a police photographer's work is very important.
Above left: A photograph of the scene of a murder, roped off for further investigation.
Above right: The exact angle at which a collision occurs can be vital evidence in road accidents.
Below left: A photograph showing the scene of a breaking and entering, with damage to the safe.

of facial 'segments' covering every racial and physical type, from which the police operator can, from the description of witnesses, build up the face of a subject jigsaw style.

Scenes of crime photography

Along with identification procedures, 'scenes of crime' work takes up a good proportion of the police photographer's time. To the layman, the phrase perhaps automatically suggests murder, but cases of robbery and burglary, malicious damage, public violence and arson all require recording photographically. Traffic fatalities and other serious accidents – pile-ups on the highways for instance, where the cause needs to be ascertained – come under the scrutiny of the forensic camera lens.

Where murder especially is concerned the photographer has first access to the body after the Police Surgeon has confirmed death. He works alongside the exhibits officer, whose task it is to gather and label evidence, and a scientist from the regional forensic laboratory. The photographer takes general and close up shots of the body *in situ*, along with the position of any bloodstains or weapons present, and any other special views which the pathologist, forensic scientist or investigating officer may want. His next port of call is the mortuary, where he will photograph the body clothed and unclothed and at various stages during the post-mortem, at the direction of the pathologist.

VTR developments

In these fields, in particular, the videotape recording (VTR) is likely to take over from the still camera fairly rapidly during the next few years. Video recordings of the autopsy on Robert Kennedy were taken in 1968, and the Los Angeles Coroner's office along with those of several major cities has continued the practice since. In the early 1970s the Connecticut State Troopers – after the

Texas Rangers the oldest state police force in America – introduced videotaping at the scene of the crime, and again the practice has spread. The photographic officer examines the scene, as it were, through the camera viewfinder, at the same time describing what he sees on tape through a throat microphone. The advantages of having an 'action replay' of activities at a murder scene or in an autopsy room are obvious. Supplementing the written notes of detective or pathologist, they provide a ready reference to dubious or unclear points. And VTR may play an active part in crime reconstruction, as a case from Baltimore in the early 1970s shows.

The Seagar case

A plump, 48 year old blonde named Iris Seagar had fallen to her death from the balcony of her penthouse apartment to the sidewalk 200 feet below. Police investigating the death found that most of her neighbours thought that Iris had committed suicide, driven to it by the drunkenness and violence of her husband. The husband, sole eyewitness, said that this was not so: she had been fiddling with a faulty airconditioner outside the window and had tipped over the guard rail. Examining the scene, the police found such an accident probable, but the insurance examiners were more cautious: the dead woman's $100,000 insurance policy, from which her husband was the sole beneficiary, naturally carried a nullifying clause in the case of suicide.

Accident, suicide – or murder? Baltimore forensic scientists constructed several dummies five feet three inches tall and 127 pounds in weight – the same size as Iris. These were dropped, thrown, pushed and tipped over the balcony, their descent filmed on video, and the films analysed frame by frame. The films showed that Mrs Seagar could not have fallen accidentally without landing within ten feet six inches from the wall of the building. In fact, she had landed in the roadway, sixteen feet eight inches out. The conclusion was that she could not have jumped that distance, but she could have been thrown: her husband confessed to having hurled her to her death in a fit of frantic, drunken rage, and was convicted of murder.

Above: Specialist photography can reveal evidence which is invisible to the naked eye. This micro-photograph shows a speck of gunpowder in fibre.
Below: Infra-red photography gives a clear image of these cheques damaged in a serious bank fire.

Photographing fingerprints

The third division into which the police photographer's work falls is that of fingerprints, still the mainstay of criminal identification 80 years after its introduction to Scotland Yard by Commissioner Sir Edward Henry. Although the study and comparison of fingerprints – dactyloscopy, to give it its technical name – is a specialist skill in itself it would be quite useless without photography. Over the past eight decades, fingerprint photographers have developed their own techniques through which they gain clear prints from any surface on which they might be deposited: rough, multicoloured, plastic – as in soap or putty – and from mirrors, bottles, convex and concave glass, leather and even the inside of rubber surgical gloves.

Striped surfaces are photographed through a filter, to 'cancel out' one colour, while multicoloured surfaces are treated with a powder which fluoresces strongly in ultra-violet radiation. Commercial anthracene, which fluoresces a bright yellow, is the most popular dusting powder in such cases. A yellow filter is used on the camera to remove both ultra-violet and visible violet radiations, 'clearing' the background and producing a crisp outline.

Ultra-violet and infra-red photography

Ultra-violet and infra-red photography also play a part in work in the forensic science laboratory and in which the scientist and photographer work as a team. Blood, semen, saliva, oils, chemicals and other substances fluoresce under one or the other influences, and photographs of the fluorescence can be used in analyzing the substances or testing for their presence on clothing, woodwork, and so on.

In the uncovering of forgery both processes are invaluable, showing up erasions or additions and 'invisible' writing. The longer wavelength radiations of infra-red are particularly useful to the officer taking observation pictures at long range, being less diffused by the atmosphere than visible light and ultra-violet radiations – hence the predominant red of a faint rainbow in a summer storm – and so giving clearer details. Infra-red cameras also have the advantage of functioning in the dark – or at least in cinemas, theatres and such places. A

Above: This micro-photograph provided crucial evidence in a murder case. The circled area contained blood, bone and hair matching the victim's.

spotlight covered with infra-red transmitting filter, giving off only a faint, dull red glow, is trained on the section of audience which is of interest. Then the camera, without filter or flash, is simply focused and activated. An infra-red flash, attached to a camera like an ordinary flash cube, can also be used to photograph a suspect indoors without drawing his attention, for no unusual light is visible.

A frequent laboratory use of infra-red photography is that of deciphering writing on burned or charred surfaces; occasionally, even identifiable fingerprints have yielded themselves for examination under infra-red rays, and they also clarify serial numbers which have been filed from the surface of engine blocks, firearms and other metal objects.

Macrophotography and photomicrography

In preparing evidence for court, two specialist branches of photography play an important part: macrophotography and photomicrography. Frequently, tiny marks – the scratches made by a house breaking tool, for instance, the hallmark on a piece of silver or the alteration on a forged document – need to be examined in detail. In many cases an ordinary negative can be 'blown up' to meet the situation quite satisfactorily, but after certain magnification the enlarged image begins to lose definition. To obtain clear images on a larger scale it is necessary to produce magnified negatives in the camera itself, usually by using a long 'bellows'-like extension and a lens of short focal length, a process known as macrophotography. Magnification up to ten times the size of the original object can be usefully obtained in this way, but beyond that the image again becomes blurred.

Experts collecting evidence from the scene of a crime often use optical aids to examine the area for tiny shreds of evidence – contact traces – left by the

BLOOD IN THE DRAINS
The Ruxton killings

There are a dozen murders in British forensic history which are 'classics' – ones which get talked about whenever pathologists or crime writers get together. Well up in this league table is the Ruxton case, and as far as forensic photography is concerned, it may well be first in its league, as the Ruxton identification pictures appear in almost every medico-legal textbook.

A lady out for a Sunday stroll had a nasty surprise when she looked over the parapet of a bridge which crossed a small stream, the Gardenholme Linn. The date was 29 September 1935 and the place was just over the Scottish border, on the road between Carlisle and Edinburgh.

She saw a human arm lying on the bank of the stream, which had been in flood until a few days earlier. The police were called and they began a search of the area which ultimately recovered no less than 70 fragments of human remains, some made up into untidy parcels with newspaper, straw, cotton wool and cloth.

These grisly finds were made over a considerable time and distance. At the end of October, a left foot was found nine miles away, and as late as November 4, a right arm and hand was discovered at the side of the road half a mile from the bridge.

The collection included two heads with parts of neck attached, two portions of trunk and 15 parts of limbs, which consisted of four upper arms, three forearms and hands, and four legs, two with feet and two without.

In addition, there was a great pile of assorted flesh, which included three female breasts, a womb and parts of the female genitalia.

Professor John Glaister of Glasgow University came to the scene and saw that the fragments had been deliberately mutilated to prevent identification. The two heads had suffered especially, the ears, eyes, noses, lips and skin having been removed. Teeth had been pulled out after death, and other identifying features such as the sex organs, bunions and finger tips had been mutilated or removed.

The revolting jigsaw was taken to the forensic department at Edinburgh University, where another well-known forensic pathologist, Professor Sir Sydney Smith, and an anatomist, Professor Brash, collaborated with John Glaister in trying to re-assemble the pieces for they were decomposed and crawling with maggots.

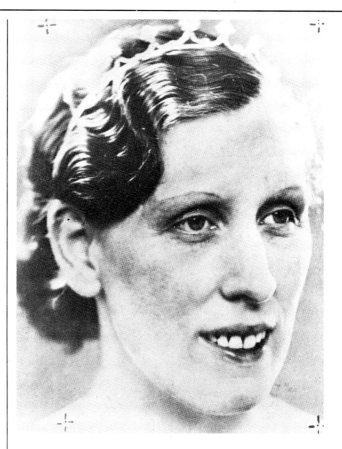

Painstakingly, they began fitting the parts together and although most of the soft tissue could not be assigned to the correct place, they managed to assemble the bony material into two female body 'groups', which they called Body Number One and Body Number Two.

While this medical work was going on, the police were carrying out a systematic and very efficient investigation, which in itself ranks alongside the pathological work as a model of detection.

The corpse pieces were found on 29 September, so it was vital to calculate when the deaths took place. The stream had subsided after a flood which lasted until 18 September, and as some of the obscene parcels had been stranded well above the normal water-mark, they must have been dumped there while the Linn was in full spate.

Though the killer had gone to such lengths to try to conceal the identity of his victims, he made some elementary mistakes.

As well as leaving breasts and other female parts, he had wrapped some parts in newspaper; the

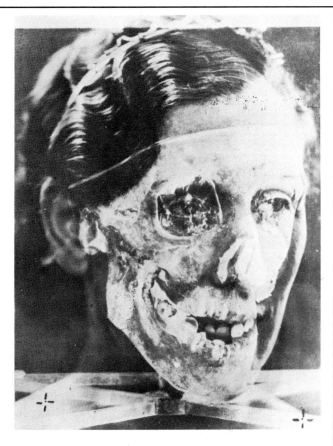

Above: *The photographic negative of Mrs Ruxton's skull fits perfectly over a photograph. This was the first time this technique was used in a case.*

latest date was on the *Sunday Graphic* for 15 September, so now the police knew that the dumping, if not the deaths, had occurred between the 15th and 18th.

A lucky break followed immediately, as part of the torn sheet of newspaper referred to the crowning of a carnival queen in Morecambe. The detectives soon found that this was a special edition for the Lancaster area — and almost simultaneously, the Chief Constable of Dumfries noticed in a Glasgow newspaper that the nursemaid to a Lancaster doctor had gone missing.

The Lancashire police were soon on the trail and began asking questions of the doctor — whose wife had also just vanished!

The general practitioner concerned was an Indian, a Parsee who had qualified in Bombay. His real name was Bukhtyar Rustomji Hakim, but he had anglicized this to Buck Ruxton.

He was 37 years old and in 1928 had taken Isabella van Ess as his common-law wife, though they had never married. Their union produced three children and a great deal of aggravation, for the doctor was insanely jealous. On two occasions, police had been called to his house because he had assaulted her and threatened to kill her, accusing her of being unfaithful to him. They had several servants, including a charlady and a local girl of 20 called Mary Rogerson.

Mrs Ruxton was last seen alive when she drove home from Blackpool on 14 September — the last day that Mary Rogerson was seen alive.

When the police began asking questions, Dr Ruxton became indignant and almost hysterical, inviting the police to search his house and abusing them for ruining his practice with their false accusations.

Meanwhile, the forensic pathologists and the anatomist were working away patiently in Edinburgh. They found that Body Number One was between 18 and 25, and was about four foot eleven tall, had eight teeth missing before death and suffered from recurrent tonsillitis, and the one recovered breast indicated a young woman who had not borne children.

Mary Rogerson, the police informed them, was 20 years old, about five feet in height, had had six teeth extracted some time before, suffered from tonsillitis and was unmarried.

She also had an appendix scar and a scar on the right thumb. Significantly, the right thumb and the abdominal skin were missing from Body Number One.

The other body was between 30 and 35, was about five foot three inches, had brown hair, had lost 15 teeth and had the remains of a bunion on the left foot. Her breasts were suggestive of a woman who had borne children.

Mrs Isabella Ruxton was almost 35, was five feet five inches tall, had brown hair, had dentures corresponding with the missing teeth and had an inflamed bunion on the left big toe.

To clinch matters, remains of palm and finger prints from Mary Rogerson's remains, obtained by delicate techniques from the rotting skin, matched numerous prints in the Ruxton house in Lancaster.

But still the doctors were not finished. They made casts of the feet of the two bodies and tried to fit them into shoes belonging to the two women. They fitted perfectly into the correct footwear, but were totally incompatible when swapped around.

Probably the most famous photograph in the science of identification was then made by Professor Brash and a detective-constable from the Edinburgh CID.

They took a photograph of the horribly mutilated head of Body Number Two – which was little more than a skull – and superimposed a negative of it over a positive print of a picture of Mrs Ruxton taken during life. The skull picture had to be enlarged and orientated to exactly the right size and angle, then adjusted so that the point of the chin, the angle of the jaw, the eyebrows, etc. were all superimposed.

And superimposed they really were, the coincidence being a perfect fit. Though this is not incontrovertible evidence of identity, it is a striking piece of confirmation – and works absolutely in the reverse direction, for if the fit had not been perfect, then it would have meant that it could not have been Mrs Ruxton's skull.

This technique, used in this way for the first time in the Ruxton case, has been employed many times since. Indeed, the Soviet forensic service say that they make positive identification with its help, having had many thousands of opportunities to practise in identifying the exhumed victims of war-time prison camps.

By the time that the medical work was over, Dr Ruxton was under arrest. He had given some blood-stained carpets to his charlady and foolishly tried to win her silence. The police heard that the bath had had a yellow tide-mark almost to the top. They dismantled the waste-pipe and found blood and remnants of flesh inside.

There was blood on the bannisters, carpets, stair-pads and on one of the doctor's suits of clothes. He had obviously used the bathroom to cut up the bodies, a process which Sydney Smith estimated would have taken at least eight hours.

No cause of death was ever discovered, due to the state of the bodies, but Buck Ruxton was found guilty at Manchester Assizes in March 1936.

He made a pathetic showing in the witness box and though his defence was conducted by Norman Birkett QC, later to become the famous judge Lord Birkett, and Sir Bernard Spilsbury advised on the medical aspects of the defence, he had no chance of acquittal and was hanged at Strangeways Prison on 12 May 1936.

He wrote a confession which was published the following Sunday in a newspaper, admitting that he killed his wife in a fit of temper because he thought she had been with another man. Mary Rogerson saw it happen and he had to silence her as well.

criminal. Similarly, a criminal may pick up traces from the scene which my have adhered to his shoes and clothing, which may later help to identify him. These substances, dust, hair, fibres and other traces can be examined under a microscope by a forensic scientist.

In order to present his findings to the court in a convenient manner, the forensic scientist has to convey exactly what he sees under the microscope. To do this, he uses the technique of photomicrography, which involves taking a photograph through the lens of the microscope. There can be little doubt that the microscope is one of the most useful tools of the forensic scientist, and photomicrography is correspondingly important.

Microscope examination often involves comparing sample substances connecting a suspect with the scene of a crime – for example fibres on a suspect's shoe may be compared under the microscope with the fibres from the carpet at the scene of a crime. Officers may find a piece of cut wire at the scene of a break-in, and later apprehend a suspect carrying a piece of equipment suitable for wire-cutting. The forensic scientist can cut a similar piece of wire with the same equipment, and then examine the striations on the cut ends through a comparison microscope. These are typical examples of the thousands of instances in which the microscope and photomicrography are used to provide evidence.

Reconstructing faces

Such painstaking work is a labour of dedication, if not exactly of love, and the technicians responsible rarely get the kudos of public acclaim. Perhaps the most dramatic, head-line making aspect of forensic photography is that which deals with the reconstruction of dead faces, whether for missing persons posters or for the benefit of the investigating officers themselves. West Yorkshire Metropolitan Police had a rare opportunity to produce a composite picture of this kind during the Yorkshire Ripper investigations.

On the night of 31 January 1978, Peter Sutcliffe killed an 18 year old part-time prostitute named Helen Rytka in Huddersfield, stripping her first before beating her about the head with a hammer and slashing her face and body.

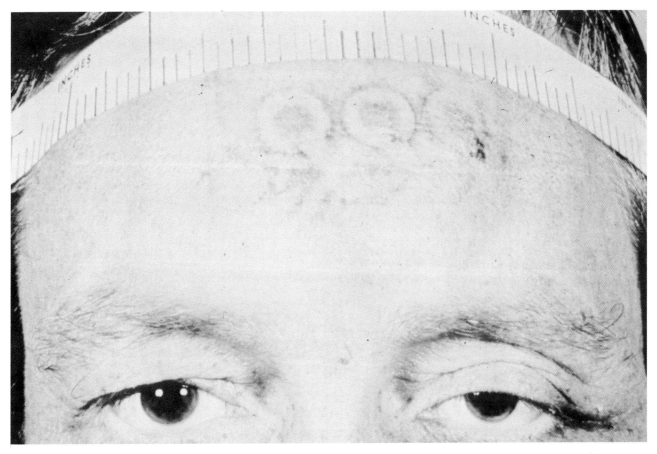

Above: *The imprint of a boot on this victim's face has been photographed for identification purposes later.*

Helen had a twin sister, Rita, who although not identical facially was of the same height and build. Police needed to trace Helen's movements immediately prior to her death, and issued a poster bearing details of the girl and her full length 'portrait'. In the macabre but effective picture the body was that of Rita Rytka, wearing her sister's discarded clothing, while the carefully touched-up face was that of Helen.

The superimposing of photographs on skulls has become almost a commonplace where decomposed corpses need to be identified. The technique was first used during the infamous Buck Ruxton case of 1935 (discussed on pages 110-112) and has varied little since then.

A Russian, the late Professor Mikhail Gerasimov, pioneered 'plastic reconstruction' work at the University of Irkutsk, adding a technique to the growing science of facial identification which,

after a slow start, is being used more and more in Britain and the United States. The Gerasimov method involves the reconstruction, in plasticine, of facial muscle onto the skull working from known constants relating to the contours of the face. The result is tinted and photographed in normal portrait style. In a test case in the early seventies, the Metropolitan Police Forensic Laboratory in London made such a portrait from the head of an unknown man who had died under a bus, despite the fact that much of his skull had been crushed.

A good picture is worth a thousand words, runs an old newspaperman's adage; but as photographic, cine, and video techniques improve and are applied to police work, it becomes an increasingly fitting motto for the forensic photographer.

FINGERPRINTS

'A thumb-print and what came of it' was the title of a chapter in Mark Twain's *Life on the Mississippi* published in 1883. This was a prophetic reference to an exciting development in criminal identification which at the time it was written was unheard of in America although there were gentle stirrings elsewhere. Mark Twain returned to the theme in his detective story, *Pudd'nhead Wilson*, which was published in 1894. The central character was a young lawyer called Wilson whose whim was to collect fingerprints. In telling the story, Twain has him using this knowledge to track down a murderer. Wilson declares in court that no one can disguise his fingerprints and that it is possible to identify a criminal by means of them. As events in the real world of crime detection were to show, Pudd'nhead Wilson was quite right.

Fingerprints are the impressions made by the ridges on the ends of the fingers and thumbs. They are unique to each individual and offer an infallible means of personal identification. The ridge patterns on the fingertips remain unaltered throughout a person's life except for gross destruction of the tissues. Even when the epidermis is destroyed by surface burns or abrasions, the original and underlying patterns return during the healing process. Thus, despite age and the ravages of disease or accident, each individual's fingerprints remain unchanged, even surviving the embalming processes of the Ancient Egyptians.

The history of fingerprints

These tell-tale marks of an individual's identity are commonly associated with criminal investigation but many countries keep fingerprint records for other reasons – to identify missing persons, victims of disasters or accidents and military personnel. Historical records reveal a number of insights regarding the individuality of fingerprints. For centuries, the Chinese used thumb impressions on document seals and early anatomists such as Marcello Malpighi (1628-1694) described the finger tip ridges. Thomas Bewick (1753-1828), the English naturalist, had his 'mark' in the form of a single finger impression printed under his signature in his books, and in 1823 the distinguished Czech physiologist, Johann Evangelist Purkinje (1787-1869), published a description of fingerprints and their types. Despite this interest in finger impressions, their full significance did not emerge until 1880. In that year, Dr Henry Faulds (1843-1930), a Scottish physician working at the Tsukiji Hospital in Tokyo, published a letter in *Nature*, the British scientific journal. He mentioned his interest in fragments of ancient pottery bearing finger impressions and suggested that fingerprints might be a possible means of identification.

Faulds's letter touched off a kindred spirit in Sir William Herschel (1833-1917) who reported that he had been using fingerprint identification in India for several years. Herschel, Chief Administrative Officer of the Hooghly district of Bengal, recognizing the individuality of the fingerprint, had used thumb impressions to identify illiterate prisoners and workers in the course of his official duties. Thus, by one of the quirks of chance, two men working independently in two far-flung countries had made the same discovery. The initial excitement created by the announcement in *Nature* sparked off a flurry of research and the first completely scientific appraisal of fingerprints was made by Sir Francis Galton (1822-1911), the influential English scientist and traveller.

Basic classification

In the course of studying anthropometry, the identification system based on body measurements devised by Alphonse Bertillon (1853-1914), Galton had corresponded with Herschel who won him over to the possibilities of identification by fingerprints. The two men concluded that fingerprints were individual and permanent and Galton set about the task of verification and classification. He established that identical fingerprints were not inherited and showed that even identical twins had different ridge patterns. He laid the ground work for a basic classification system, putting the most commonly observed features into three groups – arches, loops and whorls. Galton's book, *Fingerprints*, appeared in 1892 but it was left to another Englishman, Sir Edward Henry, to complete the task of fingerprint classification.

Henry, a doctor's son, was appointed Inspector General of Police in Bengal in 1891. He introduced anthropometry as a routine procedure for registering the identity of criminals but when he read Galton's book on fingerprints he became fascinated with the problems of classification. Henry established five basic patterns, adding tented arches to Galton's three groups and dividing loops into two classes. In 1896, he instructed the police forces under his command to abandon anthropometry in favour of dactyloscopy (the term used for fingerprinting). Success with the new method was immediate. Its application was simple and demonstrably effective as the rate of criminal identification in India improved dramatically.

Forensic uses

At the same time that Galton and Henry were perfecting their researches, a serving police officer in another continent brought the first murderer to justice with the aid of fingerprints. Juan Vucetich (1858-1925) of the Provincial Police of Buenos Aires based at La Plata, Argentina, employed Bertillon's method, but having read Galton's work quickly realized that fingerprinting was a superior method of identification. Against the wishes of his superiors, Vucetich set up a fingerprint system in the La Plata Bureau of Identification and in 1892 was given an opportunity to test his faith.

Below: *Herschel with the palmprint of a businessman, Mr Konai, which was his signature to a handwritten contract.*

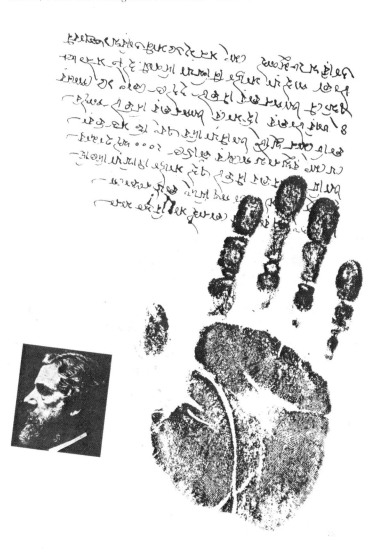

Two young children were found dead with their throats cut in their home at Necochea in Buenos Aires Province. Their mother, Francesca Rojas, who was wounded in the neck, accused a neighbour of attacking her and killing her two children. Local police were advised to look for fingerprints and their search revealed some bloody finger impressions on a door frame. The section of wood was cut out and sent to La Plata together with fingerprints taken from Rojas. The bloody prints in the murder room were found to be identical to the fingerprints of the victims' mother. Confronted with this information, Mme Rojas broke down and confessed that she murdered her children to make her free for her lover's attentions. She was convicted of murder and sentenced to life imprisonment and Vucetich was vindicated.

The Henry system

This successful use of the new method kindled fresh interest around the world, although Bertillon brooded in Paris over the impending demise of his system of identification. In 1900, Henry published his *Classification and use of fingerprints* and in the summer of that year a committee was set up in London to consider the new system of identification. Their recommendation was that the use of anthropometry in England should be dropped and Henry's system of fingerprint classification be adopted in its place. In 1901, Sir Edward Henry was appointed Acting Police Commissioner for the metropolis and Head of the Criminal Investigation Department. The Henry system was widely adopted by police forces around the world and, outside of South America, remains the most commonly used fingerprint classification.

The Vucetich system

In Argentina, Vucetich developed his own classification system which he published in 1904. His four-group system, the arch, whorl and left and right loops, was favoured by most of the Latin-American countries. While many modifications to fingerprint classification have been devised, all owe something to the pioneering efforts of Vucetich and Henry whose systems are employed by every law enforcement agency.

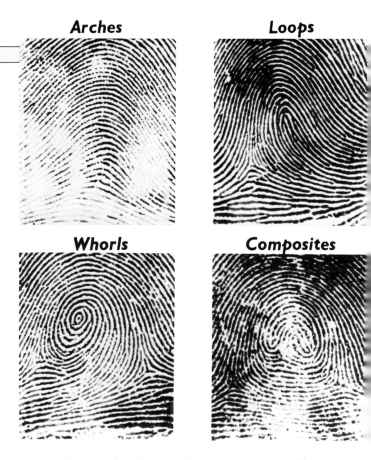

Above: *The basic classification of fingerprints, developed by Galton and put into practice by Henry.*

If further demonstration of the forensic value of fingerprints was needed, it came in 1905 with the trial in London of the Stratton brothers. An elderly man who ran a paint shop in south-east London was found dead in the adjoining parlour. He had been battered to death and his wife who had been badly injured died a few days later. Robbery was plainly the object of the assault for a metal cash-box in the shop had been prised open. What captured the attention of police officers was a clear thumbprint on the box. All those known to have handled the cash-box, including the dead couple, were fingerprinted but none of their prints matched that found at the crime scene. Police suspicion of known criminals focussed on the brothers, Alfred and Albert Stratton. Both had convictions for burglary and house-breaking and a milk-roundsman reported seeing two men hurrying from the paint-shop early on the morning of the murder. Alfred Stratton's girl friend admitted that the brothers had been out all night and when Alfred returned he destroyed his coat and dyed his shoes. With suspicion hardening, the police brought the Strattons in for questioning. Their fingerprints were taken and Alfred's right thumbprint proved a perfect match with the one on the cash-box. Photographic enlargements of both prints were produced in court and although the defence did its utmost to contest this new form of evidence, the jury was convinced that it spelled guilt for the Strattons. The brothers were convicted of murder and were subsequently hanged. Henry's system had triumphed and its acceptance into police procedure around the world was assured.

How the Henry system works

The Henry system of fingerprint classification is based on four groups of ridge patterns – arches, loops, whorls and composites. Arches are divided into two classes, plain and tented, according to their shape, and whorls and composites are grouped together. Loops are referred to as *ulnar* when they slope towards the little finger and *radial* when they slope towards the thumb. Each is designated by a capital letter. Thus, a plain arch is A, a tented arch T, a radial loop R, an ulnar loop U and a whorl W.

Loops make up about 65 per cent of all fingerprint patterns, whorls about 30 per cent and arches the remaining 5 per cent. As the proportion of loop patterns far exceeds the other categories, they are further classified according to two fixed features called the core and the delta. The core is the approximate centre of the pattern, and deltas are formed when a ridge divides. The number of ridges which lie between the core and delta is an important classification feature. Enlargement of fingerprint impressions reveals the great variety of ridge patterns in configurations which are unique to each individual. Fingerprints are classified by the shape of their patterns, by the finger positions of the pattern types and by the detailed characteristics of the ridges. The scale of the task confronting Henry is better appreciated when it is realized that more than one of the basic patterns may appear on the same pair of hands. His solution was to consider the ten fingers as a unit and he devised a simple

Below: *Fingerprints formed by perspiration, natural oil or dead skin are common, but usually invisible. These prints are called latent, because they need treatment to make them visible. Here an expert compares a latent print found at the scene of a crime with one from a suspect.*

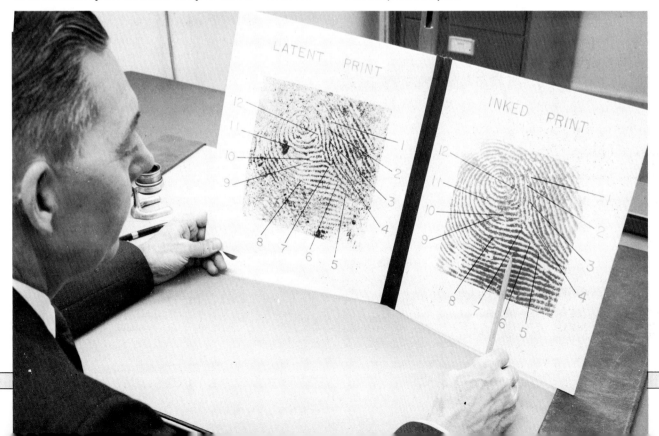

formula by which their characteristics could be expressed.

The first step in primary classification was to assign a numerical value to each of the ten digits. Thus, the right thumb is 1, the right index finger 2 and so on to the left little finger which is 10. This standard notation is printed on all fingerprint record cards used in those countries which adopted the Henry system.

1	2	3	4	5
Right Thumb	Right Index finger	Right Middle finger	Right Ring finger	Right Little finger
6	7	8	9	10
Left Thumb	Left Index finger	Left Middle finger	Left Ring finger	Left Little finger

The numbered digits are then considered in pairs: 1 and 2, 3 and 4, 5 and 6, 7 and 8 and 9 and 10. The pairs are written in the form of fractions with the even-numbered digit of each pair placed in the numerator position. Each pair is then assigned an arbitrary numerical value, giving;

pairs	$\frac{2}{1}$	$\frac{4}{3}$	$\frac{6}{5}$	$\frac{8}{7}$	$\frac{10}{9}$
numerical value	16	8	4	2	1

Whenever a whorl pattern appears in a set of fingerprints it takes on the value of the pair in which it is found. A formula is then derived by totalling the whorl pattern values for fingers 2, 4, 6, 8 and 10 and adding 1 to give the numerator, and totalling the whorl pattern values of fingers 1, 3, 5, 7 and 9 and adding 1 to give the denominator.

Thus for a set of prints with whorls in spaces 3, 7 and 10 the formula is expressed as $\frac{2}{11}$. This primary classification is further developed by adding secondary characteristics and other refinements. The capital letters A, W and L are used in secondary classification to denote the type of pattern appearing on the index fingers of each hand. The formula is further extended by the use of the small letters a, t and r denoting arches (plain or tented) in any finger or a radial loop in any but the index finger. This information is shown either to the left or the right of the secondary classification according to its position on the hand. A further letter system is used as a sub-secondary classification and refers to the ridge characteristics in loops and whorls. The ridges in whorls are traced in relationship to the deltas and are designated meeting (M), outside (O) and inside (I). An additional refinement is ridge counting in which a line is drawn from the core to the delta and the number of ridges intersected by it is counted. Henry's primary classification system made possible 1042 combinations of whorls and the primary and secondary systems together permit over a million groupings. The system allows a simple numerical formula to be derived for every combination of fingerprint patterns.

The single-fingerprint system

While the ten-finger classification proved ideal for searching collections of formal fingerprint records, the most frequently encountered crime print is the single impression. This is the chance fingerprint left involuntarily at the scene of the crime for which a search of a ten-finger collection would be a colossal task. This was recognized early on in the development of fingerprint classification and in 1930

KEY TO FILING OF PRIMARY GROUP												
A aA	rA	Aa	A-a	A--a	Aa-a	Ar	A-r	A--r	Ar-r	aAa	aA-a
A A	A	A	A	A	A	A	A	A	A	A	A
aA--a	aAa-a	aAr	aA-r	aA--r	aAr-r	rAa	rA-a	rA--a	rAa-a	rAr	rA-r
A	A	A	A	A	A	A	A	A	A	A	A
rA--r	rAr-r	A2a	A-2a	Aar	Aa-r	A-ar	Ara	Ar-a	A-ra	A2r	A-2r
A	A	A	A	A	A	A	A	A	A	A	A
aA2a	aA-2a	aAar	aAa-r	aA-ar	aAra	aAr-a	aA-ra	aA2r	aA-2r	rA2a	rA-2a
A	A	A	A	A	A	A	A	A	A	A	A
rAar	rAa-r	rA-ar	rAra	rAr-a	rA-ra	rA2r	rA-2r	A3a	A2ar	Aara	Aa2r
A	A	A	A	A	A	A	A	A	A	A	A
Ar2a	Arar	A2ra	A3r	aA3a	aA2ar	aAara	aAa2r	aAr2a	aArar	aA2ra	aA3r
A	A	A	A	A	A	A	A	A	A	A	A
rA3a	rA2ar	rAara	rAa2r	rAa2r	rAr2a	rArar	rA2ra	rA3r			
A	A	A	A	A	A	A	A	A			

Left: The standard key to the filing of the primary group of classifications, using secondary characteristics and other information.

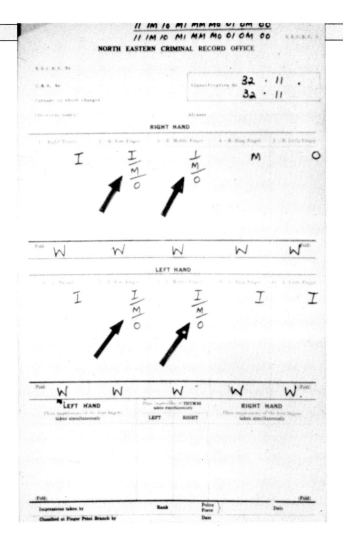

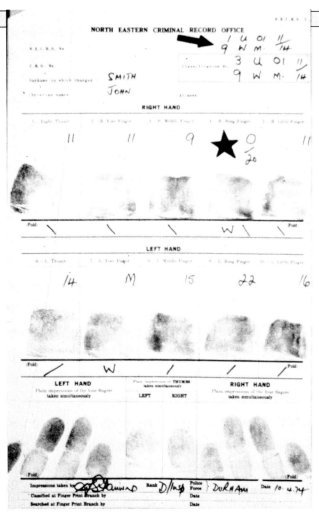

Above: *The chart on the left demonstrates the correct way of distinguishing between inside, outside and meeting whorls. The chart on the right is a standard fingerprint chart used in the UK.*

Scotland Yard adopted a single-fingerprint system. This was devised by Chief Inspector Harry Battley, Head of the Fingerprint Bureau.

The single-fingerprint system is a collection of ten numbered files each referring to individual digits as they appear on the ten-finger record card. Henry's general classification formula is used but more attention is paid to the fine details of ridges, cores and deltas. The comparison of a crime fingerprint with impressions taken from a suspect is a highly skilled job. Identification depends on showing a minimum of twelve matching characteristics in the all-important ridge patterns. Where these twelve points of comparison can be demonstrated, proof of identity is established. Evidence for use in court is presented by means of photographic enlargements with the points of comparison marked. The number of points of comparison required in the courts varies from country to country. In England, in criminal courts, 16 points are required in a single print, or 10 + 10 in two prints or two parts of the same print, for the purpose of identification.

Poroscopy

While the formal fingerprint record consists of carefully inked impressions set out in numbered boxes on a record card, fingerprints left at a crime scene are often not visible and may be fragmentary or

WHO KILLED SIR HARRY?
The Count de Marigny trial

A classic investigation of fingerprint evidence saved the life of Count Alfred de Marigny, accused of murdering his father-in-law, Sir Harry Oakes, in 1943. The incident was set on an exotic tropical island in the Bahamas, and was all the more exciting for involving the more colourful and glamorous elements of local 'high society'.

Passions ran high about the case, which was notorious not only for the particularly gruesome nature of the murder, but also because of the lurid aura of rumour and gossip centred around the Duke of Windsor's apparent part in the affair.

Sir Harry Oakes was American by birth, and a self-made millionaire. His wealth came from gold mines in Canada, and he adopted that country's citizenship in 1939.

In common with other affluent members of the international community, he lived in grand style in the Bahamas, then under the governorship of his friend, the Duke of Windsor. His knighthood was awarded under the patronage of the duke, and it was said that Sir Harry was the richest baronet in the British Empire.

On the night of 7 July 1943, he was hideously murdered. Someone came to his room and crushed his skull with four blows of a blunt, triangular-edged instrument. While he was still alive he was doused with insecticide and the bed on which he was lying was set alight. When he was found in the morning, his charred body was covered with feathers from a split pillow, and flames still licked at the mattress.

It was not difficult to think of people with a grudge against Sir Harry: he was disliked and resented by so many people that part of the problem was how to narrow down the suspects. Nothing had been stolen, so a robbery had not been the motive. Some people thought that it might be a Mafia murder: the grotesque shroud of feathers could be read as a mob warning. Others thought that it could be a voodoo revenge killing, not unknown in that part of the world, as it was whispered that the body had been castrated, but this in fact was not the case.

The Duke of Windsor took immediate personal charge of the investigation. His first step was unconventional, and puzzled many people. He chose to call in two Miami police captains, Edward Melchen and James O. Barker, to deal with the case. Edward Melchen had acted as his bodyguard from time to time, and Barker had a reputation as a fingerprint expert; they set to work at once. The Duke of Windsor told them that he wanted a quick solution to the problem, and he was rewarded by the fact that it only took them a few days to make an arrest.

The man they charged with the murder of Sir Harry Oakes was his son-in-law, Alfred de Marigny. He had married the Oakes' young daughter Nancy only days after her 18th birthday. The wedding was secret, and the couple did not inform Nancy's parents. De Marigny knew very well that they would never have consented to the match. He was from Mauritius, a suave, handsome, much-married adventurer, who had become used to living off his rich wives. Sir Harry and Lady Eunice had hoped for something better for Nancy.

Sir Harry, particularly, hated de Marigny with a violence. He was convinced that the man had only married Nancy for her money, and he periodically assured the couple that he would cut her off without a penny. He was beside himself when it seemed that his other children also liked and responded to de Marigny; Sir Harry saw him as a family-breaker.

When de Marigny was charged with murder, people in the Bahamas felt a righteous anger. They'd always known he was no good, and now they couldn't wait to see justice done and the guilty fiend hanged.

The trial opened on 13 October. Nancy de Marigny stood by her husband and had sought the help of a well-known New York private detective, Raymond Campbell Schindler. She knew that her husband had faults, but they were not the sort that characterized a murderer. Her mother, on the other hand, was sure that de Marigny, a man she had always mistrusted and who had caused such problems in the family, had finally taken the step that had ruined her life.

The prosecution had no difficulty in establishing that the two men had a bad relationship, and de Marigny certainly wasn't denying it. What they had to show, to prove their case against him, was that he had been in the room on the night of the murder — something he categorically denied. Their case rested on the evidence of a clear fingerprint that they alleged had been found on a Chinese screen by the bed.

Now in the tropics the humidity is so high that fingerprints literally melt away, so if de Marigny's print had been discovered it could not be more than

Right: *Sir Harry Oakes. His case showed that police officers could manipulate fingerprint evidence.*

24 hours old. That would make him either the murderer, or, at the very least, an accessory.

Suspicious circumstances surrounded this fingerprint, not least the fact that although it was apparently found on the day that the murder was discovered, no mention of this outstanding piece of evidence had been made for a few days. But worse was to come. Godfrey Higgs, who was leading the defence, had taken a thorough course in fingerprinting to prepare himself for the trial, and he was able to exploit to the full the fact that there was something distinctly fishy about the prosecution's case.

Schindler, the private detective brought in by Nancy, had hired his own fingerprint expert, Maurice O'Neill of New Orleans Police Department.

Together they had re-examined the evidence surrounding the fingerprint.

First of all, the damning print was a 'lift', secured by placing a piece of transparent tape over the print, then lifting it off. Then there was the strange fact that the investigators had failed to take a photograph of the site from which the fingerprint had been removed.

Higgs poured on the pressure.

Why had the fingerprint not been photographed *in situ* as was the correct and established practice? The Miami detectives' rather sheepish response was that their fingerprint camera had been broken.

O'Neill had been careful to photograph every inch of the screen, using highly sensitive ultraviolet techniques which would show up any outlines left after the surface of the prints had been eroded by the tropical climate. By using this technique, he was able to show that there was no 'shadow' trace of a print on the area of the screen where de Marigny's was alleged to have been found. Finally, there were two clear moisture marks on the lifted print exhibited as the prosecution's most serious piece of evidence.

Higgs asked Barker, the fingerprint expert, to describe where on the screen the prints had been found. Barker said that he could not remember, though when he was pressed he described a scroll-like piece of pattern. There was, in fact, no such pattern on the screen, or anything like it. The only explanation Higgs could find that would fit the moisture marks in the background of the print was that it had been lifted from a glass – and Melchen had made a point of getting de Marigny to pour him a glass of water when he first interviewed him at the start of the investigation.

As Higgs persisted with his cross-examination, Barker became more and more shifty and flustered. He had no sensible explanation for any of the points that Higgs raised, resorting to asserting that everything was a coincidence.

"This is the most outstanding case in which your expert assistance has been required, is it not?" asked Higgs, at the end of the interrogation.

"Well, it's developed into that."

"And I suggest," continued Higgs, "that in your desire for personal gain and notoriety, you have swept away truth and fabricated evidence."

It was clear that the jury thought so too, as they brought in a verdict of not guilty. The tide of opinion in the courtroom had turned in de Marigny's favour, and everyone cheered at the verdict.

Despite further private investigations, the murder was never solved.

blurred. A refinement to identification in such cases was provided by Edmond Locard (1877-1966), the pioneering French forensic scientist. He discovered that the individual sweat pore openings of the finger's ridges had their own distinguishing characteristics. There are normally between nine and eighteen pores per millimetre of ridge but the size, shape and position of the openings differ from individual to individual, and are permanent.

Developing the prints
Crime scene fingerprints fall into three categories, visible impressions left by a bloody or dirty hand, impressions left in plastic materials such as putty, tar, chocolate or soap and latent or hidden fingerprints. It is the latter, which need to be developed or visualized by means of dusting powder, which have captured the imagination of detective fiction writers. Latent prints are impressions left by the sweat-moistened ridges of the fingertips on a polished surface such as metal, glass and painted or polished wood. Their existence is determined by oblique lighting directed at suspect surfaces – detectives do not as a matter of course cover everything with dusting powder in their

Below: *Detectives take latent fingerprints by dusting from a van which had been ambushed in Croydon, UK.*

Above: *As demonstrated by the Oakes case, it is vitally important to take evidence at the scene of the crime.*

search for dabs! Once located, prints are dusted with fine aluminium powder to develop them and the impressions are then photographed in close-up and at a scale which will record their position on the item in question. It is vital that fingerprint photographs used in court can be clearly related to the objects on which they were found at the crime scene.

Latent fingerprints may also be removed from suitable smooth surfaces by a process known as lifting. Transparent adhesive tape (lifting tape) is smoothed over the dusted print which is then peeled off on the tape. The lifted print is fixed to a glossy-surface card for record purposes. Latent prints on porous surfaces such as paper, cloth, plaster and unprepared wood may be developed using iodine fumes, silver nitrate or ninhydrin spray. Once developed, a photographic record is made. Print impressions on skin may also be visualized using special techniques including X-rays.

Mass fingerprinting

British police officers investigating the brutal murder of 4 year old Anne Devanney in 1948 had in their possession the likely murderer's fingerprints but their problem was to identify their owner. The duty nurse in the children's ward at the Queen's Park Hospital, Blackburn noticed an empty cot when she did her early morning rounds on 14 May. The hospital grounds were searched and the body of the missing girl was found a short distance from the ward. She had been sexually assaulted and was dead from a savage beating.

Crime scene investigators established that the murderer had moved a bottle when he approached the child's cot and left finger impressions on its glass surface. The intruder's prints were quickly isolated

Above: *Latent fingerprints being removed from a false number plate by lifting.*

from those of the nursing staff and, armed with this evidence, the police set about fingerprinting the entire male population of Blackburn in order to find a matching set. This was an enormous undertaking but on 12 August, set number 46,253 was found to match the fingerprints on the bottle. These suspect prints belonged to Peter Griffiths, an ex-serviceman working as a flour mill packer, who was promptly arrested. He said, "I hope I get what I deserve."

The jury thought he deserved to be convicted of murder and he was duly found guilty, subsequently paying the supreme penalty for his crime.

This historic investigation did much to establish the credibility of fingerprinting in the minds of the public. In addition, it showed that no law-abiding person had anything to fear from fingerprinting. After all, 46,252 men in Blackburn had been proved innocent. In a dramatic sequel to Britain's greatest man-hunt, all the fingerprint records were publicly destroyed to demonstrate that no infringement of civil liberties could result from their use.

Palmprints and footprints

In theory, any ridged area of the hand or foot may be used as a means of identification although problems arise in keeping systematic files. Nevertheless, palmprints and footprints left at the scene of a crime afford valuable evidence, as Michael Queripel discovered to his cost in another memorable British investigation. On the night of 29 April 1955, a woman who had left her Potter s Bar home to walk the dog on the nearby golf-course was reported missing. Her body was found the following morning near the seventeenth tee. She had been battered to death with a heavy iron tee marker which lay close by with a bloody handprint clearly visible on its metal surface.

The palmprint on the murder weapon was not identifiable from criminal records so the police decided to take palmprints from the local population. Nine thousand impressions were taken for comparison with the murder print and on 19 August, a matching print was found. It was the 4,604th impression to come under the investigator's scrutiny and belonged to 17 year old local government employee, Michael Queripel. At first

Below: *The iodine fuming technique. The flask contains iodine crystals and the bulb sucks in air, thus vapourizing the iodine. This is then blown onto the fingerprints and, being sensitive to certain constituents of perspiration, gives a good purplish-brown trace on the paper.*

THE INDELIBLE FINGERPRINT
The George Ross case

The criminal's fear that he will be betrayed by his fingerprints left at the scene of the crime is reasonable enough. Everyone has watched the typical scenario in a gangster movie where the villain assiduously wipes clean any wineglasses or doorhandles that he has touched. We can assume the average hoodlum watches the same movies, and arrives at the conclusion that with a little care, he can eliminate all traces of his fingerprints.

A handkerchief would certainly do the job, and, one might think, running water flowing over the print over the course of a few days. At least, this is how one American criminal reasoned as he sat in a back-street restaurant in Cleveland. Sometimes, events take an unexpected turn, and the remarkable story of George Ross is one of the classics in fingerprint expert's lore — the case of the indelible fingerprint!

When Patrolman Forney Haas saw a large Lincoln with Californian license plates driving the wrong way down a one-way street in Cleveland, Ohio, on 8 December 1951, he had no idea that the driver was George Ross, a well-known criminal wanted for housebreaking, robbery and car-stealing. Ross was on the run and a description of him had been telexed to police across the nation: 27 years old, 5ft 9½in tall, slim, with dark brown hair and a dark complexion.

Patrolman Haas chased Ross in his patrol car and forced him to the kerb. Ross said he had not realized the street was one-way. Haas asked to see his licence, and Ross, playing for time, claimed to have left it at home. Haas insisted on seeing it, so they drove in convoy to the rooming-house at 8210 Euclid Avenue where Ross had rented a room under the name of Montgomery.

His landlady, Mrs Lottie Cooper, was sweeping the hallway when she heard men's voices shouting in one of her rooms. She heard one man say "I'm telling you my licence was in my wallet when I left. It's been stolen from here." Evidently Haas still thought he was dealing with an ordinary traffic offence. But after a few more angry exchanges, Mrs Cooper heard a shot, followed by two

more. The door opened and a man holding a smoking revolver ran past her and out into the street. Patrolman Haas was rushed to hospital but died half an hour later without regaining consciousness.

The murderer's identity was soon discovered through the abandoned car. It was believed to have been stolen in California by two criminals who had then headed east committing a string of robberies. One of them, George F. Ross, fitted the description of 'Montgomery', and when shown a picture of Ross, Mrs Cooper was fairly certain she recognized him as the escaping killer who had rushed past her.

However, Ross himself had provided the most damning evidence of his involvement in Haas's death. Before fleeing, he had grabbed Haas's service revolver — which could always be identified as his by its serial numbers — and he knew it now had his own fingerprints on it. A pistol with latent fingerprints had once earned him a prison sentence in another state. He had to get rid of it, and quickly. He was sitting in a cheap restaurant in Bedford, a suburb of Cleveland, when the ideal solution occurred to him. He went to the washrooms, dropped the revolver in one of the toilet bowls and pulled the flush. The gun sank out of sight. Now he had to get out of the area and somehow escape the furious manhunt which he knew would follow on the killing of a policeman.

The police were not far behind him. At Cleveland headquarters, the men in charge of the case, Inspector McArthur and Police Captain David E. Kerr, were studying a wall map of the country wondering which way he had gone. The phone rang: someone very like Ross had been seen stealing a parked car in the suburb of Bedford, and heading south.

For several days Ross just succeeded in evading capture. He was surprised robbing a petrol station in West Virginia, but escaped, dropping a revolver. Cleveland police were disappointed when it turned out not to be Haas's gun. Two days later, in Ellicott City in Maryland, a Chief of Police and a patrolman approached him as he slept in a car parked in a petrol station. Shots were exchanged, and Ross escaped again, though a bloodstained blanket suggested he was wounded.

Meanwhile detectives had plenty of time to assemble the known facts of Ross's background. It was a sad story of spells in institutions from an early age, and compulsive

he said he had simply stumbled across the body but later he admitted killing the woman. He pleaded guilty to the charge of murder and in October 1955 was tried at the Old Bailey. He was convicted but in view of his age was ordered by the judge to be detained in prison.

American developments

Although identification by fingerprints owed its origins to the genius of a Scotsman and three Englishmen, it was American enthusiasm which led to modern improvements and refinements. Systematic fingerprinting was adopted in the USA in thieving escalating from cars to large amounts of money. And now that absurd traffic violation had turned him into a dangerous murderer. So when a Maryland farmer named Duval gave Ross a lift on 17 December, and recognized him, he said nothing, but waited until he had dropped Ross before stopping two policemen. He drove them back to Ross, who at first said his name was Perkins, but soon admitted his identity and was arrested.

Ross claimed that he had killed Haas in self-defence, and when he came to trial on 4 February 1952 in Cleveland, his defence also pleaded that he was insane – a 'psychopathic personality' and a 'moral imbecile'. Public opinion was strongly behind the prosecution, but the missing police revolver could weaken their case.

This vital clue was in fact not missing at all. It was being kept secret by the prosecution to be used as a final, sensational piece of evidence. Soon after the murder, one of the little restaurant's customers had noticed that a toilet was stopped up. A friend of the proprietor, Fred Romito, offered to reach for the obstruction, and fished out the revolver, which had stuck in the drain.

After several days' immersion in water no fingerprints could be expected; but laboratory technicians examined it carefully all the same. There was nothing on the butt – but on the barrel they found what looked like a fingerprint. It was not a latent print, but one actually *etched* into the metal, which could be seen even with the naked eye. Various explanations were offered for this unusual phenomenon. The heavy lime content of the water, or a chemical reaction from the copper ball in the tank, were both suggested, but the most popular theory was that Ross's sweat had had an unusually high salt content, due to his nervousness and tension, and had eaten into the metal of the gun as he handled it.

The prosecution used their damning evidence cleverly. After the defence had asked again and again about the gun, and one after another, police investigators had truthfully denied having found it, the gun was finally produced just before the end of the prosecution's case. The build-up convinced the jury, in spite of Ross's story of self-defence and the psychiatric experts' claim of insanity. He was found guilty of murder on two counts, with no recommendation of mercy, and went to the electric chair on 16 January 1953.

the early 1900s and the two most important collections were those maintained by the Federal Penitentiary at Fort Leavenworth in Kansas and by the International Association of Chiefs of Police at Washington DC. These were combined to form the nucleus of the FBI's Identification Bureau which

was inaugurated in 1924 by J. Edgar Hoover. The basic Henry system of classification was used to build a collection which today holds 200 million records in civil and criminal categories. The civil category holds records on government employees, military personnel, defence employees and aliens. The FBI's Identification Bureau handles records submitted by over 1,400 agencies and deals with 30,000 or more fingerprints daily.

The FBI system
The huge scale of this collection has put the FBI at the forefront of developing classification techniques and methods of searching. The Henry system has been extended by the addition of further classification features. These are known as the major, final and key and are based on counting the ridges in

Below: *The driver of a car which mowed down a column of US soldiers in 1942 is fingerprinted on arrest.*

specified patterns on particular digits. Thus the major classification considers only the thumbs, the final deals only with the little finger and the key with the first loop encountered in a set of ten digits but excluding the little finger. The order of classification on the standard American fingerprint record is, key, major, primary, secondary, sub-secondary and final. This extension of classification allows prints in a large collection to be grouped more easily into pattern categories of specific fingers and thereby speeds up the search procedure.

The FBI's National Crime Information Center (NCIC) contains a computerized information retrieval system on wanted persons. This includes descriptive data as well as fingerprint information and the NCIC operates a fingerprint classification (FPC) procedure to assist the police and law enforcement agencies in submitting standardized entries and requests. One of the greatest problems is presented by manual searching which is an enormously time-consuming process. Machine searching methods have been developed and semi-automatic fingerprint recognition systems are being developed. The single crime fingerprint poses its special problems for identification experts faced with manual scanning which could take weeks.

Above: *An examiner uses a comparator to identify a latent fingerprint with an inked print* (left) *in the Identification Division at FBI Headquarters, Washington. The FBI holds millions of sets of fingerprints, most of them belonging to non-criminals.*

Laser technology
New technology has come to the rescue, however, in the form of laser equipment which can scan eighty fingerprint images a second on microfilm and process the data electronically. Advances are also being made in locating and recording latent fingerprints. For example, Canadian scientists have found that certain types of impressions can be located and made to fluoresce under laser illumination. Ridge characteristics are shown in fine detail and can be recorded photographically. Details of the pores are also heightened and these can be examined microscopically. This fluorescence effect results not from the natural substances found on the skin but from residues of organic substances such as motor oils, inks and paints which are associated with particular occupations.

Videofile
Computerization and electronic scanning devices

have not yet met the challenge of searching a file of millions of records for a single fingerprint but this is an area of rapidly growing innovation. In Britain, Scotland Yard has been active in the development of improved procedures. A national fingerprint computer called Videofile was introduced in 1977 which contains two and a half million prints of convicted criminals.

This system, which allows prints to be compared on a visual display screen, has speeded identification by five times. Videofile also has a scene of crime index comprising records of known criminals in the London Metropolitan area. This is used as the first step in matching the scene of crime single fingerprint. The days when it took two weeks to make manual checks of the entire print collection, as in the case of the Black Panther investigation in 1976, are rapidly disappearing.

Erasing fingerprints

A frequent preoccupation with the criminal fraternity in the face of the damning identification provided by fingerprints is how to avoid leaving them. The use of gloves and wiping prints from objects at the crime scene are two obvious precautions but some criminals have resorted to more drastic measures. The gangster John Dillinger persuaded two doctors to perform plastic surgery on his fingertips in 1934. The results were a failure and his advisers adopted another method which involved dipping his fingers in acid until the ridge patterns disappeared. This only gave temporary relief from the worries of identification for by the time he was caught by the FBI, Dillinger's ridge patterns had reappeared.

Robert Phillips, a man with an extensive criminal record, went through painful surgery to have skin transplanted from his chest onto his fingertips. When he was arrested in 1941 in Texas for failing to carry a draft card, police took fingerprint impressions from him. To their horror and to the arrested man's delight, the fingerprints bore no ridge patterns. A body search of the man calling himself Robert Pitts soon revealed the scars on his chest which explained why his fingertips were devoid of patterns. He was scornful of attempts to establish his identity without the aid of fingerprints.

His triumph proved rather hollow for the FBI's resources turned up his likely identity through other physical characteristics and sufficient ridge patterns had been left on the second phalanges of his fingers to provide confirmation. Moreover, acting on information received from the criminal underworld, police tracked down the shady doctor who confessed to carrying out the transplant operation. Both he and Robert Phillips were sentenced to long terms in prison. Such painful methods of avoiding identification quickly went out of fashion as the criminal accepted the truth of Pudd'nhead Wilson's remark that he could "unerringly identify him by his hands".

Below: *A poster to help bring John Dillinger to justice. Note the fingerprint classification.*

GET·DILLINGER!
$15,000 *Reward*

=== **A PROCLAMATION** ===

WHEREAS, One John Dillinger stands charged officially with numerous felonies including murder in several states and his banditry and depredation stamp him as an outlaw, a fugitive from justice and a vicious menace to life and property;

NOW, THEREFORE, We, Paul McNutt, Governor of Indiana; George White, Governor of Ohio; F. B. Olson, Governor of Minnesota; William A. Comstock, Governor of Michigan; and Henry Horner, Governor of Illinois, do hereby proclaim and offer a reward of Five Thousand Dollars ($5,000.00) to be paid to the person or persons who apprehend and deliver the said John Dillinger into the custody of any sheriff of any of the above-mentioned states or his duly authorized agent.

THIS IS IN ADDITION TO THE $10,000.00 OFFERED BY THE FEDERAL GOVERNMENT FOR THE ARREST OF JOHN DILLINGER.

HERE IS HIS FINGERPRINT CLASSIFICATION and DESCRIPTION. ———— **FILE THIS FOR IDENTIFICATION PURPOSES.**

John Dillinger. (w) age 30 yrs., 5-8½. 170½ lbs., gray eyes, med. chest, hair, med. comp., med. build. Dayton. O., P. D. No. 10587. O. S. E. No. 559-646.

F.P.C. (12)

M   9   R   O   O
    S   14   U   OO   8
13   10   O   O   O
u   R   w   w   w
5   11   15   I   8
u   U   u   w   u

FRONT VIEW

Be on the lookout for this desperado. He is heavily armed and usually is protected with bullet-proof vest. Take no unnecessary chances in getting this man. He is thoroughly prepared to shoot his way out of any situation.

GET HIM

DEAD

OR ALIVE

Notify any Sheriff or Chief of Police of Indiana, Ohio, Minnesota, Michigan, Illinois.

or **THIS BUREAU**

SIDE VIEW

ILLINOIS STATE BUREAU OF CRIMINAL IDENTIFICATION AND INVESTIGATION

T. P. Sullivan, Supt.   Springfield, llinois

BALLISTICS

The branch of forensic science termed, rather imprecisely, 'ballistics' is one of the newest and busiest disciplines in the scientific fight against crime: a case of necessity once again proving itself to be the mother of invention. Over the last seventy years, two world wars and long-drawn conflicts in Asia, the Middle East, Africa, South America and Northern Ireland have left the world gun-conscious, and even those untouched by personal experience of firearms know the vicarious excitement of face-to-face shoot-outs from films and television.

Above: *This illustration shows a composite photograph of two .32 cartridge cases. The one on the left is alleged to have been fired from the gun of Nicola Sacco, in the famous Sacco and Vanzetti case (page 144). The test cartridge case is on the right.*

The United States, with the right of the citizen to bear personal arms built firmly into its constitution, has perhaps suffered most from all this. In the mid-1970s the breakdown of homicide figures for a typical year in the US showed gun deaths taking up 65 per cent of the index: 51 per cent with handguns, 8 per cent with shotguns and 6 per cent with rifles. Stabbings and physical street violence together accounted for no more than 29 per cent of American murders, while that favourite crime of the Victorians, poisoning, trailed with 3 per cent.

In Europe – Northern Ireland aside – shooting fatalities are nowhere near as common, but there has been a slight increase over the past decade, enough to warrant a ballistics laboratory for every national police force. Interpol keep an extensive collection of firearms data at their headquarters near Paris, and in England and Wales the needs of the provincial forces are catered for by a busy Home Office laboratory at Nottingham.

The ballistics cases of the Metropolitan and City of London police forces are taken care of by the Metropolitan Police Forensic Science Laboratory on the banks of the Thames. In Ulster, civil and military ballistics authorities struggle to keep abreast of daily developments in the province.

What is ballistics?

In fact, the term 'ballistics' in this context is a misnomer which is used by press and police alike as a handy tag to describe the work of the firearms examiner. 'Ballistics' is simply the study of projectiles in flight and forms only part of the firearms examiner's work, which also includes the collection and evaluation of data on the many different categories and makes of firearms, their range and rate of fire, the nature of the wounds they cause, and the chemical residues they leave on gunman and victim alike.

Like those of other forensic scientists, the objects of the firearms examiner are basically three-fold: identification, measurement and comparison. In the case of a fatal shooting the police will look to him for evidence of whether they are dealing with a case of accident, suicide, or murder. But no firearms examiner works in splendid isolation; in the course of a complex investigation he may call upon the pathologist who performs the autopsy, the histologist, who specializes in human tissue, biologists to deal with bloodstains, chemists to analyse powder residue, perhaps a metallurgist to consider the makeup of a bullet, and of course the fingerprint officer who will attempt the delicate task of lifting fingerprints from the weapon.

The ideal result of all this will be that the firearms examiner can tell the police that victim A was killed by bullet B, that bullet B could only have come from pistol C, and that suspect D had possession of the gun and showed every indication of having fired the fatal shot. He may also be required to show the reason why, in simple layman's terms, to a court.

'Little short guns'

It is only since the general introduction of breech-loading, rifled firearms during the last century that the work done by the modern firearms examiner has become a practical proposition.

Robberies involving firearms are a particular problem in the USA. These dramatic scenes are of hold ups in banks in Kalamazoo (above) and Lee-Harvard (below), and were both recorded on security cameras installed in the banks.

Although the 'casques that did affright the air at Agincourt' were loaded with gunpowder and were followed in later years by the development of heavy muskets and arquebuses, portable handguns appeared only in the early years of the sixteenth century. They are said to have been invented in the Italian town of Pistoia – hence the name 'pistol' – and arrived in Britain about 1515 as German imports. We know that footpads and highwaymen quickly realized their usefulness from the words of Henry VIII himself: 'Evil disposed persons,' he wrote, 'have done detestable murders with little short guns.'

These 'little short guns' remained basically unchanged in design for the next three hundred years and more, consisting of a barrel mounted on a wooden stock which housed the trigger mechanism – the 'lock'. They were loaded by pouring a measure of powder into the muzzle of the barrel which was followed by a lead ball and a paper wad to keep the load in place; the wad was them tamped firmly with a ramrod. The pistol was 'primed' by pouring a little powder into a pan at the rear of the barrel which surrounded the 'touch-hole'. The very early models were fired by simply touching off the powder in the pan with a smouldering match, which in turn ignited the main load. Later, wheel-, snaphaunce and flint-locks used flint and steel to mechanize the firing process, and the last muzzle-loaders were 'percussion' pistols in which an explosive metal cap was placed on a nipple over the touch-hole and struck by a hammer when the trigger was pulled.

Like modern shotguns, muzzle-loading pistols were smooth bore, and the bullets used often failed to fit the inside of the barrel tightly, allowing the gases from the exploding gunpowder to escape around the sides. They made a loud noise and a lot of smoke and because of their eccentricity and individuality they were not only potentially dangerous to use but almost useless as far as a criminal investigator was concerned: almost, but not quite.

Early ballistics cases

The first recorded case of forensic firearms examination was solved by comparison – the main factor, even today, of such work. In 1784 a man named Edward Culshaw was shot in the head with a flintlock pistol, and his acquaintance, John Toms, was arrested on suspicion of the murder. In Culshaw's wound was found the wad from the pistol, which, when unfolded, proved to be a strip torn from a popular broadsheet. A matching piece was found in Toms' coat pocket, providing damning evidence.

It also provided a useful lesson for the forces of the law, for when a policeman was shot in Lincoln in 1860, it was again a wad made from newspaper which brought his killer, a man named Richardson, to justice. A singed wad found near the body bore the name of the *Times* newspaper and the date of publication, 27 March, 1854. At Richardson's home a double-barrelled pistol with one load discharged was found and examined. The remaining wad was from the same issue of the *Times,* a fact attested by the paper's editor at Lincoln Assizes, when Richardson was sentenced to death.

The first recorded case of a bullet leading to arrest and conviction – so perhaps the first true 'ballistics' case – appears in the memoirs of Henry Goddard, one of the last of the famous Bow Street Runners, the London law force which immediately preceded the Metropolitan Police. In 1835 Goddard investigated a case of shooting and discovered that the moulded lead ball taken from the wound was curiously ridged. The ridge mark obviously came from the mould. Goddard interviewed a number of gun owners under suspicion of the crime, in each case asking to see their bullet moulds. When he finally found one that fitted the murder ball, his case was solved.

Goddard's identification foreshadowed almost exactly the work done by modern firearms examiners in showing that a fired bullet is unique to one gun, but it was not until the rifling of gun barrels in the early nineteenth century became common practice that the possibility of every discharged bullet being proved individual occurred.

Rifling marks

Rifling – cutting of a spiral groove into the bore of a gun barrel to give the bullet spin and thus make its flight more accurate – was in fact a very old concept. An early 'rifle' was recorded in Italy as early as 1477, and the Nuremburg gunsmith Gaspard Kot-

Above: *Officers from the British Flying Squad are examining a group of firearms collected from professional criminals. The sawn-off, pump action shotgun is widely used.*

ter improved the technique slightly in 1520. To make rifling effective, however, the bullet had to fit the interior of the barrel tightly, which made for obvious difficulties in ramming a bullet into place from the muzzle end of the gun. A compromise was reached by the Irish duelling pistol maker Joseph Manton, who in the early nineteenth century 'half rifled' his superb saw-handled pistols: the improved accuracy caused a swift decline in the popularity of pistol duelling, or 'blazing', as a means of settling gentlemanly disputes.

The grooves and 'lands' – raised strips between the grooves – of a rifled gun barrel leave distinctive marks upon the bullet called 'striations' from the Latin 'stria'. Stria originally meant the fluting on an architectural column, and bullet striations resemble these to a remarkable degree; even air weapons leave rifling striations on their pellets. The only firearms that do not are smooth bore guns such as shotguns and antique weapons of the flintlock type, plus such home made weapons as 'replica' guns which have had their barrels bored through to render them lethal – not only, it must be said, to the victim but often to the user too.

Breech-loading weapons

The difficulties of muzzle-loading a rifled weapon were largely overcome in 1751, when 'breech-loading' sporting guns were introduced. In these, the gun barrel hinged downwards near the lock,

POINT BLANK
The Gutteridge murder

The typically English parish of Stapleford Abbotts lies in unspoiled Essex countryside in the heart of Epping Forest. Until the morning of September 27 1927 its rural peace had not been interrupted by anything approaching violent crime since the days when Dick Turpin had roamed the Ongar-Romford road 200 years previously. But from that day on the village was to hold a grim place in criminological history.

At first light a farm-worker, wending his way to work along the Stapleford Road, found a body lying in his path; by its uniform he recognized it as that of Police Constable George William Gutteridge, but he could not be sure of the face, for two heavy calibre bullets had been fired – one into each eye – at point blank range.

When the dead man's colleagues from the Essex Constabulary examined the scene, along with a police surgeon, they found that, in addition to the two bullets which had so hideously disfigured him, Gutteridge had been hit by two similar bullets in the chest.

His bicycle lay on the grass verge nearby, and his notebook and pencil were in the road beside him; the evidence indicated that Gutteridge had stopped a passing motorist for questioning, and had been gunned down. His assailant had then stood over the corpse and shot out the eyes.

Gruesome as this last act had been, there was not much mystery as to the motive behind it. In those days when education in general was still somewhat shallow, a lingering superstition persisted that the last sight a man saw was registered photographically on the retina after death: Rudyard Kipling had, in fact, published a short story about the belief.

A number of burglaries in the area seemed to provide the wider motive behind the crime: presumably Gutteridge had chanced across the culprits. And a complaint to the police earlier that morning provided the likely vehicle used by the killers. Dr Edward Richardson Lovell, of London Road, Billericay, Essex, had locked up his new Morris-Cowley saloon in the garage adjoining his house after coming from his rounds late the previous evening. At some time during the night the garage had been broken open and the car stolen.

Scotland Yard were informed and Detective Chief Inspector Berrett was put in charge of the

Above: *Robert Churchill's ballistic evidence in the Gutteridge case was the first used in a British court.*

case, while an all out search for the missing vehicle was instigated. By the evening of the same day the Morris-Cowley was found abandoned in South London. Traces of blood matching that of the dead constable were found on the driver's door and off-side running board, and on the floor under the driver's seat was found a vital clue – a Webley .455 calibre revolver shell case of Mark IV pattern.

Meanwhile an autopsy had been performed, and four discharged bullets removed from the victim's wounds. These too, were of .455 calibre, and though battered by the impact, traces of striations left by the rifling were discernible.

In the opinion of Robert Churchill, called in by Detective Chief Inspector Berrett, he should be able to match them to the murder weapon — given, of course, a chance to examine the murder weapon.

Unfortunately, after a fairly promising start, the trail during the next few days and weeks seemed to have grown cold. Berrett believed that he was looking for a thief or thieves who went armed and used a motor car during the course of crime: a relatively new breed in Britain who took their lead from the well-publicized, sedan-driving gangsters of the United States. On the other hand, if they were sophisticated enough to use these new methods, they were probably smart enough to lie low following the newspaper outcry which centred on Gutteridge's bloody end.

Almost two months after the murder, in November, a Vauxhall car was stolen from Tooting, South London, not far from where Dr Lovell's Morris had been found abandoned. There was nothing at first to connect it with the earlier crime, but underworld contacts gave the investigating officers a lead; rumour had it that it had been stolen by William Henry Kennedy, a 36 year old typesetter who was a known associate of criminals, though he had no record.

He was also said to carry a gun.

Kennedy had vanished from his usual London haunts, but shortly after Christmas, Detective Inspector Kirschner of Scotland Yard traced him to Liverpool and enlisted the aid of the Liverpool City Police in tracking him down. On January 25 1928, police surrounded a house in Copperas Hill, Liver-

Below: Frederick Browne was found guilty of shooting P C Gutteridge, and was hanged at Pentonville prison, London.

pool, and Kennedy ran out, brandishing an automatic: a Liverpool Detective Sergeant, William Guthrie Mattinson, tackled and disarmed him, and he was charged with attempted murder of the officer and theft of the Vauxhall car.

Once Kennedy was in custody, Kirschner tried psychological tactics — not, as was later suggested in court, the 'third degree.' Only the use of a gun and the theft of a car suggested any connection with the Essex killing, which had been committed not with an automatic but with an Army pattern Webley revolver. But Kirschner told the accused man that the Yard believed him to be involved, pointing out that if he himself were not guilty but turned King's Evidence, he might escape with a jail sentence.

Kennedy, who had recently married, implicated a man named Frederick Guy Browne, a 47 year old ex-convict who had a garage at Northcote Road, Clapham Junction.

Browne was interviewed by detectives and arrested on a holding charge of car theft, while his premises were searched. Four revolvers, one a Webley .455, were found in the garage, along with a stock of ammunition which included a number of Mark I and Mark IV Webley bullets. They were handed over to Robert Churchill.

On April 23 1928 the pair were tried for murder at the Old Bailey, Churchill taking the stand to tell of the painstaking work which he had put into the case. Firstly, the Mark I and Mark IV .455 ammunition had been rejected as obsolete by the Army in the early years of the First World War. It was packed with 'black powder' which had been superseded by newer propellants. Traces of a similar black powder had been taken from Gutteridge's eye wounds.

Test firing of the Webley found in Browne's possession had produced rifling marks which Churchill claimed were identical to those on the bullets removed from the constable's body, but he also showed that the breech face and firing pin of Browne's revolver had produced identical marks to those found on the base of the cartridge recovered from Dr Lovell's car — which could only have been left there by the killer.

He and army officers from Woolwich Arsenal had then test fired no less than 1,300 .455 Webley revolvers to see if the breech face tooling marks could be reproduced in any way; none matched. Both men were found guilty on the strength of this ballistics evidence — the first time it had been produced in a British court of law — and they were hanged on May 31, Browne at Pentonville and Kennedy at Wandsworth.

Left: *A microflash photograph of a police scientist firing a sawn-off shotgun to test the behaviour of the cartridge in flight.*
Opposite top: *A .455 Webley revolver, test bullets and test card.*

Opposite below: *Striations on a bullet found in a body are matched with those on a bullet fired from the gun of a suspect.*

exposing the open, near-end of the barrel – the breech. The powder was usually contained in a paper cartridge which was torn open to allow ignition from the flint and steel lock. Ordinary sporting shotguns are loaded in much the same way today, although the modern cardboard or plastic cartridge also encloses the load of shot and has a brass butt which contains a small detonator, fired when the gun hammer falls on it.

Shotguns play a dolefully large part in modern British crime since they are available legally. Of a total of 6,547 serious firearms offences committed in 1979, 430 involved the use of a shotgun, causing 39 deaths and 109 serious injuries. A further 252 cases featured 'sawn-off shotguns' which caused three deaths and 11 serious injuries. The sawn-off shotgun, its barrel radically cut down and its stock shortened to pistol grip size, is altered for convenience in carrying and concealment. At close range the bunched shot delivers a hideous wound, but because of the shortened barrel, the shot spreads outwards very rapidly, rendering the gun less lethal at a distance.

Throughout the nineteenth century the design of breech-loading rifles continued to improve; in some, the breech was exposed for loading by pulling down a lever under the stock, as in the case of the famous Winchester rifle, while in others a bolt on the top of the barrel was drawn back. The early breech-loaders were single-shot weapons, cartridges being inserted singly. By the end of the century, however, most rifles had magazines, which made them 'repeating' weapons. The action of the lever or the bolt ejected the spent cartridge, throwing it out to one side, and then extracted a new bullet from the magazine and slotted it into the breech for firing. The action of the firing pin, the extractor and ejector mechanisms all left marks on the fired cartridge which were to prove invaluable in forensic ballistics.

Hand guns

The development of hand guns also progressed in the nineteenth century. In the 1830s Samuel Colt of Hartford, Connecticut, produced the first practical revolver, bringing it to what most gunsmiths would

CUT-DOWN 410° FIRED
IN A 455 WEBLEY REVOLVER
RANGE 8'

Whereas a revolver carries five, six or up to eight shots in a cylinder which presents each cartridge to the hammer in turn, the automatic, properly called the 'self-unloading' hand gun, acts in a somewhat similar fashion to a rifle. The magazine, containing up to 14 rounds of ammunition, is slotted into the hollow handle of the weapon. A slide on the top of the barrel carries the firing pin. When the trigger is pressed, the firing pin hits the primer of the cartridge and fires the bullet, at the same time releasing a powerful force of expanding gas in the breech of the gun – up to four or five tons per square inch – which blows back the slide. The slide's action, like that of the rifle bolt, ejects the spent cartridge, extracts a new one from the magazine and slots it into firing position once more.

Forensic ballistics

The mechanical characteristics and idiosyncrasies of firearms are, of course, vital for forensic purposes, for besides the striations left on the discharged bullet, the spent cartridge case will also be marked in various ways. The extractor and ejector mechan-

agree was its perfect form in the Colt Army 1873 model, which became famous for its .45 calibre.

The calibre of a gun is the diameter of its bore between the rifling lands, measured in fractions of an inch: on the Continent calibre is measured in millimetres. Other manufacturers followed Colt's lead: Remington and Smith and Wesson in the United States, Adams and Scott-Webley in Britain, Starr, Luger, Browning and Beretta on the Continent, until revolvers were in use in every part of the world.

In the early decades of the twentieth century, the so called 'automatic' pistol began to appear.

bullet found in body

bullet from suspect's gun

the two bullets compared

isms, and sometimes even a faulty magazine, will tend to leave identifying scratch marks; the 'blow back' effect of firing will slam the cartridge back against the breech face, leaving an impression of any tooling marks which may be present on the latter; also, each firing pin will leave its own characteristic impression.

The bullet will bear the rifling marks of the barrel, which tell a very individual story. The width and number of lands and grooves, their slant or 'pitch' and whether they turn the bullet to left or right will help in narrowing down the search to a particular type and make of gun. The make of an empty shell will help here too, together with the presence or absence of a rim at its base; revolvers and shotguns normally have rimmed cartridges, which stop them sliding through the chamber or breech, while a self-loading pistol cartridge is generally rimless or semi-rimmed, bearing instead a groove to provide grip for the extractor.

Bullet wounds

But the gun and empty cartridge form only one side of the story. The other, grimmer side concerns the discharged shot and the effect it has on the flesh, blood, and bone of its victim. Obviously, bullet wounds came to the attention of medical men long before firearms examination became a separate discipline, and it is for this reason that forensic pathologists feature largely in the annals of the early days of forensic 'ballistics'.

Hans Gross, an Austrian judge who wrote a classic textbook, *Criminal Investigation*, first had his attention called to the possibilities of firearms examination by a pathologist, who removed a bullet from Gross's grandfather's head while performing an autopsy on the elder Gross in 1845. In 1799, while serving in the Austrian army, he had been shot by a ball which lodged behind his eye and was considered too dangerous to remove. Hans Gross noticed that the bullet was marked in a curious way, and that traces of powder still adhered to it. The time would surely come, he considered, when such details would be invaluable in the solving of crime scientifically.

But it was almost another 50 years before the first successful case occurred – and in retrospect,

most forensic experts would agree, the conclusions drawn were dangerously arbitrary. It was the work of Professor Alexandre Lacassagne, founder of the medico-legal faculty at Lyons University and perhaps the foremost forensic pathologist of his day. Lacassagne had been an Army medical officer and had had ample opportunity to study bullet wounds. In 1889 he turned his attention to the bullet which he had removed from the body of a murder victim. Under the microscope Lacassagne noticed seven longitudinal grooves on its surface, and correctly deduced that these had been made by the rifling – the first time, as far as is known, that such a conclusion had been reached. There were seven different grooves: therefore, he reasoned, the murder weapon must have a series of seven 'lands'. Only one weapon among several suspects had such a number, and Lacassagne plumped for this as the fatal one.

Striation analysis

Paul Jeserich, a forensic chemist at the University of Berlin, was the first to compare the striations from two bullets fired from the same weapon. In 1898 he was asked to conduct chemical tests on a suspect's pistol, during which he fired the gun. Eyeing the test-fired bullet and the alleged murder bullet casually, he noticed their similarity, and examined them more closely under a microscope. They were identical, and the case was solved without recourse to chemistry.

There were a number of other isolated cases of a similar nature during the next 20 or 30 years. One of them impressed the great American juror and author Oliver Wendell Holmes, whose comments on a case similar to that solved by Jeserich were widely quoted. Shown the identical nature of two bullets from the same gun, he said: 'I see no other way in which the jury could have learned so intelligently how a gun-barrel would have marked the lead bullet fired through it.'

Data classification

If any further progress was to be made, however, forensic scientists needed data as controls to their experiments, and the man who set about the mammoth task of providing them was Charles E. Waite,

TRACKS ON THE VELDT
The Van Niekerk/Markus Case

Brutal murders occur every day, all over the world, and South Africa is certainly no exception. However, the slaying of Bill Nelson and his friend Tom Denton at Waterval Farm on the Transvaal was particularly poignant, since they had extended great kindness and hospitality to their assassins.

In December 1925 the South African sun blazed with fierce intensity, and the outside walls of the farmhouse were beginning to crack under the midsummer heat. Bill Nelson, the 60 year old farm manager, would have made a mental note of this, because although he didn't own the estate, it was his responsibility to attend to the upkeep of the farm buildings as well as the land.

Nelson shared the farmhouse with Tom Denton, five years his junior and an ex-soldier. Denton made his living from a modestly sized general store situated on the farm estate, which catered to the native labourers working on the land. Farming life in the Transvaal was a remote and isolated business in the 1920s — even now, it would hardly be described as being at the centre of a social whirl. With neighbouring farms so far away, it was a rare occasion when visitors turned up. On Tuesday, the first day of December, the arrival of two strangers on the farm must have provided a welcome relief from routine for the two naturally kindly men.

They could have no suspicion that the following 24 hours would lead up to a situation in which South Africa's ballistics experts fought to unravel the maze of conflicting evidence surrounding what would become the famous Van Niekerk-Markus Case. Their visitors claimed to be hitch-hiking across the Transvaal in search of work, and were full of hard luck stories about their difficulties.

In fact they were ex-convicts who had met up while serving time in the same prison. They had just been released, and had decided to join forces. The elder, Van Niekerk, was an utterly hardened criminal who had spent half of his 34 years in jail; he was cunning enough to recognize the gullible good nature of Denton and Nelson, and Markus, who was ten years younger and much less experienced, followed his lead in playing on their sympathies.

Nelson generously offered them employment replastering the cracked farmhouse walls. With

South African ballistics experts helped to convict Van Niekerk (top) *and Markus* (bottom) *of murder.*

typical thoughtfulness, he told them to relax for that day, showed them to their room in the house, and gave them a hearty meal. On Wednesday, they started work on the plastering, while Denton and Nelson discussed a small shooting expedition. They decided to go off immediately and invited Van Niekerk and Markus to join them. The two were given guns, and after the day's sport they turned in for an early night's sleep.

Shortly after midnight the natives who worked on the estate were awakened by the sound of shots. They rushed from their huts and saw the two newcomers running from the farmhouse, which had been set on fire. The police were sent for and officers and a police surgeon later found the badly burned bodies of Nelson and Denton in the main bedroom.

The dead men were covered with revolver and shotgun cartridges, which had exploded in the holocaust. They had both been shot in the head. Nelson's wound had apparently been made by a revolver and Denton's by a shotgun.

In the meantime, Van Niekerk and Markus had made off across the veldt, and eventually boarded a train for Pretoria, where they arrived early in the morning on December 4th. By that time, however, the hunt was well under way.

The investigation was led by Detective-Sergeant Daniel Malan of the Pretoria CID, who used native trackers as well as uniformed officers and plainclothes-men.

It emerged that several people had been robbed or swindled by the two runaways, and came forward to provide information. One was a farmer who had been swindled by them, and Malan had the farmer's fields searched since the two men had been living on his land.

It was then that the classic clue was discovered; it was an extraordinary piece of luck for Dan Malan in the shape of a crumpled piece of paper which had been used to wipe lather from a razor.

The paper turned out to be a store receipt for two hats. It was made out to A. Van Niekerk, and a quick search of police and prison files soon divulged a huge amount of information. Witnesses had provided descriptions which were easy to link to Van Niekerk, and it was a short task to connect him with Markus, since they had left prison together, and were already a well established pair.

The killers had meanwhile left Pretoria, knowing that they were the centre of a huge manhunt, and by Sunday December 6 they had reached Queenstown, 750 miles away. As the net closed in tighter, Van Niekerk made off on his own, and was caught on a train at Cathcart, yet another 40 miles further on.

The next morning he was taken by a fast train to Queenstown, and during the journey he stunned his armed escort, Constable Lotter, with his mana-cled hands and threw himself out of an open carriage window. Lotter set off in pursuit and, after Van Niekerk had dodged the bullets that were fired at him, the constable caught up with his man and knocked him out with the butt of his empty gun.

With Van Niekerk safely in custody in Queens-town police station, the search continued for Edward Markus, who was an habitué of the town. He was soon apprehended in one of his old haunts and he was persuaded to betray Van Niekerk, whom he said he befriended in prison. He claimed that the older man had talked him into attacking and robbing their benevolent hosts while they were asleep.

"Van Niekerk walked between the beds on which the men were lying," he stated. "He was holding a lighted candle in his left hand and a revolver in his right. He shot the man on his left through the head; then did likewise to the man on his right."

He added that he and his companion stole silver from under a mattress, gold and banknotes from a trunk, and clothes from the general store. Van Niekerk, he continued, threatened to shoot him as well if he did not cooperate. And it was Van Niekerk who scattered ammunition over the murdered men, soaked the beds with paraffin and then set fire to them.

But Van Niekerk had a different story to tell when a magistrate visited him in his cell on December 12. "Both Markus and I committed the crime," he asserted. "I used a revolver and he used a shotgun, Markus shot one man through the ear. I fired next with the revolver, through the other man's temple. Then we ransacked the place."

The conflicting stories were not resolved by the police and it was left to ballistics experts to try and establish the truth of the matter. Their chance came when the two accused were tried for murder at the Palace of Justice in Pretoria in February 1926.

It was then stated that a scientist for the Crown had compared the wound in Denton's skull with a typical hole made by firing a shotgun. He dis-charged such a weapon at a wooden box and, from the size and shape of the hole, concluded that Denton definitely had been killed by a shotgun.

This meant that Markus was lying when, in court, he repeated his version of the killings. However, his counsel called another ballistics expert – Captain George Cross, Inspector of Small Arms to the South African Defence Force – into the witness box. On being shown the bullet hole in a portion of Nelson's skull, he confirmed that it had been caused by a revolver. But he disagreed that the wound in Denton's skull was that of a shotgun.

"I would not like to say it was due to a bullet wound at all," he offered, "nor how the skull came to be shattered in that way. From my experience I know that the same weapon can, in successive shots, produce different wounds." Cross also queried the use of a box to test bullet wounds in a skull.

His evidence carried great weight and convinced many of those present that Markus had been – however willingly – no more than an accomplice in the double murder. This was seized upon by Markus's counsel, who presented his client as "no more than an obedient servant, following the demands of an unbalanced man". While representing himself as acting out of fear, Marcus was unable to explain why he had planned to take his homicidal maniac friend home to meet his family! Much of his evidence was contradictory and confused, but he stuck to his assertion that Van Niekerk was mentally unbalanced.

This tallied, in part, with Van Niekerk's defence as presented by his lawyer. According to the attorney, Van Niekerk was mentally retarded, if not insane. He was not, therefore, responsible for his homicidal actions on the death night. A medical expert stated that the accused was a "moral imbecile" who should be detained in a mental hospital.

But when asked by the Attorney-General for the Transvaal, C. W. de Villiers, about the ability of such a person to "know the nature and quality of his acts", the expert replied "I have seen an imbecile of the mental age of three or four years commit an act and know it was wrong. Therefore a person of higher age must know it."

The summing-up of the judge, Mr Justice Feetham, lasted for almost three hours and hinged on the questions: Was Van Niekerk criminally responsible for his action in killing one or the other of the two men? And did Markus actively assist him in the deed – as the Crown ballistics expert suggested?

It took the jury a little over two hours to form their answers. They returned a verdict of 'guilty' on both men. On April 14 1926, Van Niekerk and Markus – who had returned food, work and kindness with treachery and death – paid for their crime on the gallows.

Above: *The inside view of a rifled gun barrel showing the 'lands' — the spiral ridges and grooves of the rifling.*

a middle aged assistant investigator in the office of the New York State prosecutor. After working successfully to clear a man accused of homicidal shooting, Waite drew up a list of all firearms manufacturers in the United States and asked them for details of every model they had ever produced – the number of rifling grooves, direction of twist, calibre and so on.

He repeated the process with European gunsmiths, and by 1922, after five years' solid toil, had a formidable bank of information at his disposal. He also realized that, because of the wearing down of machine tools, their marks on the inside of a barrel, made during the cutting of the rifling, ought to be individual if a way could be found of examining them.

He explained the problem to a physicist named John H. Fischer, who had worked on the development of the cystoscope, a medical instrument used to insert fine tubes carrying tiny lamps into the bladder and kidneys in order to facilitate their inspection without resorting to an operation. A similar instrument, decided Fischer, would be ideal for Waite's purpose. After a period of experiment, Fischer came up with the helixometer: a long hollow probe fitted with a lamp and magnifying apparatus at its tail end. With a few modifications, the helixometer is still a fixture of every firearms laboratory.

Bullet comparison microscopes

Waite had also interested a chemist and micro-photographer named Philip O. Gravelle in the problems of bullet comparison. Gravelle's contribution to their solution was equal in importance to that of Fischer. He invented the comparison microscope; objectives joined by a single viewing lens. This meant that two bullets could be placed together on the slides and easily compared for correspondence or dissimilarity.

Together, Waite, Fischer and Gravelle founded the Bureau of Forensic Ballistics in 1923, a New York based organization which was to ensure America's lead in the field for the next half century. When Waite died in 1926, his place as head of the Bureau was taken by Colonel Calvin Goddard, like the Frenchman Lacassagne an ex-Army medical officer with an abiding interest in firearms.

The Prohibition era

Colonel Goddard came onto the scene at exactly the right time, for prohibition had led to an unrivalled era of firearm-backed lawlessness. After working on several cases on behalf of the youthful Federal Bureau of Investigation, Goddard was encouraged to move West. He became founder and first director of the Scientific Crime Detection Laboratory at Northwestern University, Evanston, Illinois, which remains one of America's crime research centres; he also helped set up the FBI Ballistics Department in Washington, the largest and busiest of its kind in the world.

European developments

In Europe – in Britain in particular – firearms

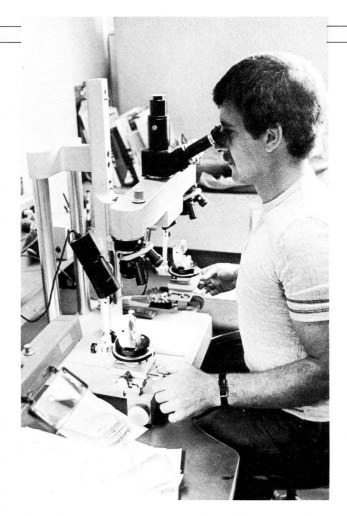

Above: *The comparison microscope in use. Its invention by Philip Gravelle revolutionized the work of bullet comparison.*

investigation remained largely in the hands of the pathologists. Professor, later Sir, Sydney Smith, founder of the medico-legal faculty at Cairo University and later Regius Professor of Forensic Medicine at Edinburgh, was one of the leading exponents, studying entrance and exit wounds, powder burns and powder 'tattooing' on human skin and other medical phenomena associated with gunfire. In the troubled Egypt of his day he had ample opportunity to study his subject at first hand, and his textbooks on the subject make fascinating reading even for a layman. As a student he had been taught by Professor Harvey Littlejohn, who had himself been a student under Dr Joseph Bell, Arthur Conan Doyle's model for Sherlock Holmes. The tradition of the great detective/scientist

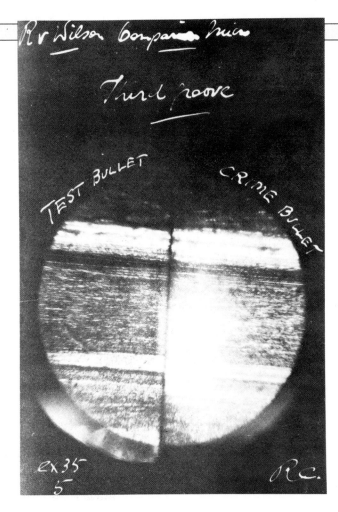

Above: *A test bullet and suspected crime bullet are examined under a comparison microscope at the third groove.*

showed through. Smith was never satisfied with simple laboratory work; wherever possible he visited a murder scene himself, using a mixture of careful deduction and imagination in order to produce results.

One typical case shows his brilliance: a young soldier was brought into hospital suffering from wounding in all four limbs, and later died. Smith thought at first that he had been involved in a 'shoot-out', but on examining the body, the site where it was found, and the soldier's clothing he was able to show that the man had been the victim of a freak accident. As he bent down to adjust his puttees the soldier's Lewis gun had gone off at a range of about a yard. The bullet had entered the outside of his left leg below the knee, come out of the other side and entered his left arm below the elbow, went through that and through his right thigh and finally all but blew off his right arm.

'One of the interesting features of this case,' Sir Sydney wrote, 'was that the bullet did comparatively little damage in the first three limbs, and only exploded and disintegrated after striking the bone of the right arm.'

Sir Bernard Spilsbury, a national British institution because of his dramatic court appearances, was a contemporary of Smith. A lifelong student of suicide, he was one of the first to point out that gunshot suicide generally bore its own distinguishing features. If a gun is fired in contact with the head, for instance, the hair is usually singed, powder and other residues are deposited on and driven into the skin, and there is usually a 'rebound' bruise at the edge of the wound. Spilsbury also demonstrated that the angle of entrance and exit, and the extent of powder staining, can indicate the position and distance of the gunman, observations he brought to bear on, for instance, the assassination of Field Marshal Sir Henry Wilson by IRA gunmen in 1922.

Robert Churchill's experiments

The first modern British firearm examiner of real expertise was Robert Churchill, a sporting gunmaker whose shop near Leicester Square was patronized by rich and titled clients. In several cases he evolved experiments which have become part of set procedure in the field of forensic ballistics. One, for example, involved the measurement of the range of shotgun fire. It began on a moonlit night in October, 1927 when a 35 year old farm labourer and poacher named Enoch Dix was caught in Whistling Copse, a spinney on the estate of Lord Temple near Bath, Somerset. Two keepers named William Walker and George Rawlings recognized him and there was an exchange of fire, during which Walker fell dying. Police arrested Dix and ordered him to strip, showing his back and thighs pitted with pellet wounds from Rawlings' gun, a 12 bore. Dix claimed that Rawlings had fired first, and that his own gun, a single barrelled .410, had discharged accidentally.

Churchill was called in and first studied the wounds on Dix's body, then test fired Rawlings' gun at a series of whitewashed metal plates, varying the range. From these he concluded that Rawlings had hit Dix at a distance of 15 yards. It followed that Dix, to be telling the truth, must have fired at the same distance, but Churchill discovered that the spread of shot from his .410 reached between 27 and 30 inches at 15 yards, whereas the wound in Walker's throat was five inches in diameter. This could only have been produced by the .410 at a range of less than five yards – point blank, in fact. It was a simple piece of deduction, but had never been used before. Today, it is standard practice in any case involving a shotgun.

The problems facing Churchill and his immediate successors, the first 'official' Home Office firearms examiners who were appointed in the late thirties and forties, are very much the same as those dealt with in modern laboratories, for gun and ammunition design has produced little of real novelty since then. The introduction of 'magnum' cartridges in the fifties – first manufactured by Remington and used to load such weapons as the Luger Blackhawk and the Smith and Wesson .44 Magnum – has meant that hand-guns are harder hitting, but their mechanism is largely unchanged and their victims suffer in much the same way as with older weapons.

Modern weapons

The wider use of pump-action shotguns, which have a magazine holding up to five cartridges, has, if anything, lightened the load of the firearms examiner, for they are fitted with extractor and ejector devices which leave markings, and because the ejectors tend to throw out the spent cases with some force the gunman, even if he is careful, is that much more likely to leave a fired, tell-tale shell case behind.

'Replica' firearms, catering to 'quick draw' enthusiasts and military 'war game' societies have, however, presented firearms examiners with new headaches over the past decade; they are made of mild steel and alloy, have blocked-off barrels and no firing pins, and because of this are sold without a licence. But because they are extremely realistic, even down to their inner mechanism they are, in criminal terms, a major innovation. In 1979,

'THOSE ANARCHIST BASTARDS'
Sacco and Vanzetti

When the law and politics become entangled, the end result can be a potent brew. Add to these ingredients a suitable setting – about 40 miles from Salem, Massachusetts, scene of the lurid witch trials of the seventeenth century – and you have the recipe for a crime reporter's dream case.

Such was the calibre of the Sacco and Vanzetti trial, which captured world headlines for seven years. The trial dramatized and focussed major issues: the 'red scare' in the USA followed close on the heels of the Russian Revolution of 1917 and the homeland of capitalism found itself harangued by a new breed of radicals, many of them poor immigrants, preaching the liberation of the downtrodden worker to shouts of "Down with the bosses". The 'New Left' of the 1920s was not only proletarian, but also attracted intellectuals, many of whom believed that Sacco and Vanzetti, the one a humble fish peddler, the other a factory worker, were being used as scapegoats by the Establishment.

The incident that began the long-drawn-out furore occurred in a small New England township. Each Friday afternoon paymaster Frederick A. Parmenter delivered a $16,000 weekly payroll to a shoe factory in South Braintree, Mass. He was accompanied by an armed guard, Alexander Berardelli, and they were invariably alert and on the look-out for trouble. Even so, at around three o'clock on 15 April 1920, they paid little or no attention to two men idly leaning against a fence near the Slater and Morrill Shoe Factory on Pearl Street.

It was not until Parmenter and Berardelli – each carrying a black money bag – were passing the loiterers that anything unusual occurred. One of the men suddenly sprang forward, took a gun from his pocket, and fired at Berardelli from almost point-blank range. As the guard crumpled to the ground, Parmenter dropped his payroll bag and ran diagonally across the busy street.

He was pursued by the gunman, who brought him down with two shots. Meanwhile, the second man bent over Berardelli and fired more bullets into him. The bandits then gathered up the money bags and jumped into a large black Buick that came tearing round the corner. Within minutes, the robbery had been successfully concluded and Parmenter and Berardelli were fatally injured. Berardelli died at once, from four .32 calibre bullets. There were also four .32 ejected cartridges beside his body. Parmenter died later, from a .32 bullet wound. The bullets and cases were identified as products of the manufacturers Winchester, Peters and Remington.

Eye-witnesses later said that a third gunman – who took no active role in the robbery – also leaped into the

Above: *The jury at the trial of Vanzetti* (left) *and Sacco* (right) *heard complex ballistics evidence.*

car, which contained two other gangsters. Of the five men involved in the stick-up, only two were described in detail. They were the two 'foreign-looking' loiterers, one of whom was clean-shaven and the other of whom wore a heavy moustache.

It was the clean-shaven man who had fired the first shot at Berardelli and then chased and killed Parmenter. For the next two weeks police scoured the area for the two killers, at least one of whom was suspected of having taken part in an attempted payroll robbery at Bridgewater near Boston the previous Christmas. Then, on the night of 5 May, two men answering to the fugitives' descriptions were spotted on a streetcar in the district.

Police officer Michael Connolly boarded the vehicle and arrested the suspects, Nicola Sacco, 29, and the mustachioed Bartolomeo Vanzetti, 32, who came from the Massachusetts coastal town of Plymouth. They were both Italian immigrants, who spoke with thick accents: and they were both armed with guns. Sacco had a .32 Colt automatic containing a full clip plus extra cartridges, variously made by Winchester, Remington and Peters. Vanzetti had a fully-loaded .38 revolver. He also carried

shotgun shells which were similar to the one left at the scene of the Bridgewater hold-up. Later they claimed they needed the weapons for self-protection as they lived in such 'bad times'.

To make things worse for them, they were in possession of 'anarchist literature', at a time when there had been a number of bomb explosions in the USA. One pamphlet taken from Sacco advertised a political meeting which he planned to address.

'Fellow workers,' it said, 'you have fought all the wars. You have worked for all the capitalists. You have wandered over all the countries. Have you harvested the fruits of your labours, the price of your victories? Does the past comfort you? Does the present smile on you? Does the future promise you anything? Have you found a piece of land where you can live like a human being?'

Ballistics experts had already stated that Parmenter and Berardelli had been killed by a Colt .32, and the police were convinced that they had taken the murder weapon from Sacco on the streetcar. But before the alleged anarchists could be tried for the double killing, Sacco was put on trial for the previous — and abortive — Bridgewater robbery. Vanzetti was able to provide an alibi for that time. Sacco was found guilty as charged and sentenced to 10-15 years imprisonment.

The judge at his trial was Webster Thayer and, ominously enough, he also presided over the trial of both Sacco and Vanzetti, which opened at Dedham, Mass, on 31 May, 1921. Those wishing to retain a due confidence in the Olympian objectivity of the law would have found it an edifying experience to overhear the comments of the officials on the case. Chief prosecuting attorney Frederick Katzmann regarded them as "those damned God-hating radicals", while Judge Webster Thayer's locker-room style boast after the trial was "Did you see what I did with those anarchist bastards the other day?" Some 60 witnesses took the stand for the prosecution and almost 100 appeared for the defence – most of whom gave conflicting evidence of identity.

Then came the turn of the ballistics examiners, whose opinions were thought to be vital to the outcome of the trial. Altogether, four pistol bullets had been removed from Berardelli's body; one from Parmenter's corpse; and another from the paymaster's clothing. For the prosecution, Captain William Proctor of the State Police, 'doubling' as an arms expert, told how he and a colleague – Charles Van Amburgh – had recently fired 14 test bullets from Sacco's automatic into a box of specially oiled sawdust.

The recovered bullets were compared with the mortal bullet taken from Berardelli's remains. The ridges and grooves made by the bullets passing through the gun barrel were thought to be more or less identical. Asked by Assistant District Attorney Harold Williams if the death bullet had been fired from Sacco's automatic, Proctor replied: "My opinion is that it is consistent with being fired by that pistol."

He was supported by Charles Van Amburgh, who told the court: "I am inclined to believe that it (the death bullet) was fired from this (Sacco's) automatic pistol." He added that a rough rust track at the bottom of the pistol barrel corresponded with rust traces found on the mortal bullet – although the barrels of all Colts tended to rust.

This was less than conclusive, and the evidence was soon challenged by the experts called by the defence. The first of them, James Burns, had spent some 30 years as a ballistics engineer with the US Cartridge Company. He felt that the death bullet could have been fired by a Colt; but it could equally have come from a Bayard, a foreign make. He, too, was asked if the mortal bullet had come from Sacco's gun, and he answered: "In my opinion, no. It doesn't compare at all."

The second defence expert, J. Henry Fitzgerald, was currently head of the testing room at the Colt Patent Firearms Company, and he seconded Burns' statement. "I can see no pitting or marks on the bullet that would correspond to a bullet coming from this gun," he declared.

It appeared to be a stalemate. However, after a surprisingly dispassionate summing up of the evidence by Thayer, the jury returned a verdict of "guilty" – murder in the first degree.

The news travelled around the world like wildfire, and immediately there was an international outcry for another trial. Organizations were set up for fund-raising, and the defence fought again and again for another chance to present their case. The controversy raged for seven years, until finally in June 1927 the State Governor of Massachusetts set up an independent committee under the eminent President of Harvard, Lawrence Lowell. Colonel Goddard, who had built up an excellent reputation as an arms expert, volunteered to examine the ballistics evidence with his new equipment, a helixometer and early comparison microscope.

The defence refused to employ Goddard's assistance, but the prosecution agreed. Goddard's findings showed that Parmenter and Berardelli had definitely been killed by shots from Sacco's gun. The Lowell committee reported back, and the inevitable end of the line was reached. On 23 August 1927, Sacco and Vanzetti went to the chair.

'replicas' were used in a total of 285 serious offences, including robbery and rape, and the fact that they can be converted efficiently into lethal weapons is attested by the eleven serious woundings and one homicide caused by them in the same year.

The only 'plus' for the firearms examiner in such cases is that a doctored replica is, by its very nature, unique in every important feature; once a bullet is matched with such a weapon there can be little question, as there sometimes is with production firearms, of evidence being inconclusive.

Current developments

If such men as Churchill, Goddard, and Waite set the basic standards of practical forensic 'ballistics' those standards are constantly being questioned in modern laboratories. It was the great Churchill, for instance, who, writing in 1933 for police consumption, advised scenes of crime officers that 'a weapon found on the scene of the crime should be lifted by passing a metal rod down the muzzle.'

Today, such a practice is absolute anathema. 'DO NOT handle by means of inserting a pencil or similar article in the barrel' stresses a Home Office pamphlet to police officers; this is because the modern helixometer and similar instruments are capable of detecting minute clues from the interior of the gun.

Again, dermal nitrate tests which, in Churchill's day, were the very latest thing in the gathering of firearm evidence have now been almost totally discontinued. When a gun is fired – particularly a revolver or a shotgun – residue from the exploding cartridge is driven out to the rear of the gun and deposited on the hands and clothing of the gunman. Swabs soaked in a one per cent solution of hydrochloric acid were used to wipe the suspect's hands, and these were analysed for the presence of nitrates. The main problem, it was recently realized, lay in the fact that nitrates are increasingly used in substances such as fertilizers, cosmetics and other everyday preparations as well as being present in cigarettes and cigars, so that the value of a swab as a positive indication of recent gun handling is lost.

But the value of 'blow back' as evidence is too great to be ignored, and new processes of analysis such as scanning electron microscopy and micro-probe analysis are being used to make minute examination of a suspect's hand swabs and clothing. High speed photography, producing photographs of bullets and residue leaving a gun at 1/3000 of a second intervals, help the examiners to bring the costly and time consuming processes to bear on the most promising areas of skin and clothing.

'But really the modern developments are merely proving theoretically what we have long practised empirically,' said a top firearms examiner. 'We still rely largely on an expert's experience in treating each case as an individual one. Each and every firearms case brings its own unique problems.'

Below: *In a classic 'crime of passion' Ruth Ellis (right) shot her lover, David Blakely, pictured with her. The glamorous blonde was the last woman to be hanged in Britain. Police in the UK do not normally associate gun crimes with women. Ellis used a Smith & Wesson .38.*

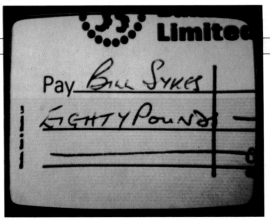

FORGERY

Welsh farmer John Harries and his wife Phoebe were inordinately proud of their small herd of dairy cattle, as most of their Carmarthenshire neighbours were well aware. The 63 year old owner of Cadno Farm and his ailing wife, nine years his junior, ran their business with meticulous efficiency, assisted by their adopted nephew Ronald, a 24 year old who was in fact a distant relative.

In October 1953, however, callers noticed that the cows were being milked irregularly and that various farm tasks had been neglected — not the Harries' style at all. Nephew Ronald was ready with an explanation: his uncle and aunt had gone off for a well earned holiday in London, leaving him in charge, and naturally he had got a little behind in his work. To cover costs during his absence, John Harries had left a cheque for £909 which Ronald presented to the bank on market day.

Above: *A cheque for eight pounds which has been increased to eighty. The forgery is revealed by examination under infra-red light.*

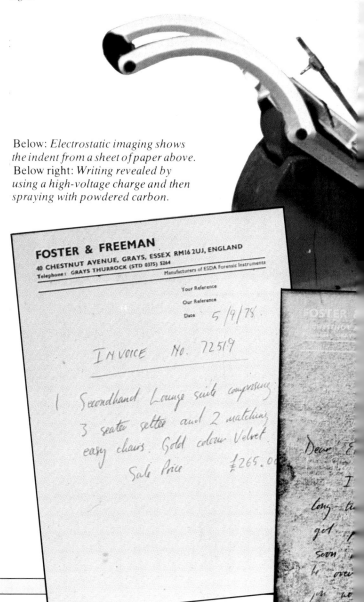

Below: *Electrostatic imaging shows the indent from a sheet of paper above.*
Below right: *Writing revealed by using a high-voltage charge and then spraying with powdered carbon.*

Below: *Using ultra-violet illumination, the obscured writing in this diary can be read clearly.*

Above left: *A small printing press of the type commonly used for forging passports and other documents. Using modern photographic reproduction techniques, the forger can produce documents which are almost indistinguishable from the real thing.*

Above right: *An infra-red document viewer. Using this piece of equipment, the forensic scientist can examine suspect documents in great detail. Matter which is invisible to the naked eye can be converted into a visual image on the visual display unit (VDU).*

The bank manager examined the cheque carefully, but could find no fault with it, other than the rather odd sum; certainly the signature tallied with his records. Nevertheless he handed it to the local police, who passed it on to a Home Office forensic document examiner. Quick tests showed that the cheque had originally been made out for £9 and that the extra words and figures had been painstakingly added in the same ink. Scotland Yard were called in, and the bodies of the missing husband and wife were found buried in a shallow grave beneath their land. Ronald Lewis Harries was hanged for their murder at Swansea Prison in March 1954.

The work of the document examiner is rarely so spectacular, although many a murderer has been brought to justice through incautious use of pen and paper. Nor is his subject matter restricted to cheques and banknotes: lottery tickets, betting slips, valuable stamps, fake passports and forged suicide notes are among the items regularly brought to his attention.

The first stage of any document's examination is a careful visual inspection of the item. The human eye is a marvellous optical instrument and can give an overall impression not attainable by even the most sophisticated electronic devices. Small variations in colour, shape and proportions give the examiner important clues which may lead towards the solution of the problem, and the document is then carefully photographed alongside an accurate scale; in some cases, particularly those involving handwriting comparisons, the remainder of the work may be conducted solely on the photograph.

A high proportion of document problems may be solved by the use of the trained eye and a few relatively simple optical aids. Thus the document examination laboratory usually has good natural light, a range of optical microscopes, sources of infra-red and ultra-violet light, an optical comparator and photographic facilities. More elaborate techniques such as radiography with soft X-rays and atomic particles, electron microscopy and laser-excited luminescence and fluorescence are becoming increasingly widely available for problems which cannot be solved by traditional methods.

Coupled with these the document examiner brings to bear a deep knowledge of paper and its qualities, watermarks, inks and paints, and searches for alterations, typewriter peculiarities, and even indented impressions not visible to the naked eye. Basically paper is made by depositing a web of fibres from a pulp onto a fine wire screen, the sheet forming as the liquid in which the pulp is suspended drains away. Paper was originally made by hand, a sheet at a time, but modern high-speed paper-making machines produce it as a continuous strip which is afterwards cut to size. In spite of new methods of mass production the essential features have not undergone any radical changes since paper-making was first practised in ancient China.

Paper components

The bulk of the world's paper is made from wood-pulp obtained by breaking down the structure of wood into its individual cells, either by chemical or mechanical means. The pulp is classified according to the method of production. Most newsprint is made from mechanical pulp, whereas better quality papers are made by chemical methods. Fibres from cotton and flax – known in the industry as rag – may also be added or may be used exclusively for special papers.

In recent times the high price and scarcity of pulp from natural sources has prompted experiments on the use of synthetic fibres, and it is likely that more and more paper will be made from synthetic materials in the future. The search for new materials is not a recent phenomenon; in the past a variety of materials and processes have been used for making paper-pulp and knowledge of the chronology of events in the history of paper-making is important for dating books and documents.

Technical as well as economic considerations influence the choice of materials. Papers made from fibrous materials alone are fairly porous and not suitable for writing or printing, so the spaces between the fibres are usually filled with a loading of very fine mineral particles mixed into the pulp. The loading makes the paper less absorbent and also increases its opacity. The surface of the paper may be modified by a coating of synthetic resin or some other material to make it suitable for special inks, such as those used in colour printing, and its 'whiteness' enhanced by the addition of optical brighteners similar to those used in detergents.

Special papers

The compositions and sources of the raw materials of pulps for high security papers such as those used in bank notes are closely guarded secrets. Bank notes probably represent the highest form of the art of paper-making since as well as being difficult to fake the paper must be tough enough to withstand constant handling without falling to pieces. Soluble

Above right: A close-up of Lincoln's portrait on a US five dollar bill. The genuine half is on the right, with all the detail clearly distinguishable. The counterfeit version is on the left. It is much less accurate, the detail has 'filled in', lines are broken, and the result looks 'smudgy'.
Right: An offset printing press, with the reverse image of a twenty dollar bill still visible on the 'blanket'.

papers, which dissolve in water, have been produced for security purposes but have also been used for illegal betting on horse races. Incriminating betting slips and accounts written on soluble paper can be destroyed easily, even during a sudden police raid, by plunging them into a bucket of water.

Examining paper

A sheet of paper has a large number of physical and chemical properties which may be used to characterize it. Although supplied in a range of sizes, all sheets tend to have the same length to breadth ratio as a result of the introduction of an internationally agreed system of standard paper sizes. Measurement of the dimensions can sometimes reveal that the sheet does not conform to the standard and may have been cut from a larger size, especially if it is not precisely rectangular. Many forgeries of official documents were detected around the time of the introduction of the international standards because they did not conform to the new sizes.

The fibrous makeup of the paper may be identified by optical microscopy after gentle disruption in dilute acid or alkali, for individual cells have features which are highly characteristic of the types of wood from which they were obtained. They retain these features even after the violent treatment to which they have been subjected during the making of the paper. Woods can be divided into *soft woods* – from coniferous trees, and *hard woods* – obtained from broad leaved deciduous trees such as oak, ash and elm. There are clear micro-anatomical differences between the conducting cells from these two types of woods, and even the species of tree can sometimes be identified. Pulps are usually made up from more than one species and the relative proportions of the components may be estimated by statistical analysis of cell counts. The species present will depend to some extent on the geographical source of the pulp and striking differences may be observed between pulps from different parts of the world, particularly those from the tropics and the Far East.

The surface mineral loadings, however, tend to show less variety than the fibrous components. China clay (kaolin) is the most widely used material, but minerals obtained from natural

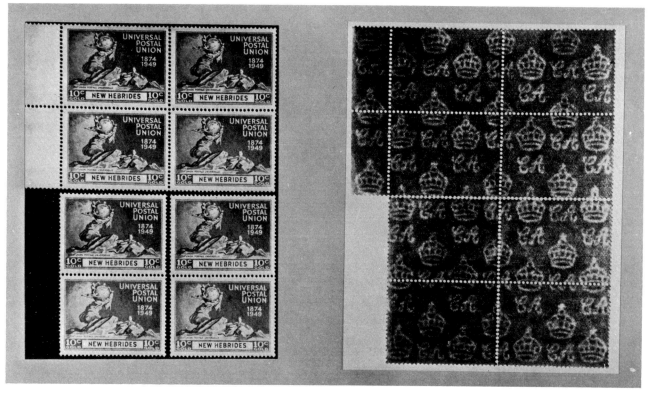

deposits of chalk and silica may sometimes be encountered. The deposits are formed by sedimentation of dead planktonic organisms from geological times. Since the skeletons of these organisms are composed of hard mineral they are perfectly preserved as micro-fossils and can be identified by high-power microscopy.

Watermarks

Next, the document examiner turns his attention to the paper's watermark. The watermark is a design formed within the fibres of the paper by a master pattern on the wire frame or on a roller called a 'dandy' which rests on top of the continuous strip emerging from a paper-making machine. Because the mark is formed at the same time as the paper itself, by brushing aside the fibres in the region of the master pattern, it is an integral part of the sheet.

Most manufacturers have their own distinctive watermark and there is a world directory which may be used for identifying the source and sometimes even the date of manufacture of a sheet of paper. Unfortunately the identification is not always

Above: The stamps on the left turned up at a dealers as a block of four and two pairs. It was claimed by the dealer that they were acquired from different sources. Examination of the watermark under transmitted light and infra-red (right), showed that the stamps were in fact from one block. This block of eight stamps had been stolen some time previously.

straightforward since major buyers of paper often have their own personal designs. Paper supplied by different manufacturers may thus bear the same mark even though it has been made in different factories. In addition the watermarks of well-known paper manufacturers may be copied by those making poor quality products.

Since the watermark is an integral part of the structure of the fibrous web it is virtually impossible to produce a convincing fake. Attempts have been made to fake marks by abrading the paper through a stencil with an india-rubber eraser but the disturbance of the fibres on the surface is clearly visible. A more ingenious method is to print the mark in olive oil with a wooden block carved to the appropriate shape. The oil diffuses into the paper making it translucent, simulating the appearance of a genuine mark when viewed in transmitted light. The patterns are easily recognized as fakes because their edges are much sharper than those of genuine watermarks.

The most difficult fakes to detect are produced by a method originally invented and patented by a paper-maker as an alternative to the traditional way of forming watermarks. The paper is moistened and pressed between two blocks, one of which bears an engraved impression of the mark. Although localized thickening and thinning of the paper in patterns is produced by this method, they differ from those made during the formation of the paper web in one important respect; such patterns result from compression of the fibres, which makes the paper thinner but does not alter its density, whereas in genuine marks the paper is thinner because the fibres have been brushed away, making it less dense than the surrounding areas.

Beta radiography
The differences in density are small and cannot be revealed by examination in visible light or even X-rays because both types of radiation penetrate thin paper easily. Beta rays, the name given to the electrons ejected during the decay of some radioactive isotopes, are less penetrating than X-rays; they are easily deflected by paper fibres and are ideal for showing small variations in density between different parts of a sheet of paper by a technique known as *beta radiography.*

The isotope source, usually *carbon-14*, is incorporated into a thin sheet of flexible plastic which can be slipped between the pages of a book. A sheet of photographic film with an emulsion sensitive to beta rays is pressed against the other side of the paper and exposed for ten hours or more, depending on the thickness of the paper. The rays penetrate the less dense fibres of the genuine marks more easily than those of the fakes and produce a correspondingly clearer image on the film.

Dating books and documents
The exposure of a series of forgeries of printed books and pamphlets produced during the latter part of the nineteenth century provides an interesting example of historical studies of paper-making.

THE HUNGARIAN CIRCLE
Oberlander and friends

It was an overcast December day at London's Limehouse Police Station and Detective Chief Superintendent Len Gillert was considering the ways of a middle-aged East End scrap metal merchant. It was not the merchant's past criminal record that interested the Chief Superintendent, but his sudden respectability in the shape of a large house in the affluent Surrey countryside, and a new and shiny silver Rolls Royce Corniche.

"Just watch him for a bit," Gillert told his officers in the Organized Crime Squad, "See what he's up to."

The scrap metal merchant proved to be a man of regular habit. Most lunchtimes found him in Soho, centre of London's night-life, progressing down Wardour Street under the watchful gaze of Detective Inspector Hilda Harris, and a police photographer.

In the following March 1976 Harris saw her merchant greet a man in the street and followed them into a cafe. The man was small, fat and spoke with a Central European accent.

"Find out who he is," instructed Gillert.

The little foreigner left the cafe and hailed a taxi. An unmarked police car followed it unobtrusively across London to the wide streets of Holland Park and No. 11 Clarendon Road.

The owner of No. 11 Clarendon Road, according to local registration, was one A.M.M. de Oberlander, and unknown to Scotland Yard. But the Yard had filed information on a Pedro Orlander and his description was very similar to Mr Oberlander's.

The Chief Superintendent checked with Interpol. Orlander had two known aliases: Ludwig Blum and Robert Weisser.

They sent a photograph of Robert Weisser, known for currency offences and forged bank documents. The photograph identified him as the occupant of the house in Clarendon Road.

Henry Oberlander was Czech born, had lived in Hungary and was known, as Weisser, to be involved in an international fraud ring that the French and German police called the Hungarian Circle, because several of them had Hungarian connections.

At Limehouse Police Station, Chief Superintendent Gillert decided to intensify his investigation. Every contact made by Oberlander and the scrap metal merchant was noted and photographed. The operations room compiled a growing catalogue of suspects, most of them with Central European or South American connections.

Gillert's team watched their travels and their use of various false passports in and out of London Airport. The police also noted frequent visits to the Thomas Cook travel agency to change large sums of foreign currency.

But, apart from breaching Britain's currency regulations and using false passports, there was no evidence of the serious crime that Gillert's instinct told him was being committed.

Then Scotland Yard's Fraud Squad turned up with six bankers' drafts, drawn against the British Bank of the Middle East, and discovered to be forgeries when they were returned to the Bank's headquarters. The payee was L. Blum, alias Weisser, and known to Gillert as Henry Oberlander.

By the summer of 1976 the file on the Hungarian Circle was growing. Oberlander and a colleague had cashed £9,000 of foreign currencies at Thomas Cook's. Scotland Yard paid for the notes, carefully noted the fingerprints on them and filed the evidence.

Meanwhile, Gillert had discovered how the Circle operated. They provided forged drafts in exchange for currency, and if the banks accepted the forgery, everyone was happy – until the banks found out. If the forgery was discovered before the bank cashed it, the victims were unlikely to be able to complain to the police as the Circle's deals were usually illegal.

And, it turned out, the international banks were equally unwilling to reveal that they had been defrauded. The forged drafts were for relatively small amounts, no more than £6000, and they preferred to keep quiet about it rather than lose their customers' confidence.

Gillert also realized that the forged bank drafts were brilliantly executed. The six British Bank of the Middle East drafts that the Fraud Squad had found were so perfect that even the bank's most experienced cashier was convinced that they were authentic.

On July 12 the Wardour Street vigil paid off again. This time the scrap metal merchant was photographed leaning against a car door looking at a map with Oberlander and another man, business consultant Louis de Saumarez Tufnell. When the photograph was enlarged the map could be identified as a small area of Malaga, Spain.

By the 18th, Tufnell was at Heathrow airport on his way to Spain. All passengers were having their hand luggage taken away for inspection, and Tufnell handed over his briefcase without complaint. In a few moments it was returned to him, checked, and Tufnell was on his way.

The check had been long enough for Gillert's officers to photocopy instructions on a land deal in Malaga and three notes of 2.7 million dollars of bankers' drafts. Two days later, Tufnell was back.

Then Oberlander and two colleagues took off for Spain. A baggage check on their return a few days later revealed documents on the land deal, a map of the land and three forged bankers' drafts for 2.7 million dollars. Whatever their plan had been the deal had obviously not come off. Gillert decided to fly to Spain to find out why.

The plot of land in Malaga was owned by a businessman called Peter Builder. The Chief Superintendent sat beside the swimming pool of his villa in Torremolinos and listened to his story.

Peter Builder had been approached by representatives of the Sheikh of Abu Dhabi (actually Oberlander and an associate) with an offer to buy his land in Malaga. After a certain amount of negotiating the price was fixed at 2.7 million US dollars. Oberlander and his colleague departed, and the Sheikh's financial adviser arrived to check out the title to the land in the person of silver-haired, old Etonian Mr Turnell (Mr Tufnell).

Mr Turnell departed in his turn and Oberlander returned, accompanied this time by another colleague who purported to be the Sheikh's personal adviser. Oberlander explained to Peter Builder that they were ready to hand over the payment in banker's drafts, but first they would require an intermediaries' commission of £130,000.

Mr Builder wanted his payment before he handed over the commission. The solution was simple, he told Oberlander, he would fly them to his Swiss bank where the drafts could be cleared immediately, and he would pay the commission.

Oberlander protested.

It would be a Saturday and the banks would be closed. No problem, Builder told them, the bank would open to deal with the matter for him. Oberlander and his colleague departed. Later he phoned Builder to suggest a delay until the next week. But Mr Builder had had enough of them and told them that the deal was off.

When he heard the Chief Superintendent's background to the Sheikh of Abu Dhabi's fictional advisers, he realized that he had been quite right. The banker's drafts were forged, so the land deal could not have gone through. But Oberlander and his Circle would have made a free £130,000 commission. Instead, Gillert had Peter Builder's testimony to prove conspiracy.

Back in London, Gillert's team were working at full pressure, and desperately needed to show something for all their time and work. One evening, a new face turned up at Oberlander's house. He was a quiet, 48 year old Argentinian, Francisco Fiocca. The Organised Crime Squad followed him to Vere Court, behind Paddington Station, and added his name and address to their file. Gillert was ready to raid all the suspects. He chose: Friday August 13.

Just after 5 am, 80 vehicles carrying 250 police officers slipped out of the Limehouse Police Station car park. By 5.45 am they were closing in on 36 different addresses. At 6 am Gillert instructed over the radio, "All personnel involved in Operation Malaga, move in now!"

The minutes ticked by very slowly at Limehouse Police Station as Gillert waited for news. Then at 6.15 the phone rang. Gillert's detective Sergeant was calling from Vere Court. "We've got the forger's den," he said.

Ten minutes later Gillert walked into Francisco Fiocca's one-room flat. He found printing presses, machines for forging bankers' drafts and rubber stamps, piles of water-marked 'security paper', certificates of birth, marriage, vaccination, immig-ration stamps, 100 passports and some 20 bank drafts. Among it all was evidence of an elaborately prepared bank swindle for £4.9 million against the Israeli Discount Bank. Everything was complete except for the signatures still to be forged on the drafts.

Oberlander's house too provided plenty of evidence: stolen tickets and cheques and 25 passports from 7 different countries and in 12 different names. Another house yielded details of a safe deposit box which turned out to contain 4 million forged Spanish pesetas and another which contained £750,000 in diamonds. The total of forged or stolen documents came close to a value of £100 million.

In December 1977, two years after Chief Superintendent Gillert had first noticed the scrap metal merchant's sudden good fortune, the 12 accused finally appeared before the Central Criminal Court in London. The police had taken 5,000 photographs, recorded statements from 482 witnesses and produced 5,800 exhibits in court. Oberlander received a 14 year sentence, and mild Francisco Fiocca, eight. The scrap metal merchant was acquitted.

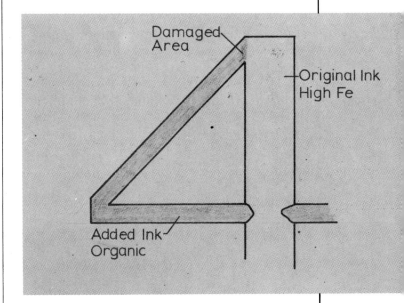

Left: *A photograph of an altered bill confiscated in the Hungarian Circle case.*
Above: *A diagram of the forgery showing the original ink, which had a high iron content, and the additional ink, which was organic.*

The forger, Thomas Wise, was a well-known editor and bookseller; his method was to select a piece of poetry or prose by a well-known living author and print copies bearing dates several years before the first known dates of publication of the pieces. The forgeries were then described as recently discovered first editions and became eagerly sought after by book collectors. Wise lent authenticity to his products by listing them in the bibliographies which he compiled and in some cases even by getting the authors themselves to sign copies.

The forgeries, which included works by Dickens and Browning, were produced after 1883, though one series all bore dates before 1850 and another dates between 1842 and 1875. Some contemporaries expressed doubts about a few of the newly discovered works, but Wise was not suspected, partly it seems because nobody thought he was clever enough to have devised and carried out such a plan. It was not until 1933, only a few years before he died, that a scientific study was made of the forgeries and Wise was exposed as the result of a neat process of detection and deduction.

Until 1861 'rag', obtained from cotton, hemp and flax and indirectly old clothing, was the only material in regular use in England for book and writing papers. Sometime before this, severe shortages had prompted a search for alternative materials; straw was found to be suitable for lower quality papers and even stinging nettles were investigated. In 1861 a successful process utilizing esparto grass was invented; commercial exploitation was rapid as supplies of rag were further reduced by the cotton shortage during the American Civil War. The next important development was the introduction of chemical pulp, first used in England in 1883. The two dates 1861 and 1883 proved vital in the unmasking of the Wise forgeries. Investigators discovered that the paper for the first series, dated before 1850, was made from esparto fibre and could not be older than 1861. Similarly the paper for the second series was made from woodpulp and could not have been used for works published before 1883.

The Vinland Map

Unfortunately paper is not always a reliable guide

Right: *The Vinland Map, showing parts of the coastlines of Greenland and North America. An old document describing the map was examined using beta-radiography. Beta rays are easily deflected by paper fibres, and this indicates whether there is any variation in density. This technique showed that the watermark on the document was genuine, which meant the paper was made around 1450. The ink on the map, however, was found to contain materials which were not in use before 1930.*

Below: *Samples of inks which have been extracted from a dubious document. By chemical analysis and comparison with a known standard ink, it is possible to detect whether part or all of the document is a forgery.*

Inks from Questione
Comparison with Standard

Standard
5075

Agreement
Page 1   Page 2   Page 3   Page 4

Standard
5075

Promissory Notes
Nov. 23, '82   Jan. 8, '63   June 20, '63

Document

Promissory Notes

Feb. 4, '58	March 3, '59	March 9, '59	May 4, '60	Nov. 3, '60

'63	May 10, '65	Oct. 27, '65	Jan. 8, '66	Jan. 18, '66	Feb. 22, '66

to date since the flyleaves and endpapers of old books provide a useful source of old paper. A really determined forger may even go as far as making the correct paper. The authenticity studies of the Vinland Map provide an example of how investigators may be misled. The map, drawn on vellum (lamb or kid-skin) shows parts of the coastlines of Greenland and North America. If it is genuine it provides support for the theory that the Vikings visited America before the voyage made by Columbus in 1492. Beta radiography of an old document describing the map indicated that the watermark was genuine and that the paper was made in 1450, proving that the map must pre-date the voyage of Columbus. Chemical analysis of ink on the map itself has revealed traces of materials which have not been found in inks made before about 1930. The true date of the map remains a mystery until an absolute dating technique – such as carbon-14 – can be used on it.

Inks

Since the ballpoint pen replaced the pen-nib the number and range of compositions of inks has increased dramatically. Further changes have been brought about by the introduction of fibre-tipped pens and most recently by pens utilizing erasable inks. Modern writing inks can be classed into fluid based types, where the fluid may be water or an organic solvent, and the oil based pastes used in ball-point pens. In both classes the colourant is a complex mixture of organic dyes. The type of ink can often be identified through microscopic examination and simple chemical tests. Accurate comparison of colour requires more complicated methods because two quite different combinations of dyes can produce inks which are very similar in colour.

In one method the dyes in the ink may be separated from each other and identified by *thin-layer chromatography*. A thin strip of paper bearing ink is cut or punched from the sheet and the ink is extracted in a suitable solvent. The solution is spotted onto a glass plate coated with a thin layer of absorbent silica. The plate is arranged vertically with its lower end immersed in a mixture of solvents and as the solvents are soaked up by the porous

THE HOWARD HUGHES HOAX
The Clifford Irving forgeries

Two things must be remembered. Howard Hughes was a very famous recluse. He was also a very famous and very powerful billionaire. At various points in a long, exceedingly idiosyncratic life he directed Hollywood movies, designed a brassière for Jane Russell, built the world's largest wooden aeroplane which he piloted on its maiden and only flight, owned TWA and sold it, owned half of Las Vegas as a kind of bizarre hobby, had the ear of President Nixon, and owned an army of private investigators.

By the time he died in 1976, Hughes was as famous as Greta Garbo, and far more eccentric. Greta Garbo lives in private, but can be seen occasionally. Howard Hughes, out of private needs and a compulsion to inhabit an environment entirely germ-free, not only lived privately; he became completely invisible, so invisible that rumours of his death followed one another constantly in the decade preceding the actual demise.

If Howard Hughes had not been terribly famous and very invisible, then Clifford Irving could not have concocted his lunatic scheme in December 1970. The tragedy for Irving is that what began as a kind of schoolboy hoax ended up as fraud and in jail sentences for him, his unfortunate wife, and Richard Suskind, an associate who did much of the research work on the scheme.

It was a simple idea. If Howard Hughes is rich and famous, and if he is constantly in the news because he is not only rich and famous but a *hermit* who never allows himself to be seen, then why not write his 'authorized' biography, basing the text on hundreds and hundreds of pages of transcribed 'interviews' with the great man, who, having met Irving in secret, will have suggested the idea to him?

This is precisely what Clifford Irving did. And it is right here that the story becomes incredible. With a hastily and very poorly forged letter from Howard Hughes to himself, Irving approached his publishers, the giant American firm, McGraw-Hill, with the proposal. Convinced by the letter — which on seeing a magazine containing a full facsimile of Hughes' handwriting Irving quickly *reforged,* though only after his editors had seen and been convinced by the first effort — McGraw-Hill okayed the deal. Ultimately it would cost them in the neighbourhood of $750,000.

It is possible to believe that Clifford Irving's initial impulse in launching his hoax was not mainly pecuniary. The whole project had a loony bravado about it that must have been deeply appealing to the author of *Fake!*, the story of the art forger Elmyr de Hory, based on taped interviews. But as soon as enormous sums of money came into the picture, exposure of the fraud was probably inevitable.

Through 1971, Irving maintained an astonishing control over the two separate aspects of what was becoming a very complex deceit. First, he and Richard Suskind, using forged letters from Hughes, and having extraordinary good luck in researching his chequered and litigious past, managed to keep not only McGraw-Hill happy, but also *LIFE* Magazine. *LIFE* had contracted to excerpt the book before publication, and Irving rifled the magazines on Hughes in his ravenous search for authentic material to feed into the faked transcripts he was supplying to a growing team of gulled editors.

Fooling them was easy enough, perhaps, given the appalling audacity of the deceit. As soon as the McGraw-Hill and *LIFE* editors began to believe that Irving was onto the real thing, they committed themselves to defend that belief. Deaf to reason they may have been as the months passed and Irving's cover stories became thinner and wilder, but they had some excuse for going along with him. After all, he was delivering the goods.

Impeccably researched, fabulous only where uncheckable, the Irving/Hughes manuscript, all 900 pages of it, is a stupendous job of work. And not only that. On two separate occasions McGraw-Hill had Irving's forgeries of Hughes' hand checked by professional experts; in no uncertain terms, both experts confirmed that the authorizations McGraw-Hill held were indeed in Hughes's own hand.

But fooling the Swiss banking authorities was something else. That was the second strand of the deceit, and it was no fun at all. Its exposure jailed his wife. Irving's use of her is the least attractive part of the story, for he involved her in a series of passport and banking frauds. She was able to gain entry to Switzerland under another name, open a bank account there as H. R. Hughes, and deposit into this account the cheques written by McGraw-Hill to Howard Hughes.

Up to the last possible moment, everything was kept top secret. But when at last *LIFE* and McGraw-Hill announced their 'scoop', all hell broke lose. Platoons of Hughes lawyers and spokesmen immediately challenged the authenticity of the text; eventually Hughes himself conducted a telephone interview with reporters who had known him when he was visible, and denied any connection between him and Irving. Too deep into the project to back out now, *LIFE* and McGraw-Hill publicly rebutted all doubts.

And who knows? If the Swiss banking authorities had not smelled a rat and begun their own investigation into the background activities of the mysterious lady in dark glasses who had opened the H. R. Hughes account, perhaps the Irving caper would have actually reached the bookstalls. It was not to be, however.

Better

Tonight — Cloudy, warmer, low in lower 20s. Saturday — Mostly cloudy, warmer, high in middle or upper 30s. Chances of precipitation: 20 per cent tonight and Saturday. See Page 33.

CHICAGO DAILY NEWS

The *Complete* Evening Newspaper

(c)1972 by Field Enterprises Inc.

97th Year, Number 36   54 Pages in 4 Sections   Friday, February 11, 1972   10 Cents   Phone 321-2000

Irving admits hoax

The boy's father refused at the conference to comment about a report that he told a federal grand jury he never met Howard Hughes. (UPI)

$ . . .
ch . . .
Di . . .

By Dave Ca . . .
and Edmun . . .

Chicago E . . .
Dick Gor . . .
charged with . . .
come tax re . . .
have listed a . . .
$94,351 for . . .
through 1969.

Gordon, 28, . . .
Circuit Court . . .
suit involving . . .
Side model, w . . .
criminal infor . . .
the Internal Re . . .
U.S. District . . .
Richard McLar . . .
issued a sum . . .
Gordon to appea . . .
on charges Feb. . . .

THE IRS crim . . .

Report he never met Hughes

Daily News Wire Services

NEW YORK — Clifford Irving once wrote a book called "Fake!" and he's being sued for that. And now, according to one report, he has virtually admitted that his Howard Hughes "autobiography" is itself a fake—a hoax involving hundreds of thousands of dollars.

The Los Angeles Times reported Friday that Irving and his research assistant, Richard R. Suskind, have told federal authorities that they never met Hughes, the bashful billionaire.

Irving's lawyer denied the report. Irving himself refused to comment.

Irving and Suskind reportedly balked at being specific unless the received assurances that Edith Irving would not be prosecuted by either U.S. or Swiss authorities.

No such promise was forthcoming, it was understood.

Clifford Irving

Irving and Suskind, sources close to the investigation told the Los Angeles newspaper Thursday, refused during a closed-door session Wednesday to spell out the details of how the manuscript was created. The session reportedly was attended by U.S. Atty. Whitney North Seymour, his top staff members and Irving's and Suskind's lawyers.

Irving had insisted repeatedly that the book was no rehash. It was, he said, based on more than 100 interviews with Hughes at various points in the Western Hemisphere.

Hughes or someone who identified himself as Hughes in a telephone interview with reporters on Jan. 7 had branded Irving's book a "totally fantastic fiction."

IRVING'S LAWYER, MAURICE NESSEN, disputed Friday's report in the Los Angeles Times.

"I deny it and I'm most concerned about stories like this," Nessen said. "I think that's all I want to say."

Asked about the report by a newsman at the Chelsea Hotel, Irving refused to comment but he said he very often hadn't "the slightest idea what the newspapers are writing about."

"First of all, so much of what I read is sheer nonsense," he said. "Some of the reports are stunning, astonishing, stunning in the sense they blow your mind."

Irving said he felt that what had happened to him in the

Turn to Back Page, this section

'nts he
come
city

rs who face ever-increas-
al estate prices.

ey stopped just short of
mending passage of a
e constitutional amend-
to grant the city the right
a local income tax.

said that the city had
the right for such a tax
the convention that
I the 1970 Constitution.

NFORTUNATELY,
n the consolidation of
publicans and indepen-
no authority was given
City of Chicago for such
he said.

think all cities should
e right to levy any kind
they feel is necessary.
are pre-empted from
so under the Con-
. We need a con-
al amendment."

ome tax "is more uni-
nd equitable" than
ms of taxes," he said.

directly, "Do you
day will ever come

A mayoral nod to lib, new library

Mayor Richard J. Daley said Friday he favors building a new main library. But he said that his wife has a right to disagree with him.

The mayor's bow to women's lib in the tightly-knit Daley family came during an impromptu meeting with reporters in his City Hall office.

It grew out of Mrs. Eleanor Daley's published comments in favor of saving and restoring the 75-year-old library structure.

"The women are entitled to their positions," said Daley. "She doesn't speak for me and I don't speak for her."

He said Mrs. Daley is free to state her views "and that is what she did."

DALEY SAID he hopes the idea of saving the old library is not totally discarded and that a newly-appointed committee would study "all phases" of the issue.

"I really believe we need a new library," said Daley.

In February 1972, the Crime Laboratory of the Postal Inspection Service at New York began a detailed examination of relevant documents from both the Swiss and US authorities and was soon convinced that forgery was involved. Meanwhile, Irving, who had not spoken to his editors for weeks, was already plea-bargaining; once the Swiss authorities had connected H. R. Hughes to his wife, the game was up.

For those interested in the pitfalls lurking in wait for handwriting experts, the whole story is of sharp interest. After all, McGraw-Hill's graphology consultants had supplied the manuscript with impeccable credentials! Only after the gaff was blown did it become transparently clear that close examination of the relevant documents — the Postal Inspection Service had about 40 to work on — would clearly demonstrate the differences between Hughes's hand and Irving's imitation of it.

The underlying motivation behind the fraud may be too complex ever to be explained. It would be far more than a mere illustration of the adage that a sucker is born every minute. Just as interesting was the eagerness to believe of everyone involved. And perhaps even more interesting than that is the manuscript itself. If Howard Hughes was a figure of myth, what better way to get at his meaning for us than to write a myth about him? On more than one publisher's shelves, the great manuscript lies gathering dust.

Above: The front page of The Chicago Daily News, dated Friday, 11th February 1972, carrying the story of Irving's fraud. The entire book centred round a forged letter from Howard Hughes, whom, it was alleged, Irving had never met. The inset shows Hughes.

coating they move upwards carrying the ink spots in the same direction. The components of the ink travel at different speeds because of differences in chemical composition and molecular structure. The individual dyes are eventually separated as a line of spots running in the same direction as the solvent. Then samples of the inks to be compared are placed side by side on the same plate together with standard dyes and pigments; similarities and differences can be observed by comparing the presence or absence of spots and by measuring the distance they have travelled along the plate.

Below: At first glance, this Egyptian statuette may appear of genuine antiquity. Examination using X-rays showed that it was made from synthetic resin filled with brass filings.

Special inks

Erasable inks contain a component which slows down the action of the ink on the paper; the pigments are suspended in a rubbery material which coats the surface of the paper at the time of writing but prevents the pigment soaking in. Another component slowly attacks the rubbery binder allowing the colourant to reach the paper; once this has happened the writing becomes permanent, but until then it can be erased by removing the rubbery binder. The advent of these inks has vastly increased the possibilities of fraud, and banks now warn their customers not to use erasable inks for writing cheques. Fortunately, unless it is made immediately after writing the erasure is not complete and traces of the ink can be detected on the paper.

Invisible inks (more correctly termed secret inks) reveal their messages only after the document has been specially treated. The simplest types are colourless organic compounds which when carefully heated will char and blacken at a temperature lower than that at which paper chars. Urine, saliva and lemon juice are the best known secret ink ingredients but a variety of other substances including water may also be used. The message is read by holding the paper close to a flame or less riskily a hot light bulb. More elaborate recipes include a starch solution which turns blue when exposed to iodine vapour, and silver nitrate which darkens on exposure to light.

Letters from prisoners of war often contained messages written in secret ink giving more realistic accounts of prison life than were permitted by the authorities. The main criminal uses still include getting messages out of prison but perhaps the most imaginative use is in gambling frauds. For example a gambler can back every horse in a race and still show a profit by ensuring that the stake shown on the slip for the winning horse is considerably more than the amount actually paid to the bookmaker. A zero written in silver nitrate based ink is added to the amount staked on each betting slip. The added numbers slowly appear as the silver nitrate darkens.

The slips for the losing horses are discarded but the winning slip now shows a tenfold increase in the bet with a corresponding increase in the amount won. Although this fraud is relatively easy to detect, by analysing the ink, many bookmakers employ procedures which prevent it altogether.

Some of the laboratory techniques used by the document examiner have even been borrowed for cheating at cards. A small spot of pale green ink is almost unnoticeable against a red background but shows up clearly when viewed through a red filter. Cards marked in this way may be skilfully inserted into a pack during the course of a game, and the concealed marks observed by a player wearing red tinted contact lenses. Experienced investigators of this type of fraud can often identify the game for which they were intended just by noting which cards in the pack have been marked.

Alterations to documents

When examining documents which may bear additions or erasures it is important to establish what was the original as well as that which has been added or removed. Even a simple alteration, for example the addition of a '0' to a '9' and 'ty' to 'nine' on a cheque, can transform the value or importance of a document. Simple erasures of pencil marks by india-rubber can be detected by dusting the surface of the paper with a fluorescent lycode powder: the particles of the powder adhere to the traces of rubber remaining on the surface. The original message can sometimes be seen by examining the indentations in oblique light but if they are faint or the original has been obscured by fresh writing some other method must be used.

The visual appearance of a document may change markedly when viewed in light of different wavelengths; for instance, inks which have intense colours in white light may be transparent to infra-red radiation and completely disappear, whereas substances such as graphite which are strong absorbers show up as very dark areas on the document. Similar effects may be observed under ultra-violet radiation. Some materials are strong emitters of infra-red radiation when they are illuminated with blue-green visible light. The eye is not sensitive to the infra-red but the effect, known as infra-red luminescence, may be observed through a device which converts the luminescence into a visible image.

Analytical instruments

The document can be examined in an instrument which incorporates several light sources and filters for selecting the wavelength of the illumination. The image is detected by a television camera incorporating a sensitive videcon tube and displayed on a black and white television monitor. Recently document examiners have started to exploit the very intense light available from high power lasers, especially in the blue-green region of the spectrum. The intense radiation has revealed features which were not previously recognized by conventional means. Laser light is not without its hazards however, since the intensity may totally destroy the colour of some inks and even burn a hole through the document.

The phenomena described may be used for

Below: *A car number plate which has been illegally altered, is revealed by the use of infra-red. If this technique fails, then lasers can be used.*

Right: *The 'S', which is the San Francisco mint-mark, on the reverse side of this 1894 US dime was found to be a fake. Pictures taken using a scanning electron microscope revealed the 'S' as a forgery. The '1894' can be seen as a smooth curve merging with the surface of the coin, whereas the 'S' was shown to be added later.*

Bottom right: *This comparison of striation marks on the edge of a bundle of forged £5 notes and on the edge of a control batch reveal that they were cut using the same guillotine. The guillotine was found at the premises where the notes were believed to have been forged.*

revealing writing which has been erased or covered by other writing. Sometimes it is also important to identify the method of erasure, particularly when chemicals have been used, and the original ink has been totally destroyed. Many commercial ink eradicators use a two stage process; potassium permanganate, a strong oxidizer, is first added to destroy any iron based pigments and is followed by a strong bleaching solution which removes the purple colouration of the permanganate in any remaining pigments. The traces of these chemicals, which soak into the paper, are identified by punching a small disc from the region of the erasure with a specially ground hypodermic needle. Traces of manganese and potassium from the permanganate and chlorine from the bleach can be detected by a technique known as X-ray spectrometry.

A prime requirement of any analytical technique used on documents is that it should be non-destructive, or at least not significantly alter the appearance of the feature of interest. Documents may have to be produced as exhibits in court and it is essential that they survive the scientific examination. The techniques of scanning electron micro-

scopy and X-ray spectroscopy fulfil this requirement because they require only a minute sample, while providing the examiner with two important types of information. Firstly, a highly magnified image of the surface of the sample can be formed; because electrons with wavelengths much shorter than those of visible light are used the image shows very fine detail, and magnifications of 100,000 times or more are obtainable. The instrument also has a much greater depth of field than an optical microscope so that very rough surfaces can be examined. As well as revealing the appearance of the sample the instrument also provides chemical information, because the impact of the electrons which have been accelerated through twenty or thirty thousand volts causes the production of X-rays whose energies are characteristic of the chemical elements present in the sample. The X-rays are collected and their energies measured in an X-ray spectrometer.

The order in which two crossed lines were written on a document can often be determined by electron microscopy. This is useful, for example, in detecting the addition of a clause to a legal document after it has been signed. Signatures are often located immediately below the last line of typing in order to prevent this happening so it is not uncommon for strokes of the handwriting to cross the typescript. The high resolution image and great depth of field show clearly whether the ink from the signature is deposited above or below the typescript, indicating which was deposited on the paper first.

Indented impressions

Impressions of writing on surfaces beneath a sheet of paper, such as on the pages in a notebook or writing pad, are difficult to decipher because no ink has been deposited and they are usually very faint. A new technique based on the processes used in photocopying machines has recently been developed for solving this problem. A very thin transparent sheet of mylar – a type of plastic – is placed on the surface of the indented document and an electrostatic charge is applied to it by passing a wire carrying several thousand volts across the surface. The indented impressions influence the distribution of charge; they are revealed by spraying the film with very fine particles of graphite or photocopying powder which adheres preferentially to the sites of the impressions. Finally the thin film is peeled away from the document and covered with a thicker transparent sheet to protect the image. One of the most notable successes of the method was a complete plan and timetable for a bank robbery left on a writing pad after the top sheet had been removed.

Typewriting

Typewriters, of course, have their own peculiarities and it follows that careful comparison of known and unknown samples of typescript should enable the document examiner to identify the machine on which the document was typed. In practice this is not always possible, but in favourable circumstances the typist as well as the machine may be identified. The make and type of machine may be identified from a reference collection which contains details of letter designs, spacings between letters and between lines, and subsidiary or special characters present on the keyboard.

Further identification may be made by examining broken letters, misalignment of the carriage and irregularities on the roller. Some of these effects may be temporary and could have been corrected by repair or servicing so it is important to distinguish them from permanent features. Similarities and differences are most obvious when the unknown and control samples are examined in a comparator. This device produces rapidly alternating images of the writing; features which are similar on both appear as steady images whereas those that differ flicker as the images change.

Future developments in document examination depend to a large extent on the nature and use of the documents themselves. Already the decline in cash transactions and increasing use of cheques and credit cards has led to a spectacular increase in the incidence of frauds involving these items. Information is now stored and transmitted electronically and can be erased without a trace and the scientific detection of computer fraud is still in its infancy. In spite of this trend in technology, however, it is likely that the use of paper and writing will continue because they are such a fundamental feature of culture and civilization.

POLICE ORGANIZATION

'If a man has knocked out the teeth of a man of the same rank, his own teeth shall be knocked out.' This unbending rule was part of the Code of law published by Hammurabi, the king of Babylon, some 2000 years BC. The code was strong on crime and punishment but relied on citizens being prepared to tell the truth on oath. In cases of doubt, trial by ordeal usually settled a person's guilt. The idea of voluntary obedience to the law was widely shared in both ancient and modern worlds and enforcement was a matter for each community.

Above: *In this method of trial by ordeal, the accused was innocent if he sank, and guilty if he floated.*

In England after the Norman Conquest, every man was held responsible for his behaviour and it was his duty to take action on any crime he saw committed. A 'hue and cry' was raised and he called on his neighbours to assist in pursuit of the miscreant. In time, families were grouped ten to a tithing and ten tithings became a hundred which was presided over by a constable, usually a nobleman, who had charge of the hundred's weapons.

Eventually, hundreds were formed into shires, areas with geographical boundaries, and the Crown appointed a shire reeve (Sheriff) to look after its interests which included law and order. The principal judicial and political institutions grew out of this system, including Common Law, which was based on custom and precedent and was the same for all members of society, trial by jury and habeas corpus which safeguarded the individual from unlawful detention.

Upholding of the law by the people because they believed in it worked effectively when society consisted of small communities in which infractions of discipline were easily observed. The steady growth of industrialization and development of large cities created a different social structure in which the old methods of regulating behaviour broke down. Faster communications and transportation aided this process and crime became more anonymous with pick-pockets and thieves of all kinds infesting the towns and highway robbers molesting travellers. The need for organized enforcement of the law had dawned.

The English police

Police organization in England dates from 1829 when Sir Robert Peel (1788-1850), the Home Secretary, established the Metropolitan Police Force. Much of the groundwork had been laid by Henry Fielding (1707-1754), the novelist, who became an unpaid police magistrate at Bow Street in 1748 at a time when London's streets were unsafe for the ordinary citizen. Bands of robbers were at large, usually at night, and their antics proved too much for the handful of parish constables who opposed them. Practically the only antidotes to crime at that time were the 'hue and cry' and the thief-takers who responded to a reward system.

The Bow Street Runners

Fielding decided to improve this situation by organizing a small group of six willing men who operated as plain-clothes detectives. These were the famous Bow Street Runners who had neither official status nor remuneration but who quickly won acclaim by ridding the streets of thieves. So successful were they that Fielding persuaded the government to pay each man a guinea a week from the Secret Service Fund to supplement his earnings as a thief-taker.

The Highwayman Act of 1692 provided a reward of £40 for the arrest and prosecution of any highwayman and a scale of fees for apprehending house-breakers, counterfeiters, army deserters and other miscreants. The most successful member of the profession of thief-takers was Jonathan Wild who sent over a hundred men to the gallows before he too trod the scaffold in 1725. Many thief-takers were themselves criminals and their inspiration had less to do with public service than with personal gain.

Above: A Bow Street Runner of 1804. They served as detectives until 1829, being replaced by 'Peelers'.
Below: Jonathan Wild on his way to Tyburn. He was a thief and receiver of stolen goods in London, and betrayed other thieves who would not share with him.

It was against this background that Henry Fielding organized his Bow Street Runners and in 1792 opened seven other offices in London each staffed with Runners. Some recognition came in 1800 when two Bow Street Runners were detailed as royal protectors following the assassination attempt on George II by James Hadfield at Drury Lane Theatre. Elsewhere in England at that time, law enforcement was carried out by constables and watchmen appointed by individual parishes. Fielding's maxim was 'quick notice and sudden pursuit', the chase being the forte of his Runners. He advertised in the newspapers urging the public to report criminal acts with speed while the trail was still warm. He showed considerable vision in setting up criminal records and advocating exchanges of information between police magistrates throughout the country.

Henry Fielding died before he could put all his ideas into practice and he was succeeded by his half brother, John, who had been blind since youth. John Fielding was a magistrate for over a quarter of a century and despite his handicap carried on his predecessor's work with great distinction. Sir John, as he later became, was also a pioneer in his own right, starting foot patrols and founding the journal *Hue and Cry* which later became the *Police Gazette*.

Between them, Henry and John Fielding established high standards for the conduct of magistrates and exhibited vision and humanity in equal proportions.

Twelve years after Sir John's death, Patrick Colquhoun (1745-1820), Lord Provost of Glasgow, retired to London where he was appointed a magistrate. He published *A Treatise on the Police of the Metropolis* which was a blueprint for police organization. He suggested that a police force be set up under the Home Office and advocated establishing a criminal record office and an official police journal.

Robert Peel's act

Thus, when the Home Secretary, Sir Robert Peel, put before Parliament in 1829 a bill 'for improving the police in and near the Metropolis', he was standing on ground that had been well prepared. Despite keen opposition, the bill became law and England's

Above: *Peel reformed the archaic penal code and simultaneously created a regular police force, the 'Peelers'* (below), *who wore beards to enhance their authority.*

Above: *Fielding, the second Bow Street magistrate after Sir Thomas de Veil was the equivalent of the present-day Metropolitan Police Commissioner.*

first official police force was created. A thousand uniformed men, nick-named 'Blue Devils' or 'Bobbies', went on patrol in London's streets. Peel had sought to ensure the impartiality of the police through their immunity from politics and by making them subject to the laws which they enforced. This independent character of the British police system is a feature which has distinguished it from the systems used in other countries.

The Metropolitan Police Force

The newly formed Metropolitan Police Force was headed by two justices of the peace or Commissioners who built up the force's strength to 3000 men. Sir Richard Mayne and Sir Charles Rowan, combining the respective disciplines of lawyer and army officer, established in practice that the police were truly servants of the public. Sir Richard said that 'the protection of life and property, the preservation of public tranquillity and the absence of

crime' would decide whether the police attained their objectives.

The extent to which the Metropolitan Police succeeded may be judged from the fact that in 1856 Parliament passed legislation making the provision of police forces throughout England and Wales compulsory. Scotland had its own legislation in the following year.

From its inception, the Metropolitan Police set up its headquarters office in Westminster in buildings entered through Great Scotland Yard. This centre of police activity in London was soon called 'Scotland Yard', a name which was to become known throughout the world as a symbol of the English policing system. The name remained even when the headquarters location was changed – it simply became New Scotland Yard.

Organizing the British police

At the same time that a police system was established throughout Britain, the Metropolitan Police Force was put under the command of a single Commissioner. He is appointed by the Crown on the advice of the Home Secretary. The Metropolitan force is the largest in the country with about a quarter of the total police manpower in the country. Its district is very large, and includes two whole counties and parts of four others.

In addition to policing the greater London area, the Metropolitan force has a number of national responsibilities. These are the maintenance of criminal records including fingerprints for the whole country, running the national bureau for Interpol, VIP protection and provision of criminal investigation expertise when required by other police forces.

The Commissioner of Police of the Metropolis has a Deputy Commissioner and four Assistant Commissioners (ACs) working under him. Each AC is responsible for a particular branch of police activity such as traffic, criminal investigation, administration and training. The Metropolitan Police area is divided into a number of districts, containing 23 divisions each under a Chief Superintendent. Up to 1829 the Bow Street Runners continued to carry out detective duties but they were disbanded in that year when the Metropolitan Police formed a small detective branch. This

Right: The growth of terrorism and bombing, such as this Whitehall blast by the IRA in March 1973, has added another dimension to police work.

became, in 1878, the Criminal Investigation Department (CID) and it is for this activity that Scotland Yard has become world famous. Over the years it has been traditional for other British police forces to 'call in the Yard' to help solve difficult cases, especially murder investigations. The Criminal Investigation Department runs a number of specialized activities including the Fingerprint and Photographic Branch, Criminal Record Office, Fraud Squad, Flying Squad and Special Branch.

Following the Police Act of 1964, the police system in England and Wales was reorganized. The great number of separate forces was reduced to 47, and later to 43, large units each under the direction of a Chief Constable. These stream-lined forces carry out law enforcement in their areas and, unlike the Metropolitan Police which answers to the Home Secretary, are subject to a local police authority. Each police force has its own CID capability and reorganization provided for improvements in training, equipment and communications, in recognition of the need to deal with developments such as inner city violence and international terrorism.

Technology and communication systems

Police organization in Britain has five major facets consisting of crime prevention; criminal investigation; traffic control; dealing with vice, gambling and narcotics; and juvenile crime. These branches of police work are aided by the use of modern communications and information systems supported by forensic science laboratory facilities. Probably the first piece of technical equipment to be introduced was the police whistle in 1884. Motorized patrols followed with motorcycles in 1921 and cars equipped with two-way radio in 1927. Two-way radio contact is used by every officer on patrol today and mobile units include river craft and helicopters. Recent legislation has added riot protection gear, CS gas, water cannon and personnel carriers. Yet the single feature which sets the British police officer apart from his opposite number elsewhere in

the world is that he is not equipped with a firearm. While this remains true in general, the growth of terrorism has necessitated the carrying of guns by officers involved in special protection duties and greater numbers of officers are being trained in the use of firearms.

Information handling is an important component of any modern organization and the use of computerized on-line search facilities greatly speeds up enquiries. The Police National Computer at Hendon, which cost £50 million to set up, puts the police officer at the scene of enquiry in touch with a wealth of information within minutes. This computer is linked with 500 terminals located at police stations throughout the country and can deal with thousands of enquiries an hour. The system houses

information on registered vehicle numbers, disqualified drivers, stolen cars, fingerprints and missing persons.

It was the speed of this information network interacting with the judgement of the man-on-the-spot which led to the capture of the Yorkshire Ripper in January 1981. Two uniformed officers in a panda car set out on a routine night patrol in Sheffield. Just before 11 pm, they saw a stationary car in what their instincts told them were suspicious circumstances. There were two occupants in the car one of whom was recognized as a prostitute. After questioning the driver, the officers radioed the vehicle's registration number to the local VDU operator for a routine check. The reply justified their suspicion for the registration number

displayed on the car in fact belonged to another vehicle. Close inspection showed that the number plates were fixed to the car with adhesive tape. The driver was taken in for further questioning and proved to be Peter Sutcliffe, the Yorkshire Ripper and killer of 13 women.

The forensic science service

The need for police work to stand closer to scientific method was first realized in Europe at the turn of the century. Important developments in police science took place in Switzerland, Germany and France. A notable event was the establishment of a police laboratory at Lyons in 1910 by Edmond Locard (1877-1966). Britain was a late entrant in this field, having a preference for the individual expert who assisted the courts with scientific evidence. The need for a forensic laboratory service with well-equipped facilities and properly-trained staff became apparent in the 1930s and the Metropolitan Police Forensic Science Laboratory was started in 1934. This, plus the six regional laboratories and the Central Research Establishment at Aldermaston, comprise the Forensic Science Service in England and Wales.

With certain exceptions, all aspects of scientific evidence are the province of these forensic laboratories. Areas excluded are fingerprints which are handled by specialized police departments, and the medical side of crime which is dealt with by police surgeons and pathologists retained by the Home Office. Trace materials collected as evidence at scenes of crime represent an enormous array of substances, mostly commonplace, which may yield important information linking a crime and suspect.

These may range from human tissues and body fluids such as skin, hair, blood and semen to such crime debris as broken glass, paint fragments, clothing fibres, bullets, cartridge cases, offensive weapons, explosives, forged documents, drugs and many other crime artefacts. There are also the impressions left by vehicle tyres, footprints and tools in association with every type of crime from arson to violent assault. In the course of a year, the Metropolitan Police Forensic Science Laboratory alone will carry out over 30,000 forensic investigations involving many specialist skills.

GETTING AWAY WITH MURDER
Brian Donald Hume

The name 'Interpol' evokes romantic associations for many people. They imagine sophisticated Maigret-like sleuths hunting their quarry across international boundaries; gum chewing New York detectives telephoning details of a suspect to London, England, in laconic 'wise guy' accents. There is some foundation for such colourful associations, of course. However, it should be admitted that the real strength of Interpol is based on the thoroughness and efficiency of its classification systems, and on its comprehensive international coverage.

These rather more prosaic qualities were to be the key factors in the downfall of a British criminal who had successfully eluded a murder verdict. Brian Donald Hume was also over-confident of the extent of his legal knowledge, and failed to take the ordinary precaution of checking a simple fact. He firmly and mistakenly believed that Switzerland was not included in the Interpol network because it did not belong to the United Nations.

The story began in January 1950. Hume appeared at London's Old Bailey charged with the murder of Stanley Setty, a shady businessman whose headless torso had been washed up on the Essex mud-flats at Tillingham. It was proved that Hume had flown in a hired light aircraft carrying two parcels around the time Setty disappeared. When questioned, Hume claimed the parcels contained parts of a printing press used to print forged food-ration coupons which he had been asked to dump at sea. Later, he elaborated this story, saying that one of the parcels made a gurgling noise when he moved it and it had crossed his mind that it might be a body — possibly that of Setty who he knew had been reported missing. Due to a technicality, Hume was found not guilty of murder, although he was convicted for being an accessory and received a twelve-year prison sentence.

Having earned all the remission to which he was entitled, Hume left prison in February 1958. In April, he changed his name to Donald Brown and in June sold his story for £2,000 to the *Sunday Pictorial* newspaper which published his confession to the murder of Stanley Setty. He claimed that he attacked Setty with a Nazi SS dagger. He had only intended to frighten him as he believed he was having an affair with his wife. In the course of this assault, it occurred to him, "— perhaps I could get away with murder." He admitted killing Setty, cutting up the body and dumping it in the English Channel from a light aircraft. The *Sunday Pictorial* obviously had a 'scoop' on its hands, and Hume was the centre of a blaze of publicity. Although he knew he could not be tried again for the same crime he decided it would be prudent to lie low for a while. He therefore disguised his appearance and with a pass-

port identifying him as John Steven Bird, chemical engineer, headed for Switzerland with the £2,000 newspaper fee in banknotes.

In Switzerland, he converted his money to US currency and travelled to North America where he enjoyed a spending spree and passed himself off as Johnny Bird, Canadian test-pilot. In July 1958 he returned to Switzerland and in Zurich resumed his relationship with his girl-friend, Trudi Sommer.

Not surprisingly, after his travels, Hume was now short of funds. His remedy was to rob a bank, and where better than England where the authorities would least expect him? He flew to England as Donald Brown, held up a bank in Brentford at gun-point, grabbed £1,300, and returned to Zurich as John Bird.

Eventually, Trudi began pressing him about marriage, and some awkward revelations occurred regarding his passport and various aliases. He decided it was time to travel again and took himself off to Canada. He returned, as before, short of funds and decided on the same solution. Indeed, he planned to rob the same London bank as before but discovered that it had moved. With the dogged determination of the committed criminal, he traced it to its new premises but was rewarded with only poor pickings amounting to £300. He further bungled his escape by leaving his raincoat on a train.

With this garment and aided by descriptions of the bank robber, police were able to connect Donald Brown to the raid and thence to Donald Hume. The only consolation for Hume was that he had seen a Police Wanted Notice which offered £1,000 reward for his capture; "it made me feel good to know I was wanted;" he remarked later. He returned to Trudi whose suspicions were aroused when she found he was carrying a gun. She pleaded with him to dispose of it but he had already decided on a further, fatal excursion into armed robbery.

On 30 January 1959, Hume walked into the Gewerbe Bank in Zurich, produced a gun and shot the cashier in the stomach. He grabbed 215 Swiss francs and was prising open a safety drawer when the wounded cashier touched off the alarm which rang in the central police station. Within minutes, police were on the scene and pursuing the robber whom the alarm bells had put to flight. Various passers-by joined in the chase and Arthur Maag, a taxi-driver, dived at his legs. Hume fired and Maag collapsed, fatally injured. Within seconds the fleeing murderer was overwhelmed by a mob of people.

Hume was taken into police custody and questioned but several hours went by before he offered any reply. Then, answering in English, he said he was John Stanilav, a civilian employee at the US Air Force in Wiesbaden. When the police provided a Polish interpreter to allow the arrested man to develop his explanation further, his deception was quickly discovered. The Zurich police sent

HUME CONFESSION

'I killed Setty...'

DONALD HUME'S ADMISSION
TO THE PICTORIAL THAT
STARTED WORLD CONTROVERSY

THERE was a blazing row when car dealer Stanley Setty and I met in my flat at Finchley-road, Golders Green, on the evening of October 4, 1949.

It was 7.35 p.m. I was livid with anger at this man for whom I had been earning money by stealing cars.

The cars I stole on his order had to match the log-books of wrecked vehicles he had already bought.

TREMBLE

BUT, furious as I was, I did not know then that seventeen minutes later I would have his dead body—and his blood—on my hands.

I began to tremble with rage when this black marketeer refused to get out.

I saw red. I yelled at him, then ran out on to the landing and snatched a dagger from the collection of war souvenirs on the wall.

DAGGER

THE handle of the dagger glinted in the light. I could see the initials "S.S."

In war, they stood for Schutz Staffel, the elite army corps of Nazi Germany.

Now those S.S. initials stood for forty-four-year-old Stanley Setty.

I dashed, dagger in hand,

I'M HOLDING A DAGGER LIKE THE ONE I USED TO KILL STANLEY SETTY

seemed to come naturally to me. We rolled over and over and my sweaty hand plunged the weapon frenziedly and repeatedly into his chest and legs.

I had to hurt him.

I aimed my blows anywhere. But Setty continued to struggle. He was as strong as an ox.

The more I stuck the dagger into him, the more he tried to push my head back and break my neck.

I tried to push Setty away from me to keep his blood off my clothes and force a gap between us.

I forced my knee into him. He grunted, but he wouldn't release his grip. It was like a vice.

WRITHE

I HELD the knife up to strike the sixth or seventh blow. I can't remember.

I plunged the blade into his ribs. I know I heard them crack.

He sank back against the sofa and slumped on the floor. He writhed and rolled over to a spot beneath the window, on his back.

Setty began to cough violently and a trickle of red came from his mouth as he heaved and panted.

I stood over him with the dagger in my hand.

And, with a feeling of triumph at winning the fight, I watched the life run from him.

I looked at the clock. It was 7.52 p.m. The fight had lasted less than two minutes—about the same time as it took you to read about it.

Now Setty lay on his back, his eyes seemed glassily fixed on the ceiling

knew that Setty had come to my flat?

I fought off my daze. My mind started clicking again.

Down in the streets outside, life was going on as usual. Carefree couples strolled arm in arm on their way to the pictures.

But at my feet a man lay dead . . . murdered by me.

I wandered unsteadily into the back room where Tony, my dog, had slept through it all. I wanted time to restore myself to an even balance. I wanted to be able to think straight.

The thought flashed through my mind that perhaps I could get away with murder.

HEAVED

FIRST, I had to get rid of all traces of the killing. Next, I had to get the body out of the way.

I went back into the lounge. Setty still lay on his back, his staring eyes fixed on the ceiling.

I got hold of him by the legs and started to drag him, being careful to keep him on his back, so that blood from his chest did not trail on the floor.

He seemed a ton weight. But I dragged him across the hall, right through the dining room and scullery of my flat, and into the breakfast room.

Then I heaved him into the coal cupboard and covered him with an old piece of felt.

TIDIED

NEXT, I tidied up the lounge and set to rights the furni-

off a detailed description of Mr Stanilav to Interpol headquarters in Paris.

Interpol's criminal classification system was put to the test and within an hour it was established that John Stanilav was identical to Donald Brown. The British authorities had notified Interpol in 1958 when Donald Hume changed his name to Brown by deed poll. Thus, the Zurich police now knew that the man they held as Stanilav was in fact Donald Hume, self-confessed murderer of Stanley Setty. Interpol also supplied the information that Hume, in the name of Brown, was wanted in London for two armed bank robberies in August and November 1958.

The extent of Hume's exploits and deception came to light when the Zurich police published his photograph. Trudi Sommer came forward to state that she knew him as John Bird, the man to whom she was engaged to be married. She produced letters which he had sent her from America and Canada. Hume, alias Brown, alias Bird and sundry other identities was sent to Regendorf prison to await trial for murder.

The trial indictment accused Hume of murder, attempted murder, armed robbery and other crimes to which he pleaded guilty. After due process, the jury convicted him and he was sentenced to life imprisonment with hard labour. Hume said nothing in his own defence but gave a characteristic display of violent struggling when being escorted from the court. Thus, nine years after he killed Setty in London, Hume was brought to book for murder.

He told the Zurich police after he was arrested that he chose Switzerland as a base for his criminal activities because it was a rich country and an ideal target for international criminals of his calibre. He also thought he would be out of the reach of Interpol in Switzerland. It was this simple mistake which finally brought him into the wide net of the international police organization.

The French police system

The British police system is unusual in being based on local control, for the pattern in most of Europe is that of national police forces responsible to central government. France has four major police organizations, the Sûreté-Nationale being the most well known. This is a civil police force with headquarters in Paris which is answerable to the Minister of the Interior. The Sûreté is responsible for maintaining law and order and providing the specialized services required for this purpose. It operates throughout France and has detection flying squads (Brigade Mobile) based in the larger provincial towns. The other police organizations in the country are a municipal force which functions in rural France, the Gendarmerie Nationale, an armed force responsible to the Minister of Defence, and the Paris Préfecture of Police.

Above: In France, unlike the UK or the USA, it is normal to use the criminal in a reconstruction of the crime. Here, the murder of a Gendarme, Neufcourt, is re-enacted in 1950. Standing by the car is the man accused of taking part.

The Paris police

Paris had its own police in 1800 largely due to the traditional interest of the French kings in the security of the capital. Like London, the French capital city had its street crime and with criminal investigation appearing ineffective, the Prefect of Police took an unusual step – he called in an escaped convict to help. Eugène-François Vidocq (1775-1857) was an unusual man whom the authorities had failed to keep in prison following his conviction for minor crimes. Vidocq's knowledge of criminal affairs was such that the detective squad which he formed to assist the police met with immediate success.

Like Henry Fielding's Bow Street Runners, this squad of detectives proved to be a force to which the street criminals readily succumbed. In 1811, Vidocq was appointed Head of the Sûreté, a position which he held until 1827 when he resigned. He served in that capacity again for a short time in 1832 and subsequently became one of the first private detectives. The former convict proved to be a pioneer in criminal investigation.

The Sûreté today is headed by a Director-General and is organized in four directorates covering counter-espionage, criminal investigation, special branch and public security. It has 17 regional headquarters throughout France whose chief officers report to the Director-General. The roles of the counter-espionage directorate and Special Branch (Brigade Spéciale) are concerned with the security of the state against treason and insurrection.

The Special Branch, a squad of specially-selected detectives, gathers intelligence for the Ministry of the Interior and also supervises betting and gaming activities. The public security function is carried out by the uniformed branch of the police service operating routine patrols, traffic regulation and communications networks.

In 1951, a special force was set up under the Director-General of the Sûreté to coordinate police action in dealing with public disturbances occasioned by strikes or emergencies. This is the Republic Security Companies (CRS) which gained a certain notoriety for meting out rough treatment in quelling riotous student behaviour in the 1960s. There are sixty CRS units stationed throughout France and a local authority can request their assistance through the head of the Sûreté. As a matter of routine, CRS officers also carry out port and frontier security duties.

The French 'CID'

The criminal investigation branch of the Sûreté is similar in many respects to Scotland Yard. It operates a detective force known as the Police Judiciaire and maintains a criminal records office, fingerprint bureau and a forensic science laboratory. The early practice of criminal investigation in France was much influenced by the anthropometric system of identification developed by Alphonse Bertillon (1883-1914) who began his career as a clerk in the Paris Préfecture of Police. Although his system of identification by body measurement was overthrown by fingerprints, he is regarded as the founder of forensic photography which he pioneered in Paris.

US police organization

The USA has the most diverse police organization in the world with as many as 40,000 individual and independent units of various sizes operating across the country. Police administration echoes the pattern of civil government and the jurisdiction of this large number of law enforcement units is variously federal, state and local. This diversity made nationwide law enforcement difficult as wanted criminals simply crossed state lines into a different area of police jurisdiction. With this in mind, Congress established the Bureau of Investigation in 1908 to provide the Department of Justice with a permanent crime investigation agency.

J. Edgar Hoover and the FBI

The early years of the Bureau's existence were not particularly distinguished owing to its restricted powers, but it was well placed for development when in 1924 the Attorney General appointed J. Edgar Hoover (1895-1972) to the position of

Below: *J. Edgar Hoover, Director of the FBI for nearly 50 years, photographed in the 1930s.*

Director. One of his first acts was to raise the standard of recruitment and from then on all agents were to be either qualified lawyers or accountants. They were dubbed G-men or 'government men'. Also in 1924, the bureau established an Identification Division with a nucleus of 800,000 fingerprints which under Hoover's direction has become the world's greatest fingerprint collection.

During the years between the two world wars, Hoover's men excelled themselves in dealing with prohibition and gang warfare and won extra powers from Congress for the fight against crime. Kidnapping was one of many criminal activities which became the province of the bureau in 1932 following the Lindbergh case which shocked the nation. In 1935 the bureau was given the appellation, Federal Bureau of Investigation (FBI), by which it is universally known today. By 1949 the FBI Director was able to state that of 261 cases of kidnapping dealt with by his agents, only two remained unsolved. Such was the success of the FBI that in 1939 the US President gave it responsibility for all internal security matters including counter-espionage and anti-sabotage measures.

Today, police jurisdiction at a national level in the USA is carried out entirely by the FBI. The bureau provides central services for all identification, technical, forensic and statistical requirements. It also plays a major role in training police personnel through the National Police Academy which was set up in 1935. The FBI has an impressive record of achievement in police science and has been at the forefront of developing new ideas.

Probably the US police at all levels are the best provided for in terms of equipment, technical facilities and communications. Considerable value is placed on crime scene investigation (CSI), for example, and many forces operate CSI units with specially-trained officers using custom-built vehicles equipped for evidence gathering. The aim is to secure physical evidence in the best condition to aid the crime laboratory.

The central crime laboratory

The FBI runs a central crime laboratory at its headquarters in Washington DC and its resources are available to any police force. The most up-to-date and highly sophisticated technical facilities are thereby available to the smallest police force. Many large police departments have their own forensic science laboratories and in every respect US police work is closely related to the 'lab'. The FBI's crime laboratory carries out upwards of 150,000 investigations a year on evidence material. An important development in criminal investigation procedures in the USA, as elsewhere, is the speed of communications.

In 1967 the FBI set up its National Crime Information Center (NCIC) in Washington DC which for the first time linked together law enforcement agencies at all levels throughout the country. The NCIC computer can be accessed on-line from numerous terminals at police departments in any state. Fingerprint and photographic identity of a suspect can be checked within minutes. The computer holds full descriptive information on wanted persons down to Social Security and driving licence numbers.

US crime levels

Criticism over political assassinations and the use of electronic surveillance methods have combined with an increase in US crime figures to put the FBI under pressure. The 1970s saw a huge increase in narcotics offences and an alarming increase in murder rates. A 70 per cent increase in homicide was reported in Miami in 1979 and 80 per cent increase in Washington DC. The attempt on President Reagan's life and the stranger-to-stranger murders committed by the Son of Sam in New York City renewed the arguments about the right of Americans to carry firearms – a right exercised by 50 million handgun owners.

International crime

The international character of much of today's crime – terrorism, fraud and drug trafficking – bears out the need for an international police organization. It was apparent as early as 1914 that the variety and speed of transportation available to the criminal needed to be matched by international cooperation between the world's police forces. Meeting in Monaco, delegates to the first interna-

Top: *Arthur Koehler, a wood technologist, examines the ladder used in the kidnapping of Charles Lindbergh's baby. He was able to match the grooves and nail holes in the ladder to the tools owned by Bruno Hauptmann (below) who had worked for the lumber firm that Koehler had painstakingly identified as the supplier of the wood which was used in the manufacture of the ladder. This evidence led to the execution of Hauptmann for the murder of the baby.*

'I HAVEN'T FALLEN OFF THE CHRISTMAS TREE' The Yorkshire Ripper hunt

The multiple murderer strikes fear in us all. Somehow, it is possible to empathize with someone who commits a homicide, in a moment of frenzy, perhaps. But one killing after another? The imagination boggles.

The Yorkshireman who killed 13 women in a distinctively brutal manner was at large for over five years in the north of England. Such was the ferocity of his assaults on his victims that he was inevitably compared with the Victorian sex killer, Jack the Ripper. As time passed, and the macabre murders continued, the West Yorkshire Metropolitan Police found the pressure mounting.

Women were afraid to go outdoors after dark; questions were tabled in Parliament by anxious MPs. Certainly, every resource of local police organization was stretched to full capacity. As nerves frayed under constant media criticism, the hunt continued. Yet how could one man evade one of the biggest dragnets ever constructed?

The actual 'catch' was an oddly routine affair. But routine is important. By investigating how and why errors are made the system of police organization is gradually improved. Yet, much as we would like to imagine the smooth efficiency of computers and card indexes clicking into motion, there is always a fascinating, random element in a case such as this.

Perhaps, in some crazed way, Peter Sutcliffe did possess some form of psychotic genius — if only in his ability to lie his way successfully through several police interviews. He certainly had more than his share of what can be normally considered to be average good luck.

His trial opened in May 1981, and attracted worldwide press coverage.

"When you speak to God it's called praying; but when God speaks to you it's called schizophrenia." Thus did a West German observer comment on the psychiatric evidence given during the proceedings. Sutcliffe, who said he had heard the voice of God instructing him to kill and who claimed that his "latent genius if unleashed would rock the nation", was sentenced to life imprisonment for the murder of 13 women. The capture of the 34-year old ex altar-boy and grave-digger followed a trail of death and mutilation.

The first murder occurred in Leeds in October 1975 and the last in the same city in November 1980. In between, the Yorkshire Ripper killed 11 other women in Huddersfield, Halifax and Manchester and attacked seven others. His hunting grounds were the red-light districts of those towns where prostitutes made easy prey. He prowled around in his car until he fixed his target and, following the routine bargaining for sex, felled her with a severe blow to the head delivered with a ballpeen hammer. He then set about his fiendish work with a knife, performing a ritualistic disfigurement of the body.

Sutcliffe was to say later that it was a miracle the police did not catch him earlier. He slipped in and out of police surveillance, enjoying the luck of the devil and building up a barrage of criticism which would later be levelled at the police. A £5 note was found in Jean Jordan's handbag after her murder in Manchester in October 1977. In the belief that she had been given the money by the killer, the police set about tracing the note. Banknote number AW 51121565 had been issued by the Midland Bank at Shipley on 27 September, a few days before the murder. It was part of a batch of £50,000 worth of notes which had been drawn by local firms to pay wages. The bank provided a list of firms who had received notes from this batch but there was no record of serial numbers that could be matched to individual withdrawals. Consequently, the police visited each company and interviewed its employees. Sutcliffe's firm was one of these and he was one of 8,300 men interviewed. His answers proved satisfactory and the heat was off.

Between March 1978 and June 1979, the police received several communications purporting to come "from the Ripper". There were three letters, two of which were sent directly to the police, and one received via a newspaper. The letters contained haunting phrases from the original Jack the Ripper letters sent to the authorities in 1888, but what seemed significant was the inclusion of details of the murder of Joan Harrison (Preston, November 1975) which had not been published.

Moreover, semen found on that victim's body was from a secretor with B-group blood, a combination found in only 6% of the population. This tied in with the sender of the letters, for the stamps had been moistened by the tongue of a secretor with B-group blood. The other communication received by the police was the tape, beginning "I'm Jack", which taunted them in a voice with a Wearside accent. This too had been sent in an envelope the flap of which had been moistened by a B-group secretor.

The police launched Project R, a massive publicity campaign unique to British criminal investigation. The "I'm Jack" tape was played in hundreds of clubs and pubs and broadcast on radio and TV. Samples of handwriting from the letters were published by the press and huge poster hoardings appeared in Leeds and elsewhere urging people to HELP US STOP THE RIPPER FROM KILLING AGAIN – LOOK AT HIS HANDWRITING, LISTEN TO HIS VOICE. In addition, photofit pictures and artists' impressions made up from descriptions given by women fortunate enough to have survived the Ripper's assaults were widely publicized. All this activity proved fruitless and the police were later criticized for misleading themselves

Above: *Peter Sutcliffe with his wife Sonia on their wedding day in 1974. She claimed she had no knowledge of his killings, and was determined to stick by him.*

over the tape. As events turned out, the Yorkshire Ripper had B-group blood but he was a non-secretor and therefore did not send the letters or tape.

On 2 January 1981, Sergeant Robert Ring and PC Robert Hydes set out on a routine panda car patrol in Sheffield. Driving along Melbourne Avenue, they spotted a parked Rover car which they thought deserved attention. The occupants were a man who gave his name as Peter Williams and a young coloured woman. Sergeant Ring thought he recognized the girl as a prostitute. "Who's she?", he asked. "My girl friend." "What's her name?" "I don't know. I haven't known her all that long." "Who are you trying to kid?" said Ring, adding "I haven't fallen off the Christmas tree."

A radio call was put in to the police computer at Hendon asking for a check on the Rover's registration number. Within two minutes Ring was informed that the number belonged not to a Rover but to a Skoda. Close examination of the number plate revealed that it was held on by adhesive tape. The driver, who had wandered off a few yards saying he was "bursting for a pee", was driven with his companion to Hammerton Road police station for questioning. The following day, Sergeant Ring returned to the scene and found a hammer and a knife which Williams, alias Peter William Sutcliffe, the Yorkshire Ripper, had hidden while ostensibly relieving himself.

The search for the mass murderer had ended but behind the jubilation of the police lurked the shadow of public criticism. Why, it was asked, with all their manpower and scientific resources, had the police let their man slip through nine different interviews and why did

The Judge praised the police. But do they deserve it? The case against them shows nothing but incompetence, stupidity and bureaucratic arrogance.

GREGORY: He expected criticism of police

HOBSON: Too little doubt over hoax

BIRDSALL: The detectives put him on file

OLDFIELD: The tape and letters obsessed him

Above: *Public criticism of Assistant Chief Constable Oldfield and Detective Chief Superintendent Hobson was strong. Although Chief Constable Gregory pointed to the difficulties of the case — too little public interest, random killings, no apparent motive — the fact remains that obsession with the Geordie tapes prevented earlier capture.*

they allow themselves to be misled over the "I'm Jack" tape?

One answer lies in the sheer magnitude of the task confronting any police force in tracking down the multiple murderer operating in different locations. In the course of their five-year investigation, which cost four million pounds, the police checked 5.2 million car registration numbers, interviewed 250,000 individuals and took 32,000 written statements. At the peak of the investigation, 250 detectives worked full-time checking every piece of information that came into their hands, including over a thousand letters a day. The police admitted making mistakes but their defence lay in the fact that they *ultimately* got their man. Despite all their previous errors, they still managed to overcome the Ripper's self-confessed 'latent genius' by alert policing plus the central computer. And, we might add, with an element of something that had so far been wholly on Peter Sutcliffe's side — sheer good luck!

Below: *Every communication had to be examined. This note, thought to be the Ripper's work, appears to deny the murder of Barbara Leach in Bradford 1979. The police believed her to be his twelfth victim.*

`Clueless`

POOR OLD OLDFIELD
WORKED IN A COLDFIELD

HOBSON HAS NO CHOICE
MISLED BY A VOICE

RELEASE OF DRURY
AROUSES FURY

BRADFORD WAS NOT ME
BUT JUST WAIT AND SEE

SHEFFIELD WILL NOT BE MISSED
NEXT ON THE LIST

`The Streetcleaner`
(T.S.)

tional criminal police congress decided to establish an organization for this purpose.

World War One prevented this coming to immediate fruition but in 1923 at Vienna, the International Criminal Police Commission (ICPC) was created. World War Two hampered progress so that it was not until 1946 that the ICPC, or Interpol as it was to become known, really came into its own. In that year, under the presidency of Monsieur F.E. Louwage, Inspector-General of the Belgian Police, Interpol became established with a headquarters office in Paris in the building occupied by the Sûreté-Nationale.

Interpol

The purpose of Interpol is to coordinate efforts against international crime by promoting mutual assistance between criminal police authorities in different countries. It was set out clearly that this objective was to be achieved within the limits of individual members' legal systems and excluded political, religious, military or racial activities.

Interpol is not a world police force but a coordinating centre for information enabling its member countries to track crime beyond national boundaries. It works by exchanging information and by identifying and securing the apprehension of wanted individuals and suspects.

Interpol rightly prides itself on the quality of its communications, an essential ingredient in international criminal investigation. Its radio-communications centre in Paris is equipped with powerful transmitters which maintain contact with 20 regional radio stations covering Europe, the Middle East, North Africa, North and South America and the Far East. Interpol staff, working in English, French and Spanish, deal with a large flow of information and enquiries, drawing on a collection which includes 175,000 files on top criminals and records of passports, car registrations, stolen property and missing persons.

Below: *The extensive archives of Interpol, based in Paris, which facilitate the capture of criminals worldwide.*

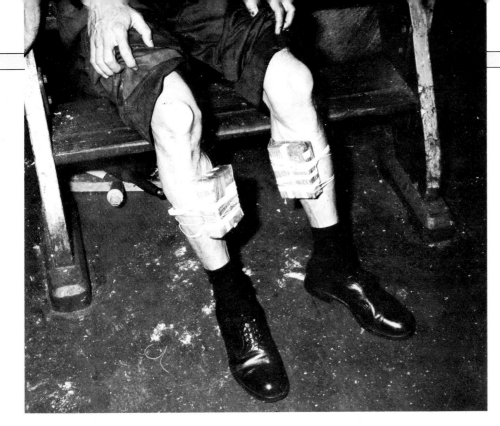

Left: *Narcotics are tied onto a sailor's legs in an attempt to smuggle them into Hong Kong. In the 1980s, dealing in drugs has become a massive business, and Hong Kong, easily accessible to the 'Golden Triangle', is one of the world's exchange centres of narcotics, besides having a serious drug problem itself.*

National Central Bureaux

Each member country has a National Central Bureau, for example Scotland Yard in Britain, which sends information of international interest to Interpol HQ and undertakes such police operations as the law permits to make searches and arrests at the request of another country. Interpol publishes an official journal, *International Criminal Police Review*, to disseminate information among its members and also seeks agreement through international agencies such as the UN on drug control and extradition procedures. In this way, over a 100 member countries are better informed in their fight against international fraud, drug trafficking and counterfeit operations.

Narcotics control

Drug trafficking is big international business and nearly a third of the enquiries dealt with by Interpol concern drug offences. The rapid growth of drug-addiction among young age groups in the western nations coupled with the implication of drug-taking in the commission of violent crime taxes the prevention and detection skills of all police organizations. The New York Police Department estimates that there are between 100,000 and 250,000 heroin users in the city. Smuggling the drugs to satisfy this appetite is big business to the tune of billions of dollars a year for the dealers. Raw heroin is imported from the 'Golden Triangle' of Thailand, Burma and Laos and from Mexico.

The US Bureau of Narcotics works closely with Interpol to plot the movements of known drug traffickers and to monitor their supply routes. National bureaux in France, Italy and Turkey have cooperated fully in an international strategy to tackle the illicit drug trade at source by raiding heroin factories. Millions of dollars worth of hard drugs are confiscated every year due to this kind of surveillance but the potential rewards for the dealers are so lucrative that this is a field of criminal activity which is likely to remain a top priority for the international police organization during the 1980s.

There is little doubt that without the benefit of Interpol's coordinating role, the world's crime problems in general and drug offences in particular, would be considerably worse than they are. Police methods have come a long way since Henry Fielding's day but his concept of rapid communications as the key to crime investigation is even more valid in today's fast-moving society.

INDEX

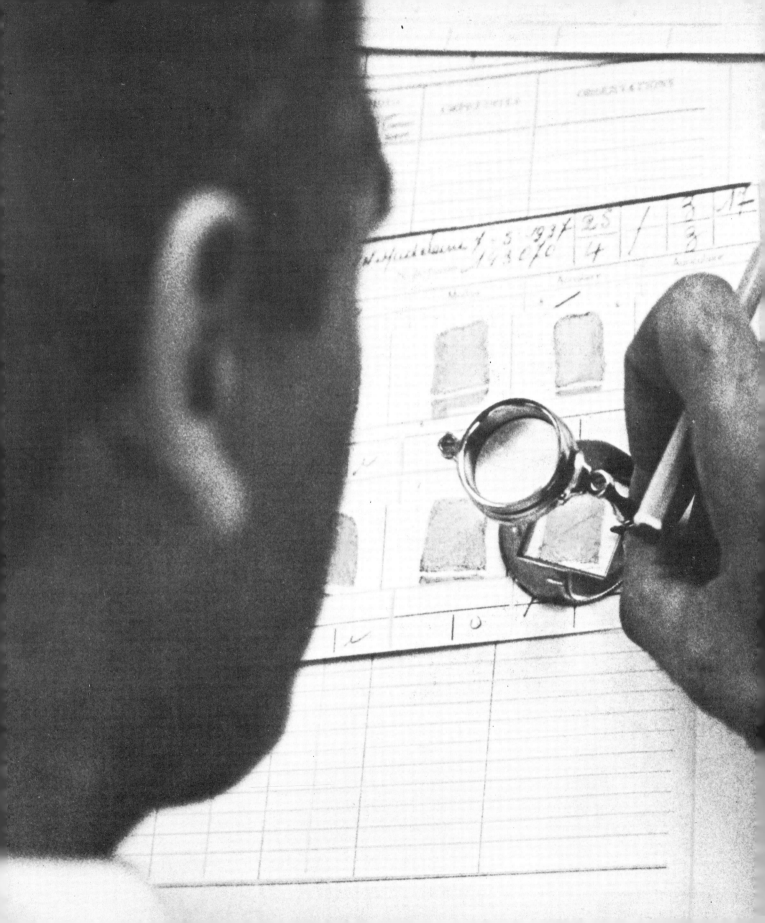